# LUXEMBOURG

AF842565

## CONSTITUTION AND CITIZENSHIP LAWS HANDBOOK

### STRATEGIC INFORMATION AND DEVELOPMENTS

**International Business Publications, USA**
**Washington DC, USA - Luxembourg**

# LUXEMBOURG

## CONSTITUTION AND CITIZENSHIP LAWS HANDBOOK

### STRATEGIC INFORMATION AND DEVELOPMENTS

**UPDATED ANNUALLY**

Cover Design: **International Business Publications, USA**

**We express our sincere appreciation to all government agencies and international organizations which provided information and other materials for this handbook**

**International Business Publications, USA**. ***has used its best efforts in collecting, analyzing and preparing data, information and materials for this unique handbook. Due to the dynamic nature and fast development of the economy and business environment, we cannot warrant that all information herein is complete and accurate. IBP does not assume and hereby disclaim any liability to any person for any loss or damage caused by possible errors or omissions in the handbook.***
***This handbook is for noncommercial use only. Use this handbook for any other purpose, included but not limited to reproducing and storing in a retrieval system by any means, electronic, photocopying or using the addresses or other information contained in this handbook for any commercial purposes requires a special written permission from the publisher.***

**2014 Edition Updated Reprint International Business Publications, USA**
**ISBN 978-14387-7935-5**

**This handbook provides basic information for starting or/and conducting business in the country. The extraordinary volume of materials covering the topic, prevents us from placing all these materials in this handbook. For more detailed information on issues related to any specific investment and business activity in the country, please contact Global Investment Center, USA**
**Please acquire the list of our business intelligence and marketing reports and other business publications. We constantly update and expand our business intelligence and marketing materials. Please contact the center for the updated list of reports on over 250 countries.**

in the USA: **Global Investment Center, USA.**
P.O.Box 15343, Washington, DC 20003
Phone: (202) 546-2103, Fax: (202) 546-3275, E-mail: rusric@erols.com

**For additional analytical, marketing and other information please contact Global Investment Center, USA**

Printed in the USA

# LUXEMBOURG

## CONSTITUTION AND CITIZENSHIP LAWS HANDBOOK

### STRATEGIC INFORMATION AND DEVELOPMENTS

## TABLE OF CONTENTS

**For additional analytical, business and investment opportunities information, please contact Global Investment & Business Center, USA at (202) 546-2103. Fax: (202) 546-3275. E-mail: rusric@erols.com**

**For additional analytical, business and investment opportunities information, please contact Global Investment & Business Center, USA at (202) 546-2103. Fax: (202) 546-3275. E-mail: rusric@erols.com**

# STRATEGIC AND DEVELOPMENT PROFILES

## STRATEGIC PROFILE

| | |
|---|---|
| Capital (and largest city) | Luxembourg 49°36′N 6°7′E49.6°N 6.117°E |
| Official language(s) | Luxembourgish (de jure since 1984), French, German |
| Demonym | Luxembourgers |
| Government | Unitary parliamentary democracy and constitutional monarchy |
| - Grand Duke | Grand Duke Henri (List) |
| - Prime minister | Jean-Claude Juncker (List) |
| | Independence |
| - From French empire (Treaty of Paris) | 9 June 1815 |
| - 1st Treaty of London | 19 April 1839 |
| - 2nd Treaty of London | 11 May 1867 |
| - End of personal union | 23 November 1890 |
| EU accession | 25 March 1957 |
| | Area |
| - Total | 2,586.4 km$^2$ (175th) 998.6 sq mi |
| - Water (%) | negligible |
| | Population |
| - 2010 estimate | 502,202[1] (170th) |
| - 2001 census | 439,539 |
| - Density | 194.1/km$^2$ (59th) 501.3/sq mi |
| GDP (PPP) | 2009 estimate |
| - Total | $38.808 billion[2] |
| - Per capita | $78,395[2] |
| GDP (nominal) | 2009 estimate |
| - Total | $51.736 billion[2] |
| - Per capita | $104,512[2] |
| HDI (2010) | ▲0.852 (very high) (24th) |
| Currency | Euro (€)[2] (EUR) |
| Time zone | CET (UTC+1) |
| - Summer (DST) | CEST (UTC+2) |
| Drives on the | right |
| ISO 3166 code | LU |
| Internet TLD | .lu[3] |
| Calling code | 352 |

**Background:** Founded in 963, Luxembourg became a grand duchy in 1815 and an independent state under the Netherlands. It lost more than half of its territory to Belgium in 1839, but gained a larger measure of autonomy. Full independence was attained in 1867. Overrun by Germany in both World Wars, it ended its neutrality in 1948 when it entered into the Benelux Customs Union and when it joined NATO the following year. In 1957, Luxembourg became one of the six founding countries of the European Economic Community (later the European Union) and in 1999 it joined the euro currency area.

## GEOGRAPHY

**Location:** Western Europe, between France and Germany
**Geographic coordinates:** 49 45 N, 6 10 E
**Map references:** Europe

**Area:**
*total:* 2,586 sq km
*land:* 2,586 sq km
*water:* 0 sq km

**Area - comparative:** slightly smaller than Rhode Island
**Land boundaries:**
*total:* 359 km
*border countries:* Belgium 148 km, France 73 km, Germany 138 km
**Coastline:** 0 km (landlocked)
**Maritime claims:** none (landlocked)
**Climate:** modified continental with mild winters, cool summers

**Terrain:** mostly gently rolling uplands with broad, shallow valleys; uplands to slightly mountainous in the north; steep slope down to Moselle flood plain in the southeast

**Elevation extremes:**
*lowest point:* Moselle River 133 m
*highest point:* Burgplatz 559 m

**Land use:**
*arable land:* 24%
*permanent crops:* 1% *permanent pastures:* 20% *forests and woodland:* 21% *other:* 34%

**Irrigated land:** 10 sq km (including Belgium) (1993 est.)
**Natural hazards:** NA
**Environment - current issues:** air and water pollution in urban areas
**Environment - international agreements:**
*party to:* Air Pollution, Air Pollution-Nitrogen Oxides, Air Pollution-Sulphur 85, Air Pollution-Sulphur 94, Air Pollution-Volatile Organic Compounds, Biodiversity, Climate Change, Desertification, Endangered Species, Hazardous Wastes, Marine Dumping, Nuclear Test Ban, Ozone Layer Protection, Ship Pollution, Tropical Timber 83, Tropical Timber 94, Wetlands
*signed, but not ratified:* Air Pollution-Persistent Organic Pollutants, Climate Change-Kyoto Protocol, Environmental Modification, Law of the Sea
**Geography - note:** landlocked

## PEOPLE

**Population:** 437,389

**For additional analytical, business and investment opportunities information, please contact Global Investment & Business Center, USA at (202) 546-2103. Fax: (202) 546-3275. E-mail: rusric@erols.com**

Base 504738 (546430) 12-81

**Emploi industriel (Industries manufacturières) par commune en 1991**

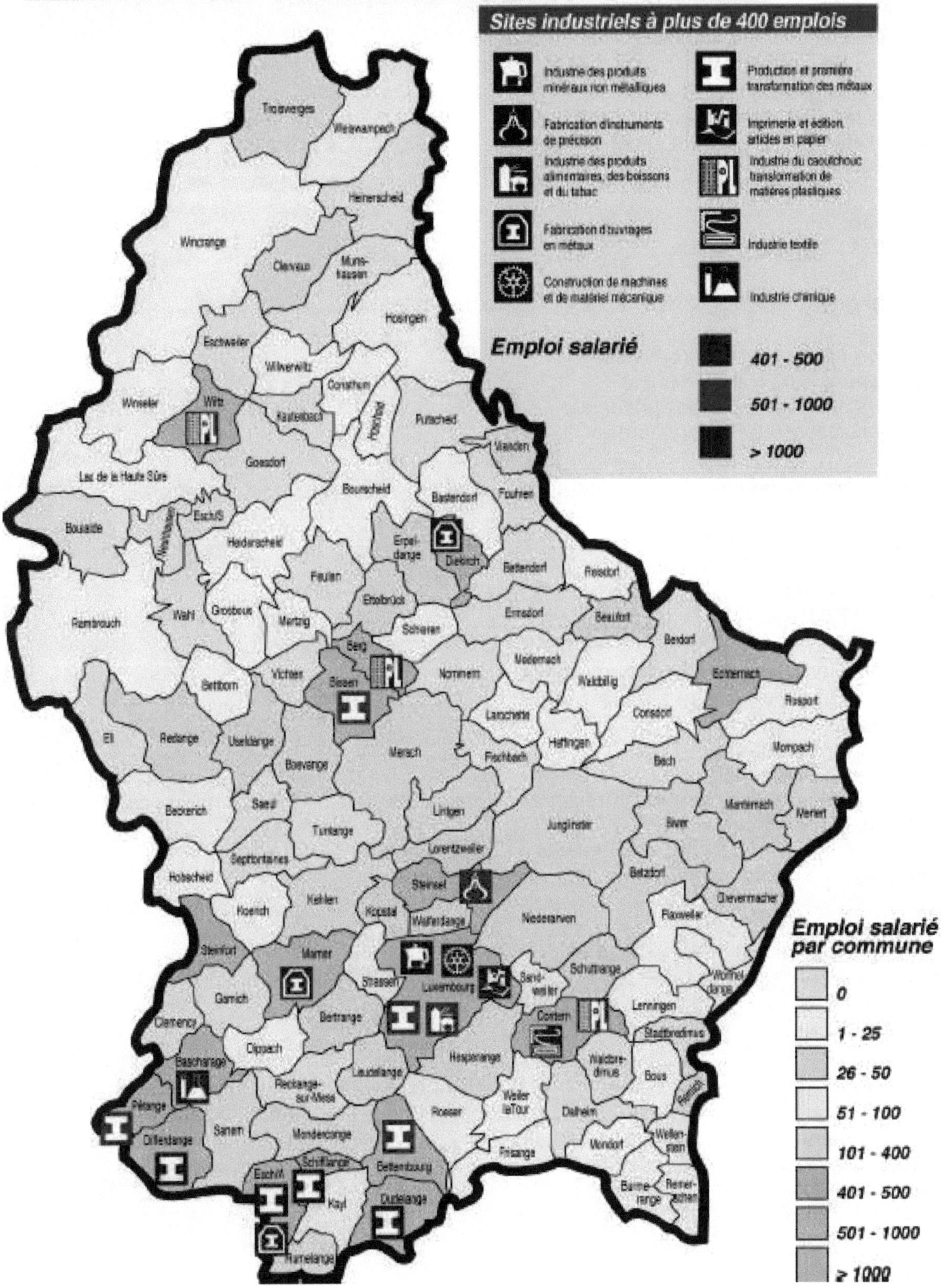

**Age structure:**
*0-14 years:* 19% (male 42,375; female 40,109)
*15-64 years:* 67% (male 148,205; female 145,325)
*65 years and over:* 14% (male 24,446; female 36,929)

**Population growth rate:** 1.27%
**Birth rate:** 12.45 births/1,000 population
**Death rate:** 8.91 deaths/1,000 population
**Net migration rate:** 9.21 migrant(s)/1,000 population

**Sex ratio:**
*at birth:* 1.03 male(s)/female

**Natural resources:** iron ore (no longer exploited), arable land

*under 15 years:* 1.06 male(s)/female
*15-64 years:* 1.02 male(s)/female
*65 years and over:* 0.66 male(s)/female
*total population:* 0.97 male(s)/female

**Infant mortality rate:** 4.83 deaths/1,000 live births

**Life expectancy at birth:**
*total population:* 77.13 years
*male:* 73.84 years
*female:* 80.63 years

**Total fertility rate:** 1.7 children born/woman

**Nationality:**
*noun:* Luxembourger(s)
*adjective:* Luxembourg
**Ethnic groups:** Celtic base (with French and German blend), Portuguese, Italian, and European (guest and worker residents)
**Religions:** Roman Catholic 97%, Protestant and Jewish 3%
**Languages:** Luxembourgian, German, French, English

**Literacy:**
*definition:* age 15 and over can read and write
*total population:* 100%
*male:* 100%
*female:* 100%

## GOVERNMENT

**Country name:**
*conventional long form:* Grand Duchy of Luxembourg
*conventional short form:* Luxembourg
*local long form:* Grand-Duche de Luxembourg
*local short form:* Luxembourg

**Data code:** LU

**Government type:** constitutional monarchy
**Capital:** Luxembourg
**Administrative divisions:** 3 districts; Diekirch, Grevenmacher, Luxembourg
**Independence:** 1839 (from the Netherlands)
**National holiday:** National Day, 23 June (1921) (public celebration of the Grand Duke's birthday)
**Constitution:** 17 October 1868, occasional revisions
**Legal system:** based on civil law system; accepts compulsory ICJ jurisdiction
**Suffrage:** 18 years of age; universal and compulsory

**Executive branch:**
*chief of state:* Grand Duke HENRI (since 7 October 2000); Heir Apparent Prince GUILLAUME (son of the monarch, born 11 November 1981)
*head of government:* Prime Minister Jean-Claude JUNCKER (since 1 January 1995) and Vice Prime Minister Jean ASSELBORN (since 31 July 2004)
*cabinet:* Council of Ministers recommended by the prime minister and appointed by the monarch
*elections:* none; the monarch is hereditary; following popular elections to the Chamber of Deputies, the leader of the majority party or the leader of the majority coalition is usually appointed prime minister by the monarch; the deputy prime minister is appointed by the monarch; they are responsible to the Chamber of Deputies
*note:* government coalition - CSV and LSAP

**Legislative branch:**

unicameral Chamber of Deputies or Chambre des Deputes (60 seats; members elected by popular vote to serve five-year terms)
elections: last held on 7 June 2009 (next to be held by June 2014)
election results: percent of vote by party - CSV 38%, LSAP 21.6%, DP 15%, Green Party 11.7%, ADR 8.1%, The Left 3.3%, other 2.3%; seats by party - CSV 26, LSAP 13, DP 9, Green Party 7, ADR 4, The Left 1
*note:*there is also a Council of State that serves as an advisory body to the Chamber of Deputies; the Council of State has 21 members appointed by the Grand Duke on the advice of the prime minister

**Political parties and leaders:** Action Committee for Democracy and Pension Rights or ADR [Robert MEHLEN]; Christian Social People's Party or CSV [Erna HENNICOT-SCHOEPGES]; Democratic Party or DP [Lydie POLFER]; Green Party [Jean HUSS]; Luxembourg Socialist Workers' Party or LSAP [Jean ASSELBORN]; Marxist and Reformed Communist Party DEI LENK (the Left) [Andre HOFFMAN]; other minor parties

**Political pressure groups and leaders:** ABBL (bankers' association); ALEBA (financial sector trade union); Centrale Paysanne (federation of agricultural producers); CEP (professional sector chamber); CGFP (trade union representing civil service); Chambre de Commerce (Chamber of Commerce); Chambre des Metiers (Chamber of Artisans); FEDIL (federation of industrialists); LCGP (center-right trade union); OGBL (center-left trade union)

**International organization participation:** ACCT, Australia Group, Benelux, CCC, CE, EAPC, EBRD, ECE, EIB, EMU, EU, FAO, IAEA, IBRD, ICAO, ICC, ICFTU, ICRM, IDA, IEA, IFAD, IFC, IFRCS, ILO, IMF, IMO, Intelsat, Interpol, IOC, IOM, ISO, ITU, NATO, NEA, NSG, OECD, OPCW, OSCE, PCA, UN, UNCTAD, UNESCO, UNIDO, UPU, WCL, WEU, WHO, WIPO, WMO, WTrO, ZC

**Diplomatic representation in the US:**
*chief of mission:* Ambassador Arlette CONZEMIUS
*chancery:* 2200 Massachusetts Avenue NW, Washington, DC 20006

*telephone:* [1] (202) 265-4171
*FAX:* [1] (202) 328-8270
*consulate(s) general:* New York and San Francisco

**Diplomatic representation from the US:**
*chief of mission:* Ambassador James C. HORMEL
*embassy:* 22 Boulevard Emmanuel-Servais, L-2535 Luxembourg City
*mailing address:* American Embassy Luxembourg, Unit 1410, APO AE 09126-1410 (official mail); American Embassy Luxembourg, PSC 9, Box 9500, APO AE 09123 (personal mail)
*telephone:* [352] 46 01 23
*FAX:* [352] 46 14 01

**Flag description:** three equal horizontal bands of red (top), white, and light blue; similar to the flag of the Netherlands, which uses a darker blue and is shorter; design was based on the flag of France

## ECONOMY

| | |
|---|---|
| **Economy - overview:** | This stable, high-income economy - benefiting from its proximity to France, Belgium, and Germany - features solid growth, low inflation, and low unemployment. The industrial sector, initially dominated by steel, has become increasingly diversified to include chemicals, rubber, and other products. Growth in the financial sector, which now accounts for about 28% of GDP, has more than compensated for the decline in steel. Most banks are foreign-owned and have extensive foreign dealings. Agriculture is based on small family-owned farms. The economy depends on foreign and cross-border workers for about 60% of its labor force. Although Luxembourg, like all EU members, has suffered from the global economic slump, the country enjoys an extraordinarily high standard of living - GDP per capita ranks second in the world. |
| **GDP (purchasing power parity):** | $33.87 billion |
| **GDP (official exchange rate):** | $34.53 billion |
| **GDP - real growth rate:** | 6.2% |
| **GDP - per capita (PPP):** | $71,400 |
| **GDP - composition by sector:** | *agriculture:* 1%<br>*industry:* 13%<br>*services:* 86% |
| **Labor force:** | 203,000 of whom 121,600 are foreign cross-border workers commuting primarily from France, Belgium, and Germany |
| **Labor force - by occupation:** | *agriculture:* 1%<br>*industry:* 13%<br>*services:* 86% |
| **Unemployment rate:** | 4.1% |
| **Population below** | NA% |

| | |
|---|---|
| **poverty line:** | |
| **Household income or consumption by percentage share:** | *lowest 10%:* NA%<br>*highest 10%:* NA% |
| **Inflation rate (consumer prices):** | 2.7% |
| **Investment (gross fixed):** | 18.3% of GDP |
| **Budget:** | *revenues:* $18.68 billion<br>*expenditures:* $18.65 billion |
| **Agriculture - products:** | wine, grapes, barley, oats, potatoes, wheat, fruits; dairy products, livestock products |
| **Industries:** | banking and financial services, iron and steel, information technology, telecommunications, cargo transportation, food processing, chemicals, metal products, engineering, tires, glass, aluminum, tourism |
| **Electricity - production:** | 3.156 billion kWh |
| **Electricity - consumption:** | 6.315 billion kWh |
| **Electricity - exports:** | 3.131 billion kWh |
| **Electricity - imports:** | 6.392 billion kWh |
| **Oil - production:** | 0 bbl/day |
| **Oil - consumption:** | 62,420 bbl/day |
| **Oil - exports:** | 283 bbl/day |
| **Oil - imports:** | 61,070 bbl/day |
| **Oil - proved reserves:** | 0 bbl |
| **Natural gas - production:** | 0 cu m |
| **Natural gas - consumption:** | 1.356 billion cu m |
| **Natural gas - exports:** | 0 cu m |
| **Natural gas - imports:** | 1.356 billion cu m |
| **Current account balance:** | $4.387 billion |

**Exports:** $16.57 billion f.o.b.

**Exports - commodities:** machinery and equipment, steel products, chemicals, rubber products, glass

**Exports - partners:** Germany 19.3%, France 15.5%, Italy 9.5%, UK 9.5%, Belgium 8.8%, Spain 5.3%, Netherlands 4.5%

**Imports:** $20.86 billion c.i.f.

**Imports - commodities:** minerals, metals, foodstuffs, quality consumer goods

**Imports - partners:** Belgium 26.3%, Germany 20.1%, China 16.7%, France 8.5%, UK 5.5%, Netherlands 4.2%

**Economic aid - donor:** ODA, $235.6 million

**Reserves of foreign exchange and gold:** $265.1 million

**Debt - external:** $NA

**Stock of direct foreign investment - at home:** $NA

**Stock of direct foreign investment - abroad:** $NA

**Market value of publicly traded shares:** $51.25 billion

**Currency (code):** euro (EUR)
*note:* on 1 January 1999, the European Monetary Union introduced the euro as a common currency to be used by financial institutions of member countries; on 1 January 2002, the euro became the sole currency for everyday transactions within the member countries

**Exchange rates:** euros per US dollar - 0.7964 (2006), 0.8041 (2005), 0.8054 (2004), 0.886 (2003), 1.0626 (2002)

**Fiscal year:** calendar year

## COMMUNICATIONS

**Telephones - main lines in use:** 360,100

**Telephones - mobile cellular:** 539,000

**Telephone system:** *general assessment:* highly developed, completely automated and efficient system, mainly buried cables
*domestic:* nationwide cellular telephone system; buried cable

**For additional analytical, business and investment opportunities information, please contact Global Investment & Business Center, USA at (202) 546-2103. Fax: (202) 546-3275. E-mail: rusric@erols.com**

*international:* country code - 352; 3 channels leased on TAT-6 coaxial submarine cable (Europe to North America)

**Radio broadcast stations:** AM 2, FM 9, shortwave 2

**Television broadcast stations:** 5

**Internet country code:** .lu

**Internet hosts:** 70,465

**Internet users:** 270,800

## TRANSPORTATION

**Railways:**
*total:* 274 km
*standard gauge:* 274 km 1.435-m gauge (242 km electrified; 178 km double track)

**Highways:**
*total:* 5,166 km
*paved:* 5,166 km (including 118 km of expressways)
*unpaved:* 0 km
**Waterways:** 37 km; Moselle
**Pipelines:** petroleum products 48 km
**Ports and harbors:** Mertert
**Merchant marine:**
*total:* 48 ships (1,000 GRT or over) totaling 1,283,738 GRT/1,872,071 DWT
*ships by type:* bulk 2, chemical tanker 10, container 1, liquified gas 18, passenger 4, petroleum tanker 6, roll-on/roll-off 7
**Airports:** 2
**Airports - with paved runways:**
*total:* 1 *over 3,047 m:* 1
**Airports - with unpaved runways:**
*total:* 1 *under 914 m:* 1

## MILITARY

**Military branches:** Army; note - the new government abolished the Gendarmerie
**Military manpower - military age:** 19 years of age
**Military manpower - availability:**
*males age 15-49:* 111,882
**Military manpower - fit for military service:**
*males age 15-49:* 92,238
**Military manpower - reaching military age annually:**
*males:* 2,563
**Military expenditures - dollar figure:** $131 million
**Military expenditures - percent of GDP:** 1%

**For additional analytical, business and investment opportunities information, please contact Global Investment & Business Center, USA at (202) 546-2103. Fax: (202) 546-3275. E-mail: rusric@erols.com**

# STRATEGIC INFORMATION ON THE COUNTRY

The Grand Duchy of Luxembourg, a constitutional monarchy, is an independent sovereign state, tucked between Belgium, France and Germany (cf **Luxembourg in Europe map**). The country is 84 km (51 miles) long and 52 km (32 miles) wide, encompassing an area of 2586 square kilometres (999 square miles) with a population of 435 700 inhabitants (official estimate Jan 1, 2000).

## GEOGRAPHY

### REGIONS

The "Eisléck" or 'Oesling' in the north, which is part of the Ardennes, on the western rim of the Eifel, and covers one-third of the territory. It is a wooded country of great scenic beauty. Highest point: 555 metres (1823 feet).
The 'Good country' in the centre and the south, covering the remainder of the territory, is mainly rolling farmland and woods. Average height: 270 metres (900 feet). Culminating point 426 metres (1400 feet). It is bordered in the east by the wine-producing valley of the Moselle, and in the extreme south west by a narrow strip of red earth which forms the Luxembourg iron-ore basin.

### RIVER NETWORK:

The 4 most important rivers are:

The Moselle, the Sûre, the Our, and the Alzette

The other rivers are:

The Mess, the Mamer, the Eisch, the Attert and the Wark in the West;
The Wiltz, the Clerve and the Blees in the North;
The Ernz Blanche, the Ernz Noire, the Syr and the Gander in the East;
The Petrusse is a very small river that crosses Luxembourg city, and meets the Alzette.

### CLIMATE:

The Grand Duchy of Luxembourg enjoys a temperate climate without extremes. The sea (some 200 miles distant) has but a moderating influence on the weather. The air is clean, beneficial and health giving. Rainfalls: 31 inches.

**LUXEMBOURG CLIMATE AVERAGES**

| | Temperature Day (°C) | Temperature Night (°C) | Sunshine (hours) | Rain (days) |
|---|---|---|---|---|
| January | 5 | 0 | 2 | 12 |
| February | 6 | 0 | 3 | 10 |
| March | 10 | 2 | 4 | 11 |
| April | 13 | 4 | 6 | 12 |
| May | 19 | 8 | 7 | 10 |
| June | 21 | 10 | 7 | 11 |

| | | | | |
|---|---|---|---|---|
| July | 23 | 12 | 6 | 11 |
| August | 22 | 12 | 6 | 11 |
| September | 20 | 10 | 5 | 10 |
| October | 14 | 7 | 4 | 12 |
| November | 8 | 2 | 2 | 12 |
| December | 6 | 1 | 1 | 13 |

Luxembourg's Statistics Office (Statec) gives averages for the years from 1951 to 1990 (in Luxembourg-City) as follows:

| Average 1951-1990 | January | April | July | October | 12 months |
|---|---|---|---|---|---|
| Temperature (Degrees C) | | | | | |
| Average | 0.8 | 8.3 | 17.5 | 9.5 | 9.0 |
| Maximum | 9.5 | 22.0 | 30.7 | 20.7 | 20.5 |
| Minimum | -9.5 | -2.2 | 6.9 | -0.4 | -1.3 |
| Relative Humidity (%) | 89.0 | 74.0 | 73.0 | 86.0 | 81.0 |
| Hours of Sunshine | 38.6 | 158.7 | 200.5 | 94.7 | 1430.0 |
| Rainfall (mm) | 69.0 | 50.6 | 62.9 | 63.8 | 782.2 |

## COMMUNICATIONS:

Air: International airport in Luxembourg: **Findel Airport** 3.5 miles north-east of the capital Luxembourg City (49°37' N, 6°13' E) at an altitude of 1234 feet.

National airline : Luxair with regular flights to: Agadir, Alicante, Amsterdam, Athens, Barcelona, Copenhagen, Djerba, Faro, Frankfurt, Geneva, Hamburg, London, Madrid, Malaga, Munich, Nice, Palma, Paris, Rhodes, Rome, Strasbourg, Saarbrücken, Tenerife, and Vienna.
Other airlines link Luxembourg to: Boston, Brussels, Budapest, Chicago, Hamburg, Havana, Leningrad, Lima, Lisbon, Milan, New York, Orlando, Reykjavik, Washington, Zurich, to name but the major destinations.

Rail: C.F.L. (=Chemins de Fer Luxembourgeois [Luxembourg Railways]) with electrified railways and buses covering the whole country.
Road: The road network is very good all over the country. All roads and motorways are toll-free.
River: The Moselle is canalised (since 1964) and links the Grand Duchy of Luxembourg to the large European Waterways.

# HISTORY

The written history of Lucilinburhuc (i.e. Luxembourg) starts in the year 963, when Siegfried, Count of the Ardennes, and founder of the Luxembourg Dynasty, had a castle built on the territory of the present-day capital of Luxembourg. This castle was the origin of the establishment of a town, which later was to develop into a formidable fortress, known by the name of 'Gibraltar of the North'. At its height, the fortress was girdled by three ring-walls studded with 24 forts, and linked underground by a 23 kilometre network of Casemates. In 1994, Luxembourg City was listed as a UNESCO World Heritage

After a long period of foreign sovereignty (Burgundian/ Spanish/ French/ Austrian / ...), the Congress of Vienna settled the destiny of the country, by raising it to the rank of Grand Duchy, and by giving it as personal property to the King of the Netherlands William I of Orange-Nassau. The personal union between Luxembourg and the Netherlands lasted until 1890. During this period the political independence and autonomy were strengthened, and the democratic institutions were developed.

The 11th of May 1867 is one of the most important dates in national history. The Treaty of London reaffirmed Luxembourg's territorial integrity, and the political autonomy which had already been granted by the Treaty of Vienna of 1839.

Furthermore, Luxembourg was declared perpetually neutral, and the great powers agreed to guarantee and to protect the neutrality of the Grand Duchy.

Since 1890, when the Crown of the Grand Duchy passed to the elder branch of the House of Nassau, Luxembourg has had its own Dynasty. The present ruler, H.R.H. Grand Duke Henri, succeeded his father, Grand Duke Jean to the throne in October 2000, after having been appointed as "Lieutenant-Représentant" -the Grand Duke's official deputy- on March 3, 1998, as provided for by Article 42 of the Luxembourg Constitution.

Grand Duke Jean's mother, Grand Duchess Charlotte, Duchess of Nassau, Princess of Bourbon Parma, died in 1985. Grand Duke Jean and his wife Grand Duchess Joséphine-Charlotte, the sister to Albert, King of the Belgians, have five children Henri, Jean, Guillaume, Marie-Astrid, and Margaretha. (See also Grand-Ducal Family Tree and/or The Grand-Ducal Family)

Executive power is in the hands of the Grand Duke and a Cabinet of 12 ministers. The legislative power rests with a Parliament (Chamber of Deputies) elected by men and women over 18, all of whom in Luxembourg have the right and duty to vote.

Despite its neutrality, Luxembourg was occupied twice by German troops during the two World Wars. The Battle of the Bulge was to a great extent fought on Luxembourg territory. In 1948, the country gave up its neutrality, to join the various economic, political, and military organisations of Europe. Already forming a close economic union with Belgium since 1921, the Grand Duchy is a founder member of the EU, and was host to the first European institutions in 1953.

At present the following European Union institutions are based in Luxembourg:

The Commission of the European Community, including the Statistical Office (EUROSTAT) and the Publications Office,
The Court of Justice of the European Communities,
The general Secretariat of the European Parliament,
The European Investment Bank,
The European Court of Auditors.

The Official Publications Office
The Nuclear Safety Administration,
The Directorate-General of 'Credits and Investments',

In addition, various other European Organisations (among which EFTA) also have offices in Luxembourg. Moreover, the sessions of the Council of Ministers take place in Luxembourg three months in the year. (April, June and October).

## ECONOMY

It was the discovery of the iron ore around 1850 which marked the turning point for Luxembourg and meant its economic take-off. An important steel industry came into being in the south-western corner of the country, drawing tens of thousands of foreign workers into the ore mines and steel factories, and bringing prosperity to the whole country.

The steel exports constitute one quarter of the value of the Luxembourg export trade. The ARBED group alone (Acieries Réunies de Burbach-Eich-Dudelange), produces 90% of the whole Luxembourg steel output. In spite of severe labour-shedding during the eighties, ARBED remains the largest private employer in the country. ARBED is the fifth largest steel complex in Europe, and the thirteenth largest in the Western world.

Since the end of World War II, great efforts have been made to bring diversity into the former monolithic industry. Aluminium, glass, cement, tyres, magnetic tapes and computer manufacturers have established plants, dams have been built in Esch-sur-Sûre and Rosport; Vianden houses Europe's second largest pumping station producing peak hydro-electricity; the ASTRA satellites are controlled from Luxembourg.

Tax rebates, help in obtaining credits, and a host of other incentives are offered to companies intending to set up plant in the Grand Duchy. However, despite these continuing efforts, Luxembourg's industrial labour is dropping in numbers, marking a slide into the service sector.

Luxembourg plays a major role as a prominent international financial centre. Numerous banks and important investment trusts have settled in the capital, as the fiscal legislation, which dates back to 1929, favours Banks and Holding Companies.

Luxembourg as an international centre numbers more than 12000 domiciled Holding Companies, some 1300 investment funds, and 220 banks which represent the greatest banking concentration in the European Community. More recently still, Luxembourg has reaffirmed its importance as a centre for Eurobonds with a big emphasis in ECUs, and the future seems likely to attract more and more investment funds in European Currency Units to this comparatively young, but steadily growing centre.

In parallel with the growth of private banking, which year on year emerges as the core activity for Luxembourg's banks, the development of other sectors, such as Investment Fund Promotion and Services, as well as Life Insurance are reinforcing Luxembourg's claim to be Europe's premier centre for all forms of Personal Investment business. Tourism contributes significantly to the National Accounts.

Its economic structure and its geographical position have necessarily led Luxembourg into a close co-operation with other countries, and particularly with Belgium since 1921, and with Belgium and the Netherlands since the second World War, with the creation of **BENELUX**, an economic Union which was the first step towards the present larger European Community.

**For additional analytical, business and investment opportunities information, please contact Global Investment & Business Center, USA at (202) 546-2103. Fax: (202) 546-3275. E-mail: rusric@erols.com**

## CURRENCY

The Grand Duchy of Luxembourg has its own currency, the **Luxembourg Franc**.
It has the same rate as the Belgian franc, and both are commonly and widely used in the country.

To help you in guesstimating the value of your currency against the Belgian/Luxembourg Franc, here's an exchange table valid on October 17, 2000.

| Currency | You sell | You buy |
|---|---|---|
| 1 Pound Sterling | 65.86 | 71.47 |
| 1 U.S. Dollar | 45.50 | 49.32 |
| 1 Irish Punt | 49.17 | 53.27 |
| 1 German Mark | 19.80 | 21.45 |
| 1 French Franc | 5.90 | 6.39 |
| 1 Dutch Guilder | 17.57 | 19.03 |
| 100 Italian Lire | 2.00 | 2.16 |
| 1 Swiss Franc | 25.65 | 27.81 |
| 1 Austrian Schilling | 2.81 | 3.04 |
| 100 Spanish Pesetas | 23.27 | 25.21 |
| 1 Finish Markka | 6.51 | 7.05 |
| 1 Danish Krone | 5.19 | 5.63 |
| 1 Swedish Krona | 4.54 | 4.92 |
| 1 Norwegian Kroner | 4.83 | 5.24 |
| 1 Canadian Dollar | 29.96 | 32.50 |
| 1 South African Rand | 6.01 | 6.53 |
| 100 Portuguese Escudos | 19.31 | 20.92 |
| 100 Japanese Yen | 42.10 | 45.65 |
| 1 Euro | 40.3399 | |

Note that Luxembourg will use the **Euro** as of 2002.

## POPULATION & LANGUAGES

Of the country's 418 300 inhabitants (1st Jan. 1997), some 90,000 live in Luxembourg-city and its immediate surroundings. The number of foreign residents in Luxembourg has already exceeded 32 % of the population. It is the highest proportion of foreigners of any EU country.

'**Lëtzebuergesch**' is the everyday spoken language of the people, and the symbol of the Luxembourgers national identity. Since the creation of a dictionary, and a grammar, this former Mosel-Frankish dialect is now recognised as the national language (since 1984), while both French and German remain the official languages. 'Lëtzebuergesch' or Luxembourgish is taught in schools and in language courses mostly addressed to the resident foreigners. Although of Germanic origin (around 11th century), Lëtzebuergesch has sufficiently differentiated itself from its parent language, so as no longer to be understood by most Germans. Indeed many French words (and a dash of English, for good measure) have been adopted into the language and were transformed, sometimes beyond recognition.

Both German and French culture meet in Luxembourg. Franco-German bilinguism, without any language differences, is a typical aspect of the country's social structure. If both German and French are used in the press, in political and in religious life, French is nevertheless the official language of the administration, jurisdiction, parliament, education, and of some literary circles. Public offices though are held to answer -wherever possible- in the language they are addressed in.

This peculiar language situation is a direct result of the size of the country, and its historic associations with both France and Germany. When going abroad -which after all, is not very far- the Luxembourgers have to speak other languages, simply because their own is not understood elsewhere.

Thus it comes as no surprise that many Luxembourgers speak English too. This is obviously more the case in the capital and in other centres, than in rural areas, where there is hardly a need for more than 2 foreign languages.

**For additional analytical, business and investment opportunities information, please contact Global Investment & Business Center, USA at (202) 546-2103. Fax: (202) 546-3275. E-mail: rusric@erols.com**

# IMPORTANT INFORMATION FOR UNDERSTANDING LUXEMBOURG[1]

**Official Name: Grand Duchy of Luxembourg**

## BASIC FACTS

National holiday: 23 June

Geography - Area: 2,586 sq. km Of which: agricultural: 49% wooded: 34%

Neighbouring countries: Germany, Belgium and France

Main towns: Luxembourg and Esch-sur-Alzette

Administrative subdivisions: 3 districts (Luxembourg, Diekirch and Grevenmacher) 12 cantons, 118 town council areas (communes)

Climate Temperate - From May to mid-October, the temperatures are particularly pleasant. Whereas May and June are the sunniest months, July and August are the hottest. In September and October Luxembourg often experiences his own "Indian Summer".

Population - Total population:

451,600 inhabitants, 81,800 of whom live in the City of Luxembourg. Over 174,200 (38.6%) people out of the total population are foreigners. (Source: STATEC January 2004)

The capital - City of Luxembourg Languages

National language: luxembourgish (lëtzebuergesch)

Administrative languages: French, German and Luxembourgish

Government - Form of government:

constitutional monarchy under a system of parliamentary democracy

Head of State: HRH Grand Duke Henri (since October 7, 2000)

Head of government: Jean-Claude Juncker, Prime Minister

Parties in power in the government:

coalition between the Christian-Social Party (CSV) and the Socialist Workers' Party of Luxembourg (LSAP)

Parties represented in the Chamber of Deputies:

[1] US STATE DEPARTMENT PROFILE

Christian-Social Party (CSV), Socialist Workers' Party of Luxembourg (LSAP), Democratic Party of Luxembourg (DP), The Greens (Déi Gréng), Action Committee for Democracy and Fair Pensions (ADR)

## ECONOMY

Currency: Euro

Unemployment Rate in Luxembourg increased to 6.60 percent in March of 2013 from 6.40 percent in February of 2013. Unemployment Rate in Luxembourg is reported by the STATEC Luxembourg. Historically, from 1982 until 2013, Luxembourg Unemployment Rate averaged 3.33 Percent reaching an all time high of 6.60 Percent in December of 2011 and a record low of 1.40 Percent in March of 1991. In Luxembourg, the unemployment rate measures the number of people actively looking for a job as a percentage of the labour force. This page includes a chart with historical data for Luxembourg Unemployment Rate.

Inflation rate: 2.0%

GDP (real growth rate): 2.1%

Number of banks 169 (Source: Statec)

Useful addresses :

Service information et presse du Gouvernement (Government Information and Press Service) 33, boulevard Roosevelt, L-2450 Luxembourg Tel.: (+352) 478 21 81, Fax: (+352) 47 02 85 www.gouvernement.lu www.luxembourg.lu info@sip.etat.lu

Service central de la statistique et des études économiques (STATEC) (Central Statistics and Economic Studies Service) 13, rue Erasme, bâtiment Pierre Werner,

B.P. 304, L-2013 Luxembourg Tel.: (+352) 478 42 52, Fax: (+352) 46 42 89 www.statec.lu info@statec.etat.lu

Ministère de l'Economie (Ministry of Economy)

6, boulevard Royal, L-2449 Luxembourg Tel.: (+352) 478 41 06, Fax: (+352) 46 04 48 www.eco.public.lu

Office national du Tourisme (National Tourist Office)

68-70, bvd. de la Pétrusse, B.P. 1001, L-1010 Luxembourg Tel.: (+352) 42 82 82 10, Fax: (+352) 42 82 82 38 www.ont.lu info@ont.lu

Service information et presse du gouvernement 33, bd Roosevelt L-2450 Luxembourg Tel.: (+352) 478-2181 Fax: (+352) 47 02 85 www.gouvernement.lu www.gouvernement.lu edition@sip.etat.lu

Languages

The linguistic situation in Luxembourg is characterized by the practice and recognition of three official languages – Luxembourgish, French and German. German is taught from the very first school year, while French is taught the following years. Moreover, German is the main language for primary education, as well as for the first few years of secondary classical and secondary technical education. French, however, is used predominantly in secondary classical education. The number of hours devoted to language teaching accounts for 50% of the total of subjects taught during the entire schooling. During these years, Luxembourgish remains the main teaching language.

Religion

Religious studies and moral and social education are compulsory in primary and secondary school.

The school system

Early education is aimed at children from the age of three. It helps children to socialize and immigrant children to integrate properly. This project was introduced for the start of the new school year 2000-2001. Early education is not compulsory. Preschool education is compulsory for children over four years of age on 1 September of the current year, in accordance with the grand-ducal regulation of 2 September 1992. Primary education takes six years and is intended for children having reached the age of six by 1 September of the current year. Post-primary education takes six or seven years depending on the orientation chosen and is split into two sections secondary education, which concentrates on classical subjects and prepares students for university, and technical secondary education, which offers practical and vocational training.

The University of Luxembourg commenced activity at the start of the academic year 2003/2004. It is the legal successor to the various higher education establishments it replaces. Teaching and research are organised in faculties, and interdisciplinary centres dealing with subjects that simultaneously relate to several disciplines. A complete university cycle has three study levels, each leading to a different degree. The first level is concluded with a Bachelor's Degree, the second a Master's Degree and the third a Doctorate. The period of study for the first two levels is five years. In principle, the period for the third level is at least three years. One of the University's vocations is to contribute to the initial and then continuing educational training of teachers for the Luxembourg school system. Another is to provide the necessary link between teaching and research activities. For that reason, it is involved in fundamental, applied and technological research. Research activities are carried out through projects implemented by virtue of agreements reached with national and international research institutions, organisations, companies and establishments.

Useful addresses:

Ministère de la Culture, de l'Enseignement supérieur et de la Recherche (Ministry of Culture, Higher Education and Research) 20, Montée de la Pétrusse, L-2273 Luxembourg Tel.: (+352) 478 66 19, Fax: (+352) 29 21 86 www.ltam.lu/culture

Ministère de l'Education nationale, de la Formation professionnelle et des Sports (Ministry of National Education, Vocational Training and Sport) 29, rue Aldringen, L-1118 Luxembourg Tel.: (+352) 478-5100, Fax: (+352) 478-5113 www.men.lu/ info@men.lu

Institut national pour le développement de la formation professionnelle continue (National Institute for the Development of Further Vocational Training)

38 rue de l'Avenir, L-1147 Luxembourg Tel.: (+352) 46 96 12 1, Fax: (+352) 46 96 20 www.lifelong-learning.lu info@lifelong-learning.lu

Université du Luxembourg

162a, avenue de la Faïencerie, L-1511 Luxembourg Tel.: (+352) 46 66 44-1, Fax: (+352) 46 66 44-506 www.uni.lu

Centre de psychologie et d'orientation scolaire (CPOS) (Psychology and Educational Guidance Centre)

280, route de Longwy, L-1940 Luxembourg Tel.: (+352) 45 64 64-1, Fax: (+352) 45 45 44 www.cpos.lu

Centre de documentation et d'information sur les études supérieures (CEDIES) 211, route d'Esch, L-1471 Luxembourg Tel.: (+352) 478 86 50, Fax: (+352) 45 56 56 cedies@mcesr.etat.lu

Service information et presse du gouvernement 33, bd Roosevelt L-2450 Luxembourg Tel.: (+352) 478-2181 Fax: (+352) 47 02 85 www.gouvernement.lu www.gouvernement.lu edition@sip.etat.lu

Forests cover almost 40% of the land. The country covers an area of 2,586 sq. km, 1,758 sq. km of which is in Gutland and the remaining 828 sq. km in Oesling. Its total population in January 2004 was 451,600.

The capital

The City of Luxembourg has a population of 81.800. Visitors never fail to be surprised by the contrast between the modern upper city, perched on a rocky plateau that's a modern sheer drop, and the three lower old towns, Grund ("the Bottom"), Clausen and Pfaffenthal. The European quarter that is home to the European institutions has been spreading over the Kirchberg plateau to the north-west of the city since the 1960s. The City of Luxembourg is at an altitude of 300 m above sea level.

The regions

The variety of Luxembourg's landscapes is one of its main attractions, despite being divided into just two main regions, Oesling and Gutland.

• The Oesling, in the north, is part of the Ardennes massif and borders Germany's Eifel plateau. This wooded region occupies a third of the country and attracts many tourists. It is also the highest region in Luxembourg, rising to some 560 m (Wilwerdange). Oesling has a harsh climate and is an area of highland villages, lakes and rivers with oak and pine forests covering its steep slopes. Its main towns are Wiltz, Vianden and Clervaux.

- The Troisvierges plateau, to the north of the Oesling, is mainly arable land and has few forests. It is the coldest and wettest area in Luxembourg.

-The Ardennes plateau, traversed by rivers below the Wiltz basin, is the area most typical of the Oesling. Its landscapes are rich in contrasts of form and colour, plateau and forest.

**For additional analytical, business and investment opportunities information, please contact Global Investment & Business Center, USA at (202) 546-2103. Fax: (202) 546-3275. E-mail: rusric@erols.com**

The area where the Oesling and the Gutland meet is one of the country's foremost agricultural regions thanks to its rich and varied soils.

• The Gutland occupies the south and centre of Luxembourg and forms the rest of the country (68%). It is mainly open countryside and forests. Its has six main regions:

- Luxembourg's Sandstone plateau is the dominating feature of Gutland. It includes some of Luxembourg's finest forests. The capital is its only town.

-Marly depressions are the most widespread and typical landscapes in Gutland. Extending to the foot of the Dogger hills and Luxembourg Sandstone, they are made up of sweeping valleys. More than two thirds of the area are given over to farming.

-The Moselle valley is the most imposing valley in Luxembourg, owing to its size and the variety of its countryside. It is one of the main magnets attracting visitors to the country, largely due to its winemaking activities.

-Petite Suisse ("Little Switzerland") or "Müllerthal" lies to the north of the Moselle valley, on the border with Germany. Its main town, Echternach, is one of the oldest in Luxembourg.

-The Terres Rouges ("Red Lands") are located to the south of the marly depressions. Here industry has moulded the landscape, iron ore having been extracted from the red land. Its main towns are Esch-sur-Alzette, the second largest in Luxembourg, Dudelange and Differdange.

-The Valley of the Seven Castles is a 24-km area that includes the châteaux of Mersch, Schoenfels and Hollenfels, the two châteaux of Ansembourg and the châteaux of Septfontaines and Koerich. These castles are set in a landscape of meadows and old villages, making them the perfect settings for many enchanting walks.

Climate

Luxembourg does not have a clearly defined climate: it varies between the oceanic climate of the Atlantic zone (small seasonal differences and mild, wet winters) and the continental climate of the eastern European plains (strong seasonal differences, harsh winters and wet summers). The oceanic influence brings rain in every season, while the continental influence brings a biting dry cold in the winter. The average temperature ranges between 0°C in January and 17°C in July. The difference in temperature between the north and south rarely exceeds 2°C.

The river system

The four largest rivers in the Grand Duchy are the Moselle, Sûre, Our and Alzette. The others are: the Mess, Mamer, Eisch, Attert and Wark in west; the Wiltz, Clerve and Blees in the north ; and the White Ernz, the Black Ernz, Syr and Gander in the east. The Pétrusse is a stream that crosses the City of Luxembourg, before flowing into the Alzette. With the exception of the Chiers, which leaves the south-west of the country on its way to the Meuse basin, Luxembourg's rivers are tributaries of the Rhine basin by way of the Moselle.

Administrative division

The country is divided into three districts (Luxembourg, Diekirch and Grevenmacher), 12 cantons, 118 town council areas (communes) and four constituencies. The district of Luxembourg comprises the cantons of Luxembourg, Capellen, Esch-sur-Alzette and Mersch; the district of

Diekirch comprises those of Diekirch, Clervaux, Redange, Vianden and Wiltz, and the district of Grevenmacher includes those of Grevenmacher, Echternach and Remich. The district commissioners have a monitoring role and act as intermediaries between the government and local authorities.

Useful addresses:

Ministère de l'Environnement (Ministry of the Environment) 18, Montée de la Pétrusse, L-2327 Luxembourg Tel.: (+352) 478 68 24, Fax: (+352) 40 04 10 www.mev.etat.lu

Office national du Tourisme (National Tourist Office) 68-70 bd. De la Pétrusse, B.P. 1001, L-1010 Luxembourg Tel.: (+352) 42 82 82 10, Fax: (+352) 42 82 82 38 www.ont.lu info@ont.lu

Luxembourg City Tourist Office Place d'Armes, L-2011 Luxembourg Tel.: (+352) 22 28 09, Fax: (+352) 46 70 70 www.lcto.lu touristinfo@lcto.lu

Ministère des Classes moyennes, du Tourisme et du Logement (Ministry of Small and Medium-sized Businesses and the Self-Employed, of Tourism and of Housing) 6, avenue Emile Reuter, L-2420 Luxembourg Tel.: (+352) 478 47 06, Fax: (+352) 47 40 11 (tourisme) www.mdt.public.lu info@mdt.public.lu

Musée national d'histoire naturelle (Museum of Natural History) 25, rue Münster, L-2160 Luxembourg Tel.: (+352) 46 22 331, Fax: (+352) 47 51 52 www.mnhn.lu musee-info@mnhn.lu

Administration du cadastre et de la topographie (Land Registry & Topography Department) 54, avenue Gaston Diderich, L-1420 Luxembourg Tel.: (+352) 44 90 11, Fax: (+352) 449 01 333 www.act.etat.lu

Service information et presse du gouvernement 33, bd Roosevelt L-2450 Luxembourg Tel.: (+352) 478-2181 Fax: (+352) 47 02 85 www.gouvernement.lu www.gouvernement.lu edition@sip.etat.lu

Sigefroid became the owner of a rock on which he had a fortified castle built. A city grew around this site and then a country... so that Sigefroid is considered the founder of Luxembourg. Luxembourg remained a relatively independent principality attached to the German Empire until 1354. The country then lost its status as earldom and was elevated to that of duchy, also and importantly acquiring the earldom of Chiny. From the 13th century, Luxembourg started to develop into a true principality.

From the dukes of Burgundy to the Netherlands

The dynasty of the counts of Luxembourg died out in 1437 and the flame passed on to the Hapsburgs of Spain. Luxembourg's acquisition by Philip the Good of Burgundy in 1443 proved decisive in its destiny. Incorporated in the Burgundian state and then in the Netherlands, Luxembourg became an intermediary between the kingdom of France and the German Empire. The death of Charles the Bold, Philip the Good's son, put an end to the Burgundian era, and the principalities of the North passed to the Austrian Hapsburgs in 1715. They formed a confederation called the Netherlands, to which Luxembourg belonged until 1839. Luxembourg was incorporated into the French Republic in 1795, and was given the name Département des Forêts (Department of the Forests). It had already been under French occupation during the reign of Louis XIV, during which time Vauban fortified the City of Luxembourg.

Luxembourg as an independent country

The Congress of Vienna elevated the Duchy of Luxembourg to the rank of Grand Duchy in 1815, theoretically making it independent, while linking it by personal union to the Netherlands. The two were recognized as separate countries but ruled by the same sovereign: William I of Orange-Nassau, King of the Netherlands, Grand Duke of Luxembourg.

The 1839 Treaty of London marked the starting point of Luxembourg's history as an independent country. It cut Luxembourg in two, giving the French-speaking half to Belgium, while the German-speaking half continued to form the Grand Duchy. It was from that moment on that Luxembourg's national identity truly came to be forged, in particular with the appearance of its first national anthem in 1859. But Luxembourg realized it could not be self-sufficient. So William II integrated it into a customs union with Germany, the Zollverein in 1842.

The progress of the Grand Duchy up to World War II

The country enjoyed strong economic growth during this period, with the discovery of mining fields and the building of railways to carry coal (Luxembourg forms a large coal basin with Lorraine). The rising demand for labour led to heavy immigration. The personal union between Luxembourg and the Netherlands ended in 1890 with the death of the last male descendant of the Orange-Nassau line, and the crown passed to the Nassau-Weilburg branch, the only Nassovian line with a male descendant. It was then that Luxembourg finally gained its own dynasty, with Grand Duke Adolf as the country's first representative. Germany's unsuccessful attempt to annex Luxembourg in 1914, which risked violating the neutrality the country had enjoyed since 1867, incited Luxembourg to gain its independence and to leave the Zollverein. The Grand Duchy thus entered into an economic union with Belgium in 1921, known as the Belgo-Luxembourg Economic Union (BLEU). It subsequently adopted the Belgian franc as the Union's currency, while keeping the Luxembourg franc in limited issue.

The interwar years

The economic depression of the immediate postwar years was followed by a period of prosperity. But from 1929, Luxembourg was affected by the world economic crisis. In the steel sector, it looked, above all, to France as a supplier of iron ore, and to Germany as a market for its steel products.

World War II and reconstruction within the European Union

During the Second World War, Luxembourg suffered forced germanization at the hands of its German occupier. Moreover, 2% of the total population lost their lives during World War II (1.5% in France). This trauma was the source of a powerful desire for regeneration. Economic opening to the outside world became the Grand Duchy's priority. Needing to form part of a larger market, Luxembourg abandoned its neutrality, becoming a founding member of UNO in 1945 and a member of NATO in 1949. The Belgo-Luxembourg Economic Union (BLEU), which had come to an end under the occupation, was reinstated after the liberation. Luxembourg became a member of the European Coal and Steel Community (ECSC) in 1951 - since the steel industry accounted for 75% of its industrial output - and of the European Economic Community (EEC) in 1957. The ECSC became the foundation for a new period of growth, while membership of the EEC marked the starting point of economic expansion. As the first workplace of the ECSC, the City of Luxembourg became one of the three headquarters of the European Union, alongside Strasbourg and Brussels. The birth of a large financial centre, accompanied by the intensification of Luxembourg's integration in the European Union, made it one of Europe's most cosmopolitan cities from the 1960s onwards. Luxembourg's financial centre also enabled the country to

**For additional analytical, business and investment opportunities information, please contact Global Investment & Business Center, USA at (202) 546-2103. Fax: (202) 546-3275. E-mail: rusric@erols.com**

overcome the 1974-75 steel crisis. Today, Luxembourg is strongly represented on the international stage, where it plays an active role, particularly in the field of cooperation with aid to developing countries. Foreigners account for 38.6% of Luxembourg's population. It is also considered a microcosm of Europe and a model of opening to the outside world. Moreover, thanks to its small size, Luxembourg enjoys a well-deserved image as a peaceful country on a "human scale".

Useful addresses:

Ministère de la Culture, de l'Enseignement Supérieur et de la Recherche (Ministry of Culture, Higher Education and Research)

20, Montée de la Pétrusse, L-2273 Luxembourg Tel.: (+352) 478 66 19, Fax: (+352) 40 24 27 www.ltam.lu/culture

Archives nationales du Luxembourg (Luxembourg National Archives)

Plateau du Saint-Esprit, L-2010 Luxembourg Tel.: (+352) 478 66 61, Fax: (+352) 47 46 92 www.an.etat.lu archives nationales@an.etat.lu

Musée national d'histoire et d'art (National Museum of History and Art)

Marché-aux-Poissons, L-2345 Luxembourg Tel.: (+352) 47 93 30-1, Fax: (+352) 93 20 271 www.mnha.lu musee@mnha.etat.lu

Musée d'histoire de la Ville de Luxembourg (Museum of the History of the City of Luxembourg)

14, rue du Saint-Esprit, L-2090 Luxembourg Tel.: (+352) 47 96 45 00, Fax: (+352) 47 17 07 www.musee-hist.lu musee-hist@musee-hist.lu

Bibliothèque nationale de Luxembourg (National Library of Luxembourg)

37, boulevard F.D. Roosevelt, L-2450 Luxembourg Tel.: (+352) 22 97 55 1, Fax: (+352) 47 56 72 www.bnl.lu bib.nat@bi.etat.lu

Service information et presse du gouvernement 33, bd Roosevelt L-2450 Luxembourg Tel.: (+352) 478-2181 Fax: (+352) 47 02 85

www.gouvernement.lu

www.gouvernement.lu edition@sip.etat.lu

## THE CURRENT SITUATION

The current linguistic situation in Luxembourg follows the logical thread of the country's history. Hierarchical bilingualism still reigns, but acquired a new significance from the time of the constitutional amendment of 1948. In effect, this amendment gave the legislator the power to determine the linguistic regime by law. This new option led the Parliament to vote a law in 1984 which, at first glance, changes nothing to the traditional situation of bilingualism. However, for the first time, the Parliament officially acknowledged the linguistic identity of Luxembourgish by determining it as a national language. The law of 1984 recognizes the three languages of Luxembourg - Luxembourgish, French and German - as official languages. This parity is slightly moderated in a provision of the above law (Article 3), which mentions that citizens must use the three languages "in as far as possible". It has to be admitted that French remains the language of legislation (Article 2), since the origins of this legislation are founded in the Napoleonic Code.

Bilingualism or trilingualism?

Bilingualism having been transformed into official trilingualism, no one would dare to suppress French and German in order to promote Luxembourgish. The importance of French and German is not just political, but represents the national identity borne of the co-existence between the Romance and Germanic worlds. By maintaining these two languages, Luxembourg remains the symbol of a meeting place between Romance and Germanic culture, as well as many other cultures nowadays. The recognition of Luxembourgish serves to reinforce and enrich traditional bilingualism.

The socio-political dimension of trilingualism

It is mainly during pre-school education that teachers speak Luxembourgish to their pupils. Young children learn to read and write in German from the first year of primary school, and then learn to read and write in French from the second year onwards. Luxembourgish is only taught for one hour per week only during the early years of secondary school. Linguistic practice in schools also reflects the situation of the country in terms of language use, characterized by an openness towards Europe in terms of politics and higher education. Indeed, the number of hours devoted to language-learning during the whole of a student's school career and over all sectors of education represents 50% of the total for all subjects. On the political level, this perfect command of two major European languages has enabled Luxembourg to integrate easily into the European structure and even to become a unifying and progressionist force. At university level, trilingualism enables Luxembourg students to pursue university studies in any French-, German-or English-speaking country. Indeed, English is taught intensively in secondary school in addition to other optional languages, such as Latin, Spanish or Italian. This linguistic situation favours adaptation among incomers from abroad to daily life in Luxembourg, since they may also express themselves in French or German. Trilingualism thus represents both openness towards the outside and the desire to receive those from outside in Luxembourg.

Some words in "Lëtzebuergesch"

Useful addresses:

Moien Hello

Äddi Goodbye

Wéi geet et? How are you ?

Mir geet et gutt/schlecht I'm feeling fine/ bad

Wou ass...? Where is...?

... de Bäcker? ... the bakery ?

Ministère de l'Education nationale, de la Formation professionnelle et des Sports (Ministry of National Education, Vocational Training and Sports)

29, rue Aldringen, L-1118 Luxembourg Tel.: (+352) 478-5100, Fax: (+352) 478-5113 www.men.lu info@men.lu

Ministère de la Culture, de l'Enseignement supérieur et de la Recherche (Ministry of Culture, Higher Education and Research)

20, Montée de la Pétrusse, L-2273 Luxembourg Tel.: (+352) 478 66 19, Fax: (+352) 40 24 27 www.ltam.lu/culture

Institut Grand-Ducal, section de linguistique, d'ethnologie et d'onomastique (Grand-Ducal Institute, Languages Section)

2a, rue Kalchesbruck, L-1852 Luxembourg Tel.: (+352) 478 27 90, Fax: (+352) 478 27 92 www.igd-leo.lu leo.contact@igd-leo.lu

Centre national de Littérature (National Literature Centre)

2, rue Emmanuel Servais, L-7565 Mersch Tel.: (+352) 32 69 55-1, Fax: (+352) 32 70 90 www.cnl.public.lu info@cnl.public.lu

Conseil permanent de la langue luxembourgeoise (Permanent Council of the Luxembourgish Language) www.cpll.lu cpll.contact@cpll.lu

... de Metzler ? ... the butcher's ?

... e gudde Restaurant ? ... a good Restaurant? ... d'Gare? ... the train station ? ... d'Bank? ... the bank ?

... de Kino? ... the cinema/movie theater ? ... de Flughafen? ... the airport? Wéivill kascht dat? How much does it cost?

Kann ech de Menu kréien? Could you please give me the menu?

Merci Thank you

Jo Yes

Neen No

Watglift? I beg your pardon?

Gär geschitt! You are welcome! Pardon Sorry Ech hun en Zëmmer reservéiert I have booked a room

Service information et presse du gouvernement 33, bd Roosevelt L-2450 Luxembourg Tel.: (+352) 478-2181 Fax: (+352) 47 02 85 www.gouvernement.lu www.gouvernement.lu edition@sip.etat.lu

## POPULATION

Today it stands at 451,600. In other words, it has more than doubled in the space of a century. However, this growth has been uneven and can be divided into four main periods: a phase of decline during the first four decades, a (slight) baby boom between 1950 and 1960, a very rapid decline which became stable between 1960 and 1980, and a renewed growth phase since the 1990s due to an increase in the birthrate, which is largely the result of a rise in immigration.

A plural society

Before the First World War, much of the country's population tended to emigrate overseas, mainly for economic reasons. However, industrialization, since the end of the 19th century, has gradually turned Luxembourg from a country of emigration into a country of immigration. In the past 30 years, immigration has increased considerably. Today, more than a third of the population is non-Luxembourgish (over 174,600, or approximately 38.6% of the population). The well-integrated foreign residents and cross-border workers account for much of the active population. More than 150 nationalities are cohabiting in Luxembourg. The main communities present in Luxembourg are the Portuguese and Italians, followed by the French, Belgians and Germans. Today, over 50% of the population of Luxembourg City is foreign.

less goes hand in hand with an increase of the number of people aged 65 or over, while the intermediary age group has remained stable. Furthermore, the number of people aged 65 or over has quadrupled this century.

- Decrease in family size: At the last census in 1991, more than a quarter of private households were made up of people living on their own. In 2003, the average fertility rate was 1.63 children per woman. In 2003, the total number of births decreased by 0.8% in comparison with 2002. The foreign birthrate rose by 4.9% and accounts for 52.5% of the total number of births.

- Population and employment: Employment rose steadily during the second half of the 20th century. The European institutions settled in Luxembourg in the 1950s and, ten tears later, Luxembourg became a major financial centre. The past 15 years have witnessed a sharp rise in the number of cross-border workers and an increase in female employment.

## LUXEMBOURG NATIONALITY

Normally, nationality is determined by birth. Each year, however, more than 1,000 foreign nationals obtain Luxembourg nationality through option or naturalization. Those who already have ties with Luxembourg either by birth or blood can obtain Luxembourg nationality between the ages of 18 and 25, through a declaration of option under one of the following conditions: they must have been born in Luxembourg by foreign parents, be married to a Luxembourger, have completed their entire education in Luxembourg or have resided in Luxembourg for the past five years. They will also have to give up their original nationality. Foreigners can also obtain Luxembourg nationality through naturalization, if they are above the age of 18 and have resided in Luxembourg for at least five years. Besides, they must have an active and passive knowledge of one of the three official languages (German, French, Luxembourgish). Thus, a foreigner who masters perfectly French will have to prove that he has a basic knowledge of Luxembourgish. On the contrary, a person who masters Luxembourgish will not be required to know French or German to be eligible to obtain Luxembourgish nationality.

Useful addresses:

Ministère de la Famille, de la Solidarité sociale et de la Jeunesse (Ministry of Family Affairs, Social Support and Youth) 12-14, avenue Emile Reuter, L-2420 Luxembourg Tel.: (+352) 478 65 06, Fax: (+352) 478 65 70

Ministère de l'Egalité des chances (Ministry for Equal Opportunities)

33, boulevard Prince-Henri, L-1724 Luxembourg Tel.: (+352) 478 58 14, Fax: (+352) 24 18 86 www.mega.public.lu info@mega.public.lu

Ministère du Travail et de l'Emploi (Ministry of Labour and Employment)

26, rue Sainte-Zithe, L-2763 Luxembourg Tel.: (+352) 478 61 06, Fax: (+352) 478 63 25 www.mt.etat.lu

Ministère de la Justice (Ministry of Justice)

13, rue Erasme, bâtiment Pierre Werner, L-1468 Luxembourg-Kirchberg Tel.: (+352) 478 45 06, Fax: (+352) 22 76 61 www.mj.public.lu

Service central de la statistique et des etudes économiques (STATEC) (Central Service for Statistics and Economic Studies)

13, rue Erasme, bâtiment Pierre Werner,

B.P. 304, L-2013 Luxembourg Tél.: (+352) 478 42 52, Fax: (+352) 46 42 89 www.statec.lu info@statec.etat.lu

Service information et presse du gouvernement 33, bd Roosevelt L-2450 Luxembourg Tel.: (+352) 478-2181 Fax: (+352) 47 02 85 www.gouvernement.lu

Today, the flag of Luxembourg consists of three bands in red, white and sky-blue, arranged horizontally. Even though the flags of Luxembourg and the Netherlands are very similar, the distinctive element of the Dutch flag is the band in ultramarine. The majority of modern tricolour flags are derived to a greater or lesser degree from the tricolour of the first French Republic. Even the ancient Dutch flag was only officially defined as being in red, white and blue in 1795, under French influence, by the Batavian Republic. Therefore, we can only guess whether the colours of Luxembourg are really national or derived from the Dutch flag after 1815. On the other hand, it is probable that the people of Luxembourg accepted the colours of the Dutch flag because they were those of their coat of arms. The flag of Luxembourg, as well as the state coats of arms, have enjoyed legal protection only since 1972. The red colour corresponds to the norm Pantone 032C and the blue colour to the norm Pantone 299C. (source : Memorial A n°73 of 09.16.1993)

The national anthem

The national anthem is made up of the first and last verses of the song "Ons Heemecht" ("Our homeland") from 1859, a text by the poet Michel Lentz, set to music by Jean-Antoine Zinnen. It was played in public for the first time at a grand ceremony in Ettelbruck in 1864. Unlike the Marseillaise, which is an invitation to combat, the national anthem of Luxembourg is an ardent call for peace. This anthem expresses all the joy of a country which had finally found independence in an atmosphere of harmony and prosperity. The "Wilhelmus", the authem of the grand-ducal family, is played when one of the members of the family arrives at or leaves a ceremony.

During the long reign of Grand Duchess Charlotte from 1919 to 1964, this celebration always took place in mid-winter, on 23 January, on the sovereign's birthday. In 1961, in particular due to the weather at that time of year, it was decided to transfer the public celebration of the sovereign's birthday, and thus National Day, to the 23 June of each year. Festivities commence on the evening before. Since 23 December 1961, the National-Day celebrations have been laid down in a grand-ducal decree. The term "national festival" does not figure in the legal texts, the day being described instead as "day of the official celebration of the anniversary of the birth of the Grand Duke".

The coats of arms

The coats of arms of the Grand Duchy of Luxembourg are on three scales: small, medium and large. The origins of the coats of arms of the State of Luxembourg date back to the Middle Ages. They were established around 1235 by Count Henry V of Luxembourg. The coats of arms are essentially composed of a barrully of silver and azure in ten parts and a lion gules, armed, langued and crowned with gold, its tail forked and looped. From 1123, Count William of Luxembourg wore a barred banner on his equestrian seal. The majority of the descendants of the first House of Luxembourg used a barrully, while the descendants of the House of Namur bore a lion. The coats of arms have enjoyed legal protection since 1972. The law of 17 June 1993 amended and supplemented the law of 1972.

Useful addresses:

Commission héraldique (Heraldry Commission)

4, rue Jules Wilhelm, L-2728 Luxembourg Fax: (+352) 42 27 97

Ministère de la Culture, de l'Enseignement supérieur et de la Recherche (Ministry of Culture, Higher Education and Research)

20, Montée de la Pétrusse, L-2273 Luxembourg Tel.: (+352) 478 66 19, Fax: (+352) 40 21 86 www.ltam.lu/culture

Archives nationales (National Archives)

Plateau du Saint-Esprit, L-2012 Luxembourg Tel.: (+352) 478 66 60, Fax: (+352) 47 46 92 www.an.etat.lu archives.nationales@an.etat.lu

Service information et presse du gouvernement 33, bd Roosevelt L-2450 Luxembourg Tel.: (+352) 478-2181 Fax: (+352) 47 02 85

## BASIC PROFILE

## HISTORY

The language of Luxembourg is Luxembourgish, a blend of old German and Frankish elements. The official language of the civil service, law, and parliament is French, although criminal and legal debates are conducted partly in Luxembourgish and police case files are recorded in

German. German is the primary language of the press. French and German are taught in the schools, with German spoken mainly at the primary level and French at the secondary level.

June 9, 1815, after 400 years of domination by various European nations, Luxembourg was made a grand duchy by the Congress of Vienna. It was granted political autonomy in 1838 under King William I of the Netherlands, who also was the Grand Duke of Luxembourg. The country considers 1835 to be its year of independence. In 1867, Luxembourg was recognized as independent and guaranteed perpetual neutrality. After being occupied by Germany in both World Wars, however, Luxembourg abandoned neutrality and became a charter member of the North Atlantic Treaty Organization (NATO) in 1949.

The present sovereign, Grand Duke Jean, succeeded his mother, Grand Duchess Charlotte, on November 12, 1964. Grand Duke Jean's eldest son, Prince Henri, was appointed "Lieutenant Représentant" (Hereditary Grand Duke) on March 4, 1998. On December 24, 1999, Prime Minister Juncker announced Grand Duke Jean's decision to abdicate the throne in September 2000, in favor of Prince Henri who assumed the title and constitutional duties of Grand Duke.

## GOVERNMENT

Luxembourg has a parliamentary form of government with a constitutional monarchy by inheritance. Under the constitution of 1868, as amended, executive power is exercised by the Grand Duke and the Council of Government (cabinet), which consists of a prime minister and several other ministers. The prime minister is the leader of the political party or coalition of parties having the most seats in parliament.

Legislative power is vested in the Chamber of Deputies, elected directly to 5-year terms. A second body, the "Conseil d'Etat" (Council of State), composed of 21 ordinary citizens appointed by the Grand Duke, advises the Chamber of Deputies in the drafting of legislation. The responsibilities of the members of the Conseil d'Etat are extracurricular to their normal professional duties.

Luxembourg law is a composite of local practice, legal tradition, and French, Belgian, and German systems. The apex of the judicial system is the superior court, whose judges are appointed by the Grand Duke.

### PRINCIPAL GOVERNMENT OFFICIALS

Chief of State -- Grand Duke Jean of Luxembourg

Grand Duke, **HENRI**
Prime Min., **Jean-Claude JUNCKER**
Dep. Prime Min., **Jean ASSELBORN**
Min. of Admin. Simplification, **Octavie MODERT**
Min. of Agriculture, Viticulture, & Rural Development, **Romain SCHNEIDER**
Min. of Civil Service & Admin. Reform, **Francois BILTGEN**
Min. for Communications, **Francois BILTGEN**
Min. of Culture, **Octavie MODERT**
Min. of Defense, **Jean-Marie HALSDORF**
Min. for Development Cooperation & Humanitarian Affairs, **Marie-Josee JACOBS**
Min. of Economy & Foreign Trade, **Etienne SCHNEIDER**
Min. of Equality of Opportunity, **Francoise HETTO-GAASCH**
Min. of Family & Integration, **Marie-Josee JACOBS**
Min. of Finance, **Luc FRIEDEN**

**For additional analytical, business and investment opportunities information, please contact Global Investment & Business Center, USA at (202) 546-2103. Fax: (202) 546-3275. E-mail: rusric@erols.com**

Min. of Foreign Affairs, **Jean ASSELBORN**
Min. of Health & of Social Security, **Mars DI BARTOLOMEO**
Min. of Higher Education & Research, **Francois BILTGEN**
Min. of Housing, **Marco SCHANK**
Min. of Interior, **Jean-Marie HALSDORF**
Min. of Justice, **Francois BILTGEN**
Min. of Labor, Employment, & Immigration, **Nicolas SCHMIT**
Min. of the Middle Class & Tourism, **Francoise HETTO-GAASCH**
Min. of National Education & Professional Training, **Mady DELVAUX-STEHRES**
Min. of Public Works, **Claude WISELER**
Min. of Relations With Parliament, **Octavie MODERT**
Min. of Religious Sects, **Francois BILTGEN**
Min. of Sports, **Romain SCHNEIDER**
Min. of State, **Jean-Claude JUNCKER**
Min. of Treasury, **Jean-Claude JUNCKER**
Chmn., Luxembourg Central Bank, **Gaston REINESCH**
Ambassador to the US, **Jean-Louis WOLZFELD**
Permanent Representative to the UN, New York, **Sylvie LUCAS**

Luxembourg maintains an embassy in the United States at 2200 Massachusetts Avenue, NW, Washington, DC 20006 (tel. 202-265-4171). Consulates or honorary consulates are located in many U.S. cities.

## POLITICAL CONDITIONS

Since the end of World War II, the Christian Social Party (CSV) has usually been the dominant partner in governing coalitions. The Roman Catholic-oriented CSV resembles Christian Democratic parties in other west European countries and enjoys broad popular support. However, in June 1999, national elections ushered in a new government. For the first time since 1974, the Socialist Party (LSAP) ceded its junior coalition position with the long-reigning CSV majority to the Liberal Democrat Party (DP).

The DP is a center party, drawing support from the professions, merchants, and urban middle class. Like other west European liberal parties, it advocates both social legislation and minimum government involvement in the economy. It also is strongly pro-NATO. In the opposition since 1984, the DP had been a partner in the three previous consecutive coalition governments.

The Communist Party (PCL), which received 10%-18% of the vote in national elections from World War II to the 1960s, won only two seats in the 1984 elections, one in 1989, and none in 1994. Its small remaining support lies in the "steel belt" of the industrialized south.

The Green Party has received growing support since it was officially formed in 1983. It opposes both nuclear weapons and nuclear power and supports environmental and ecological preservation measures. This party generally opposes Luxembourg's military policies, including its membership in NATO.

National elections are held at least every 5 years and municipal elections every 6 years. In the June 1999 parliamentary elections, the CSV won 19, the DP 15, the LSAP 13, the ADR (a single-issue party that emerged from the LSAP focused on pension rights) 6, the "Greens" 5, and the PCL 1. Hence, for the first time since 1974, the Socialists (LSAP) ceded their junior coalition position with the long-reigning Christian Socialist (CSV) majority to the Liberal Democrats. Jean-

Claude Juncker (CSV) remained for a second 5-year term as Prime Minister, and Lydie Polfer (DP), the former Luxembourg City mayor, was named Vice Prime Minister and Foreign Minister.

Somewhat unexpectedly, the Socialists gained ground in the October 10, 1999 municipal elections, with candidates taking 34% of municipal seats nationwide, including seven town mayorships. In Luxembourg City, the Grand Duchy's largest municipality, the electorate followed its postwar voting pattern and chose Liberal Democrat Paul Helminger, who had been named to finish Lydie Polfer's term when she became Foreign Minister.

## ECONOMY

Although Luxembourg in tourist literature is aptly called the "Green Heart of Europe," its pastoral land coexists with a highly industrialized and export-intensive economy. Luxembourg enjoys a degree of economic prosperity almost unique among industrialized democracies.

In 1876, English metallurgist Sidney Thomas invented a refining process that led to the development of the steel industry in Luxembourg and the founding of the Arbed company in 1911 -- now the second-largest steel producer in Europe. The iron and steel industry, located along the French border, is the most important single sector of the economy. Steel accounts for 29% of all exports (excluding services), 1.8% of GDP, 22% of industrial employment, and 3.9% of the work force.

The restructuring of the industry and increasing government ownership in Arbed (31%) began as early as 1974. As a result of timely modernization of facilities, cutbacks in production and employment, government assumption of portions of Arbed's debt, and recent cyclical recovery of the international demand for steel, the company is again profitable. Its productivity is among the highest in the world. U.S. markets account for about 6% of Arbed's output. The company specializes in production of large architectural steel beams and specialized value-added products.

There has been, however, a relative decline in the steel sector, offset by Luxembourg's emergence as a financial center. Banking is especially important. In 1997, there were 215 banks in Luxembourg, with 21,000 employees. Political stability, good communications, easy access to other European centers, skilled multilingual staff, and a tradition of banking secrecy have all contributed to the growth of the financial sector. Germany accounts for the largest-single grouping of banks, with Scandinavian, Japanese, and major U.S. banks also heavily represented. Total assets exceeded $200 billion at the end of 1996, of which some 81% was denominated in foreign currencies, primarily U.S. dollars and German marks. More than 9,000 holding companies are established in Luxembourg. The European Investment Bank -- the financial institution of the European Union -- also is located there.

Government policies promote the development of Luxembourg as an audiovisual and communications center. Radio-Television-Luxembourg is Europe's premier private radio and television broadcaster. The government-backed Luxembourg satellite company "Societe Europeenne des Satellites" (SES) was created in 1986 to install and operate a satellite telecommunications system for transmission of television programs throughout Europe. The first SES "ASTRA" satellite, a 16-channel RCA 4000, was launched by Ariane Rocket in December 1988. SES presently operates five satellites with two more to be launched before the year 2000.

Luxembourg offers a favorable climate to foreign investment. Successive governments have effectively attracted new investment in medium, light, and high-tech industry. Incentives cover taxes, construction, and plant equipment. U.S. firms are among the most prominent foreign investors, producing tires (Goodyear), chemicals (Dupont), glass (Guardian Industries), and a wide range of industrial equipment. The current value of U.S. direct investment is almost $1.4 billion, on a per capita basis -- the highest level of U.S. direct investment outside of North America.

Labor relations have been peaceful since the 1930s. Most industrial workers are organized by unions linked to one of the major political parties. Representatives of business, unions, and government participate in the conduct of major labor negotiations.

Foreign investors often cite Luxembourg's labor relations as a primary reason for locating in the Grand Duchy. Unemployment in 1999 averaged less than 2.8% of the work force.

Luxembourg's small but productive agricultural sector provides employment for about 1%-3% of the work force. Most farmers are engaged in dairy and meat production. Vineyards in the Moselle Valley annually produce about 15 million liters of dry white wine, most of which is consumed locally.

Luxembourg's trade account has run a persistent deficit over the last decade, but the country enjoys an overall balance-of-payment surplus, due to revenues from financial services. Government finances are strong, and budgets are normally in surplus.

## FOREIGN RELATIONS

Luxembourg has long been a prominent supporter of European political and economic integration. In efforts foreshadowing European integration, Luxembourg and Belgium in 1921 formed the Belgium-Luxembourg Economic Union (BLEU) to create an inter-exchangeable currency and a common customs regime. Luxembourg is a member of the Benelux Economic Union and was one of the founding members of the European Economic Community (now the European Union). It also participates in the Schengen Group, whose goal is the free movement of citizens among member states. At the same time, Luxembourgers have consistently recognized that European unity makes sense only in the context of a dynamic, transatlantic relationship and have traditionally pursued a pro-NATO, pro-U.S. foreign policy.

Luxembourg is the site of the European Court of Justice, the European Court of Auditors, and other vital EU organs. The Secretariat of the European Parliament is located in Luxembourg, but the Parliament usually meets in nearby Strasbourg.

## DEFENSE

The Luxembourg army is under civilian control. Responsibility for defense matters is vested in the Minister of Cooperation, Humanitarian Action and Defense, Charles Goerens, under the Ministry of Foreign Affairs, Trade, Cooperation and Defense.

Luxembourg has no navy or air force. A 1967 law made the army an all-volunteer force with current strength of approximatel 450 professional soldiers, about 340 enlisted recruits and 100 civilians, and a total budget of $120 million. Luxembourg has participated in the European Corps (EUROCORPS) since 1994, has contributed troops to the UNPROFOR and IFOR missions in former Yugoslavia, and participates with a small contingent in the current NATO SFOR mission in Bosnia. The Luxembourg army is integrated into the Multinational Beluga Force under Belgian command. Luxembourg has financially supported international peacekeeping missions during the 1991 Gulf war, in Rwanda and, more recently, Albania. The army also has participated in humanitarian relief missions such as setting up refugee camps for Kurds and providing emergency supplies to Albania.

# U.S. RELATIONS

Bilateral relations between the United States and Luxembourg are excellent, both historically and through common membership in the Organization for Cooperation and Economic Development (OECD), OSCE, and NATO. More than 5,000 American soldiers, including Gen. George S. Patton, are buried at the American Military Cemetery near the capital.

### PRINCIPAL U.S. OFFICIALS

Ambassador--Ann Wagner
Deputy Chief of Mission--Steve Kraft
Management Officer--Jay Parker
Political/Economic Chief--Tom Boughter
Public Affairs Officer--Anthony Clare
Regional Security Officer--Jeff Rusinek
Economic Officer--Jason Chiodi
Vice-Consul/Political Officer--Caroline Savage
Commercial Assistant--Carla Rosen-Vacher

The U.S. Embassy in Luxembourg is located at 22 Boulevard Emmanuel Servais, L-2535 Luxembourg City (tel. 352-460-123).

# TRAVEL AND BUSINESS INFORMATION

The U.S. Department of State's Consular Information Program provides Consular Information Sheets, Travel Warnings, and Public Announcements. **Consular Information Sheets** exist for all countries and include information on entry requirements, currency regulations, health conditions, areas of instability, crime and security, political disturbances, and the addresses of the U.S. posts in the country.

**Travel Warnings** are issued when the State Department recommends that Americans avoid travel to a certain country. **Public Announcements** are issued as a means to disseminate information quickly about terrorist threats and other relatively short-term conditions overseas which pose significant risks to the security of American travelers. Free copies of this information are available by calling the Bureau of Consular Affairs at 202-647-5225 or via the fax-on-demand system: 202-647-3000. Consular Information Sheets and Travel Warnings also are available on the Consular Affairs Internet home page: http://travel.state.gov. Consular Affairs Tips for Travelers publication series, which contain information on obtaining passports and planning a safe trip abroad are on the internet and hard copies can be purchased from the Superintendent of Documents, U.S. Government Printing Office, telephone: 202-512-1800; fax 202-512-2250.

Emergency information concerning Americans traveling abroad may be obtained from the Office of Overseas Citizens Services at (202) 647-5225. For after-hours emergencies, Sundays and holidays, call 202-647-4000.

Passport information can be obtained by calling the National Passport Information Center's automated system ($.35 per minute) or live operators 8 a.m. to 8 p.m. (EST) Monday-Friday ($1.05 per minute). The number is 1-900-225-5674 (TDD: 1-900-225-7778). Major credit card users (for a flat rate of $4.95) may call 1-888-362-8668 (TDD: 1-888-498-3648). It also is available on the internet.

Travelers can check the latest health information with the U.S. Centers for Disease Control and Prevention in Atlanta, Georgia. A hotline at 877-FYI-TRIP (877-394-8747) and a web site at http://www.cdc.gov/travel/index.htm give the most recent health advisories, immunization recommendations or requirements, and advice on food and drinking water safety for regions and countries. A booklet entitled Health Information for International Travel (HHS publication number CDC-95-8280) is available from the U.S. Government Printing Office, Washington, DC 20402, tel. (202) 512-1800.

Information on travel conditions, visa requirements, currency and customs regulations, legal holidays, and other items of interest to travelers also may be obtained before your departure from a country's embassy and/or consulates in the U.S. (for this country, see "Principal Government Officials" listing in this publication).

U.S. citizens who are long-term visitors or traveling in dangerous areas are encouraged to register at the U.S. embassy upon arrival in a country (see "Principal U.S. Embassy Officials" listing in this publication). This may help family members contact you in case of an emergency.

**For additional analytical, business and investment opportunities information, please contact Global Investment & Business Center, USA at (202) 546-2103. Fax: (202) 546-3275. E-mail: rusric@erols.com**

# POLITICAL AND GOVERNMENT SYSTEM

## GOVERNMENT COMPOSITION AND FUNCTIONS

The Government has a right of initiative in legislative matters known as governmental initiative, which allows it to table draft bills. After being examined by the Council of State, draft bills are put to the vote before Parliament, where the Government normally holds a majority. After the parliamentary vote, the Grand Duke exercises his rights of assent and of enactment.The legislative procedure concludes with the publication of the legislative text in the compendium of legislation known as the Mémorial, whereupon the text acquires its legal status.

The Council of State is composed of 21 Councillors. State Councillors are formally appointed and dismissed by the Grand Duke on proposal by the Government, Parliament or the Council of State.

In Luxembourg's unicameral system, the Council of State exerts the moderating influence of a second legislative assembly. It is required to voice its opinion on all items of legislation, namely on all draft and private bills tabled before the Chamber prior to voting by the deputies. Its opinion must entail a thorough examination to ensure compliance by the draft texts with the Constitution, international conventions and the rule of law.The role of the Council of State is one of persuasion rather than enforcement and is therefore advisory in nature.

### THE GRAND DUCAL PALACE

Its main tasks include:

› giving its opinion on all draft and private bills;

› examining any draft Grand Ducal regulation submitted to it;

› deciding whether to waive the second constitutional vote, that is to say the second parliamentary vote cast at least three months after the first vote by Parliament. Its refusal of the waiver is tantamount to halt the legislative process for a period of three months but does not amount to a right of veto.

### EXECUTIVE POWER

The Grand Duke is the head of state. His inviolable status means that he cannot be charged or prosecuted. The Grand Duke enjoys complete political immunity. Political responsibility lies with ministers. Indeed, any measure taken by the Grand Duke in the exercise of his constitutional powers must be countersigned by a member of the Government who assumes full responsibility. Moreover, any legislative document signed by the Grand Duke must have been submitted for prior consideration to the cabinet.

Formally, the Constitution grants the Grand Duke the right to freely organise his Government, i.e. to appoint ministers and secretaries of state, to establish ministerial departments and to confer powers on them. The number of ministerial departments generally exceeds the number of members of the Government called upon to serve in office, so a single minister normally holds more than one portfolio.

In practice, the Grand Duke chooses the Prime Minister on the basis of election results; the Prime Minister himself then proposes the members of the Government. The Government appointed by the Grand Duke presents its political programme to Parliament which takes a vote of confidence, thereby giving the newly appointed Government a parliamentary majority on which it can rely.

Under the Constitution, the Grand Duke has the right to remove any member of the Government from office but, in practice, the resignation of a minister or of the whole Government is tendered by the Prime Minister to the Grand Duke who accepts it.

**THE JUDICIARY**

Under the Constitution, courts and tribunals are responsible for exercising judicial power.They are independent in the exercise of their functions.There are two branches of jurisdiction in Luxembourg: the judicial order and the administrative order. The Constitutional Court ranks on top of the judicial hierarchy.

**THE JUDICIAL ORDER**

1.The Magistrates Courts

This is the first rank of the judicial hierarchy.The three magistrates' courts have their seats in Luxembourg, Esch-sur-Alzette and Diekirch. They have jurisdiction over minor cases, as defined by law, in civil and commercial matters.

2. The District Courts

The country is divided into the two judicial districts of Luxembourg and Diekirch, each of which has a district court. These courts hear and determine civil, commercial and criminal cases in the criminal or correctional division. In civil and commercial cases, they have jurisdiction over all cases not expressly assigned by law to another court.

Finally, the section known as the Juvenile and Guardianship Court has jurisdiction over child protection cases, as determined by law.

3. The Supreme Court of Justice

This court has its seat in the City of Luxembourg and includes:

- a Court of Cassation, consisting of a chamber in which five judges sit;

- a Court of Appeals, divided into chambers where some thirty appeal-court judges sit.

The Supreme Court of Justice meets in a general assembly primarily to rule on jurisdictional conflicts and disciplinary measures against judges. The general assembly also hears charges by Parliament against members of the Government.

Public Prosecutor's Department

The members of the Public Prosecution Office are headed by the State Public Prosecutor and are responsible for representing the State in the Courts and Tribunals. Accordingly, the Public Prosecution Office reports to the Minister of Justice.The chief task of the members of the Public Prosecution Office is to investigate crimes, offences and misdemeanours, enforce the law and ensure that judgements are enforced. The prosecutors within the Public Prosecutor's Department

**For additional analytical, business and investment opportunities information, please contact Global Investment & Business Center, USA at (202) 546-2103. Fax: (202) 546-3275. E-mail: rusric@erols.com**

are assisted in their work by judicial police officers who record the committing of a criminal offence, trace the culprits and gather evidence.

The Administrative Courts

The administrative courts are assigned by the Constitution to deal with administrative and fiscal cases.

The Administrative Tribunal hears and determines in the first instance appeals against any administrative decisions where no other recourse is admissible under the laws and regulations. It rules on appeals to set aside or alter a decision.

Supreme administrative jurisdiction lies with the Administrative Court. It is an appeal body which primarily hears cases brought against the decisions of other administrative courts, or arbitrates disputes between the Government and the Audit Court.

The Constitutional Court

The Constitutional Court is composed of nine members and sits in Luxembourg.As its name suggests, it rules on the conformity of laws with the Constitution, apart from those laws approving treaties. The public has no direct recourse to the Court. The Court exercises control ex post and cases are referred to it for preliminary rulings.

## POLITICAL INSTITITIONS

Two types of legislative initiative are distinguishable:

the draft bill. The preliminary draft of a law is drawn up by the relevant Ministry, approved by the cabinet and then submitted to the Council of State for its opinion. It is then submitted to Parliament.

the private bill. One or more MPs may table a private bill, which is submitted to the Conference of Presidents of the Parliament, which decides on its referral to committee. The text of the proposal is submitted to the Council of State for its opinion and sent to the Government for its position.

Once the Council of State has given its opinion, the private bill is sent to the relevant parliamentary committee which examines it and reports to the Chamber.

The debate in plenary session of Parliament is conducted in two stages: a general discussion and a discussion article by article. Any deputy may propose amendments.

In Luxembourg's unicameral system, once Parliament has voted on the draft, it must vote a second time on the whole text after a period of at least three months. It can however dispense with this vote if the Council of State accepts the waiver. If the latter does not give its consent, Parliament must hold a second vote after a minimum period of three months.

The law finally adopted by Parliament enters into force only after it has been granted royal assent, enacted by the Grand Duke and published in the Mémorial (Official Journal)

**For additional analytical, business and investment opportunities information, please contact Global Investment & Business Center, USA at (202) 546-2103. Fax: (202) 546-3275. E-mail: rusric@erols.com**

## PARLIAMENT

60 MPs are elected every 5 years. If Parliament is dissolved, new elections are held within 3 months of the dissolution.

Elections are direct and by secret ballot. MPs are elected on the basis of a mixed one-person-one-vote suffrage and a party list system with proportional representation. Any Luxembourg citizen who satisfies the legal conditions is entitled to participate in the elections. Voting is compulsory for voters on the electoral registers.

To qualify as a voter, a person must be a Luxembourg national, at least 18 years old and enjoy civic and political rights, which means never having been convicted of a criminal offence.

To stand for election, a person must be at least 18 years old, be domiciled in the Grand Duchy and satisfy the same conditions as those applicable to voters.

The office of MP is incompatible with the duties of Government member, judge or member of the Council of State.

Electoral Constituencies

There are 4 electoral constituencies:

› the SOUTHERN constituency (the cantons of Eschsur-Alzette and Capellen), with 23 Deputies › the EASTERN constituency (the cantons of Grevenmacher, Remich and Echternach), with 7 MPs › the CENTRAL constituency (the cantons of Luxembourg and Mersch), with 21 Deputies

› the NORTHERN constituency (the cantons of Diekirch, Redange, Wiltz, Clervaux and Vianden), with 9 MPs.

Allocation of Seats

Elections are held using a party-list system. The distribution of votes is peculiar to Luxembourg law. Voters in fact have a choice: they have as many votes on one or more lists as there are seats to fill per constituency; they can either put all their electoral weight behind the one list or give their preferential votes to the candidates of their choice.

The allocation of seats complies with the rules of proportional representation and conforms to the principle of the smallest electoral quotient. This system ensures that small political groups are fairly represented.

The Political Parties Parliament represented in

Christian Social Party (CSV)

Democratic Party (DP)

Luxembourg Socialist

Workers' Party (LSAP)

Action Committee for Democracy

and Fair Pensions (ADR)

The Greens

The Left

North Centre South East

about...political institutions / Service Information et Presse du gouvernement luxembourgeois / www.gouvernement.lu

The Communes

There are no provinces or departments in the Grand Duchy.The only political subdivision of the country is the commune.

The commune is a legal entity. It manages its assets and raises taxes through local representatives, overseen by the central authority represented by the Minister of the Interior.

There are 118 communes. Each commune has a communal council directly elected for a six-year term by those inhabitants of the commune who are entitled to vote. The day-to-day management of the commune falls to the mayor, or indeed the municipal council, bodies emanating from the communal council.

In principle, elections are held according to the relative majority system. However, if the number of inhabitants exceeds 3,000, elections are held by party list with proportional representation, along the lines of general elections.

Acting through the Government, the Grand Duke has the right to dissolve the communal council, in which case elections are called within three months of its dissolution.

To be eligible to vote in communal elections, one must satisfy the following conditions: › be 18 years old on the day of the election; › enjoy civic rights and not have forfeited voting rights in the member state or in the state of origin;

› for Luxembourg nationals, be domiciled in the Grand Duchy;

› for foreign nationals, be domiciled in the Grand Duchy and have lived there for at least 5 years, at the time of application for registration on the electoral roll.

To stand for election, one must be Luxembourg citizens or nationals of another European Union member state, at least 18 years old and have been habitually resident in the commune for six months and have been domiciled in the Grand Duchy for at least 5 years.

European Elections

Since 1979, the representatives of the Grand Duchy of Luxembourg in the European Parliament have been directly elected for a five-year term.The Grand Duchy is entitled to 6 representatives in the European Parliament. The date of European elections is set by Grand Ducal regulation. This regulation may choose the same date for European Parliament elections and general elections Parliament, as is usually the case.

Nationals of the European Union have the right to vote, actively or passively, even if they are not living in their country of origin.A series of conditions are attached to this voting right.

To be eligible to vote, one must:

› be a national of Luxembourg or of another member state of the European Union;

› be at least 18 years of age on the election day;

› enjoy civic rights and not have forfeited the right to vote in the member state of origin;

› for Luxembourg nationals, be domiciled in the Grand Duchy; however, Luxembourg nationals domiciled abroad are entitled to a postal vote;

› for nationals of another member state of the European Union, be domiciled in the Grand Duchy and have lived there for at least five years of the past six years, at the time of application for registration on the electoral roll.

To stand for election, one must:

› be a national of Luxembourg or of another member state of the European Union;

› enjoy civic rights and not have forfeited political rights in the Grand Duchy of Luxembourg or in the member state of residence or in the member state of origin;

› be at least 18 years of age on the election day;

› for Luxembourg nationals, be domiciled in the Grand Duchy;

› for nationals of another member state of the European Union, be domiciled in Luxembourg and have lived there for at least 5 years, at the time the list of candidates was submitted.

## FORMATION OF THE GOVERNMENT

The Constitution grants the Grand Duke the right to organize his government freely, i.e. to create ministries, divide up ministerial departments, and appoint their members. The diversity and number of ministerial departments considerably exceeds the number of government members called to the departmental office, and thus the same minister may frequently hold several portfolios. In practice, the Grand Duke chooses on the basis of the election results the mediator and/or the formateur of the government, who generally becomes Prime Minister. The formateur presents to the Grand Duke the team constituting the members of government. Generally, these are leading political figures forming part of the political groups represented in the Chamber of Deputies. On rare occasions it happened that someone who was not member of Parliament as appointed member of Government. The Grand Duke undertakes the appointment and swearing-in of the government members. the appointed government presents its political programme to the Chamber of Deputies, which expresses its confidence by voting in favour. Thus, the government has a parliamentary majority upon which it may rely. On the basis of the Constitution, the Grand Duke is entitled to remove any member of government from office, but in practice it is more often the case that a minister, or indeed the entire government, tender their resignation to the Grand Duke.

The government's Ministerial Council (cabinet meeting)

The government is obliged to deliberate in Council on all matters which must be submitted for a decision by the Grand Duke. Each member of government is entitled to instigate a decision by the Council on matters of his department. The Prime Minister is entitled to refer to the Council any matter affecting the government of the Grand Duchy. The decisions of the government's Ministerial Council are taken by a majority of votes. Where there is a parity of votes on matters to be decided by the Council, the Prime Minister has the casting vote. If a matter is considered urgent, it suffices for two members of government to be present and in agreement for a decision to be taken. However, they must report their decision to the next meeting of the Council.

## RESPONSIBILITY OF MINISTERS

Ministerial responsibility is inseparable from the absence of responsibility of the Grand Duke. For an act of the Grand Duke to take effect, it must be countersigned by a member of government who assumes entire responsibility for such an act. The Constitution provides, in a general manner, for the responsibility of ministers. This responsibility is general with regard to acts having a direct or indirect relationship with ministerial functions. It may be legal, i.e. criminal or civil, as well as political. The ministers are responsible for acts of which they themselves are the authors, either individually or collectively. Responsibility for any measure taken in the Council is incumbent upon all the members of government involved in adopting such measure. However, a minister who has a dissenting vote recorded in the minutes of the Council session is exempt from responsibility.

The government as a whole and the ministers individually are politically responsible for their acts before the Chamber of Deputies. The political responsibility of ministers may be subject to sanction consisting of the obligation to cease their functions when the Chamber no longer grants them confidence (motion of censure). It is customary for ministers to resign the first time they receive a hostile vote from the Chamber. On no account can a verbal or written order from the Grand Duke release a minister from his responsibility. Indeed, the responsibility of ministers would become illusory and deprived of all sanction if the Grand Duke could cover such responsibility by asserting his own inviolability. On the basis of the Constitution, only the Chamber is entitled to indict ministers. Indictments admitted against ministers for acts committed in the exercise of their functions are brought before the Supreme Court of Justice sitting in plenary session. To avoid the criminal responsibility of ministers becoming purely theoretical, the Constitution establishes an exception to the Grand Duke's right of pardon, stating that a convicted minister may only be pardoned upon a request from the Chamber.

The composition of the government

| Grand Duke | HENRI |
|---|---|
| Prime Min. | Jean-Claude JUNCKER |
| Dep. Prime Min. | Jean ASSELBORN |
| Min. of Admin. Simplification | Octavie MODERT |
| Min. of Agriculture, Viticulture, & Rural Development | Romain SCHNEIDER |
| Min. of Civil Service & Admin. Reform | Francois BILTGEN |
| Min. for Communications | Francois BILTGEN |
| Min. of Culture | Octavie MODERT |
| Min. of Defense | Jean-Marie HALSDORF |
| Min. for Development Cooperation & Humanitarian Affairs | Marie-Josee JACOBS |

| | |
|---|---|
| Min. of Economy & Foreign Trade | Etienne SCHNEIDER |
| Min. of Equality of Opportunity | Francoise HETTO-GAASCH |
| Min. of Family & Integration | Marie-Josee JACOBS |
| Min. of Finance | Luc FRIEDEN |
| Min. of Foreign Affairs | Jean ASSELBORN |
| Min. of Health & of Social Security | Mars DI BARTOLOMEO |
| Min. of Higher Education & Research | Francois BILTGEN |
| Min. of Housing | Marco SCHANK |
| Min. of Interior | Jean-Marie HALSDORF |
| Min. of Justice | Francois BILTGEN |
| Min. of Labor, Employment, & Immigration | Nicolas SCHMIT |
| Min. of the Middle Class & Tourism | Francoise HETTO-GAASCH |
| Min. of National Education & Professional Training | Mady DELVAUX-STEHRES |
| Min. of Public Works | Claude WISELER |
| Min. of Relations With Parliament | Octavie MODERT |
| Min. of Religious Sects | Francois BILTGEN |
| Min. of Sports | Romain SCHNEIDER |
| Min. of State | Jean-Claude JUNCKER |
| Min. of Treasury | Jean-Claude JUNCKER |
| Chmn., Luxembourg Central Bank | Gaston REINESCH |
| Ambassador to the US | Jean-Louis WOLZFELD |
| Permanent Representative to the UN, New York | Sylvie LUCAS |

State Secretary for the Relations with Parliament State Secretary for Agriculture, Viticulture and Rural Development State Secretary for Culture, Higher Education and Research

Service information et presse du gouvernement 33, bd Roosevelt L-2450 Luxembourg Tel.: (+352) 478-2181 Fax: (+352) 47 02 85 www.gouvernement.lu edition@sip.etat.lu

**PRINT MEDIA**

In spite of the EU's open borders, the Grand Duchy is a "small, hermetic market" for press products (Léon Zeches, director and chief editor of the "Luxemburger Wort").Thanks to their knowledge of languages, Luxembourgers can read newspapers from many different countries, but they still rely on the domestic newspapers for local news, from golden weddings and work reunions to cheque presentations at the children's day nursery – whatever the event, the local press are keen and prolific reporters.

Anyone wishing to read all the products of the Luxembourg press will need to be multilingual. Luxembourg is officially a tri-lingual country,with Luxembourgish,German and French as its administrative languages.There are even weekly newspapers in Portuguese ("Contacto" and "Correiro") as well as a monthly business magazine ("Business") and a weekly paper ("Luxembourg News") in English. Anyone wishing to partake of the leading national newspapers will need to be familiar with German and French at least. Articles in both languages sit side by side and no translations are provided.The author's choice of language is dictated partly by his or her preference and knowledge and partly by the subject. Culture and business are traditionally French-orientated, while German is usually the language of choice for local news and national affairs.

There has been a rekindling of interest among Luxembourg publishers recently in targeting the country's French-speaking community, with publications including a special weekly ("Le Jeudi") and a daily newspaper ("La Voix du Luxembourg"). In the period between the middle of the nineteenth century and the Second World War there were several French newspapers, and for the following 40 years this niche was filled by the local edition of the Metz "Républician Lorrain". This newspaper ceased to exist in November 2001, when it was replaced by an independent Luxembourg publication,"Le Quotidien", a joint venture with a Luxembourg publishing company.

Among the weekly newspapers,"Revue" and "d'Lëtzebuerger Land" can look back over half a century of history. More recent publications include "Télécran" and "Woxx".A wide range of domestic titles caters for diverse special interests,from cars and women's interests to the new economy.There is also a broad spectrum of specialist publications from parties, associations and trade unions, with around 400 titles appearing each year.

Although astonishing in economic terms, the market has been shared by several daily newspapers for decades – "Luxemburger Wort" (founded in 1848),"tageblatt" (1913), "Zeitung vum Lëtzebuerger Vollek" (1946), "Journal" (1948) and, more recently, "La Voix" (2001) and "Le Quotidien" (2001).They are produced by a number of different printers.Only the aid provided by the state prevents newspapers from going out of business. In terms of the level of sales needed to run at a profit, there should be room for only one of these newspapers on the market.The provision of direct subsidies to the press and a number of indirect measures (low delivery charges, high tariffs for official announcements) not only enable the continued existence of these newspapers,but also their low price,which accounts for the high sales and avid consumption by the public. Almost all newspapers now have their own website.

The first Luxembourg publication is generally believed to have been a Catholic monthly called "La Clef du cabinet des princes", which first appeared in 1704 and was produced by the local printer André Chevalier from 1714.Already banned in Luxembourg in 1788, it finally disappeared from the market in 1794 in the wake of the turmoil caused by the French Revolution. Countless local newspapers stepped in to fill the gap, with over 200 titles appearing up to the time of the Second World War. In 1948, UNESCO counted 82 titles in Luxembourg.The most significant arrivals were in 1848 (the year in which censorship was dropped,although the new freedom was soon to be restricted again by the Press Law of 1868) with the appearance of the "Luxemburger Wort" and in 1913 with the "tageblatt", both of which are still the country's leading newspapers.

terprise. The newspaper must appear at least once a week. It must employ at least five full-time editors. The publication must be of general interest and contain reports on political,economic,social and cultural events in one of the three national languages. It must finance itself through advertising and sales and be freely available for sale to the public.

One third of the aid granted consists of a fixed basic amount and the remainder is calculated on the basis of the number of pages produced per year.The number of copies sold is not taken into account.The total circulation, according to official figures, has remained at a constant level for a number of years despite competition from television and the internet.

-Advertising revenue is the second key line of support, and for this reason the state continues to set a limit on the advertising income of the country's one national television station in order to protect the newspaper market.

However, the latest government programme of the Christian Social-Liberal coalition of August 1999 provides for a general approval for advertisement financing for private stations.

A handful of arts newspapers are subsidized separately through direct grants from the Ministry of Culture.

The weekly satirical newspaper “Den neie Feierkrop”, published as a co-operative venture since 1993, holds a special position among the country’s press products. The title “De Feierkrôp” first appeared on 4 September 1948 as a satirical supplement to the communist “Zeitung vum Lëtzebuerger Vollek”.The origins of journalistic satire in Luxembourg can be found in the middle of the nineteenth century with newspapers such as “D’Wäschfra” and “De Letzeburger Kladderadatsch”.

Press Council

Thirty-five countries of the world, of which half are in Europe, have a press council.

In Luxembourg, this institution was inaugurated on 20 December 1979. In its capacity as a national authority, this professional body controls the issue of press cards to full-time journalists. Around 300 active and retired journalists are currently registered.

The Press Council, which is composed equally of representatives from publishers and the journalistic profession, provides a platform for the discussion of common concerns and acts as a complaints watchdog for readers and viewers. It has the authority to take action on its own initiative to deal with breaches of the journalistic code of conduct.

Press legislation

Freedom of speech, information and the press is guaranteed byArticle 24 of the Constitution:“La liberté de manifester ses opinions par la parole en toutes matières et la liberté de la presse sont garanties,sauf la répression des délits commis à l’occasion de l’exercise de ces libertés. La censure ne pourra jamais être établie. Il ne peut être exigé de cautionnement des écrivains, éditeurs ou imprimeurs ...” (Freedom of speech in all matters and freedom of the press is guaranteed, subject to the repression of offences committed in the exercise of these freedoms. No censorship may ever be introduced. Security may not be demanded of writers, publishers or printers.)

The current Press Law dates back to 20 July 1869.It has long been considered in need of reform and, in 2001, the Ministry responsible for the media submitted a preliminary draft for a new law, which is still under discussion.

Important issues to be resolved are the protection of sources, the right to refuse to give evidence in legal proceedings, freedom of access to information, the provision of an up-to-date citation right, an effective right of reply, the question of a disciplinary council, protection of the private sphere, and the criminal liability of publishers and journalists.

The interests of journalists are represented by three associations in Luxembourg. On 7 No

Service Information et Presse

the work of today’s authority is the 1991 Media Law. The duties of the “Service Information et Presse” include national and international public relations, the provision of support for journalists, publication of information material, co-ordination of the Government’s internet presence and preparation of press conferences.

Radio and television for Luxembourg

**For additional analytical, business and investment opportunities information, please contact Global Investment & Business Center, USA at (202) 546-2103. Fax: (202) 546-3275. E-mail: rusric@erols.com**

On 19 September 1959, "Radio Lëtzebuerg" made its first broadcast on the VHF frequency 92.5 MHz. Its air time was originally limited to two blocks,12.30 to 13.30 and 18.30 to 19.00,but was gradually increased over the years, and since 1996 "RTL Radio Lëtzebuerg", as it is now known, has provided a round-the-clock programme.

In the wake of the liberalization of the media in 1993, a second national radio station called "honnert,7 – de soziokulturelle radio", a public corporation, hit the airwaves. Luxembourg also has four regional radio stations (Ara, DNR, Eldoradio and Radio Latina) and over a dozen local stations.

On 21 September 1969, a three-quarter hour television programme in the Luxembourgish language called "Hei Elei, Kuck Elei" (from the libretto of the Luxembourg operetta "Mum Séis") went out for the first time.This programme, a review with its own editing team produced by the French "Télé-Luxembourg", was broadcast on Sundays until October 1991,when,at the suggestion of the Government, the format was changed to a one-hour daily live programme repeated at intervals until midnight.The programme is watched on average by approximately 70 per cent of Luxembourgish-speaking households. Special events, such as the accession to the throne of the new sovereign in October 2000 and major sporting events, are broadcast live. In autumn 2001, RTL extended its programmes for Luxembourg to 18 hours and has also offered special youth entertainment programmes since that time.

Under the terms of its franchise, which was last renewed by the Government in 1994, this private station is committed to neutrality and fulfils the public information functions of a public broadcasting corporation. In return, the Government foregoes its franchise fee. As over a third of the country's 440,000 inhabitants are foreign nationals, the state provides funding for a French translation of the daily TV news programme, which is broadcast simultaneously on the second stereo channel. There are no licence fees for the public.

A number of regional TV channels broadcast programmes by cable and satellite. Under the current regulations, these channels must be financed exclusively through sponsorship contracts.The "Uelzechtkanal", a regional channel in the south, is produced by students. "Nordliicht TV","MusicFestival","De Kueb TV" and the upcoming music and youth format "Tango TV" are all private projects. Other projects include a dedicated channel for live broadcasts from the Chamber of Deputies. In November 2000, SelecTV, Luxembourg's first digital subscription channel, went into operation with its own cable network. Digital channels for special interests such as fashion, cars and tourism, available only by satellite, are another recent development. These theme channels are licensed in Luxembourg and cater for a foreign viewing audience.

The issue of short-range broadcasting licences is controlled by an independent committee, the "Commission indépendante de la radiodiffusion". Members' mandates are renewed at regular intervals.The Commission also assists the Government in an advisory capacity in the issue of all other types of licence.

Compliance with the regulations governing TV and radio programmes broadcast from Luxembourg is monitored by the "Conseil national des programmes" (CNP), which was established in 1991.This committee,whose status as a broadcasting council is comparable to that of the "Conseil supérieur de l'audiovisuel" in France or the German Land media institutions, is composed of honorary representatives of the major socio-political sectors. Following a reorganization in 2001,the committee now has a higher level of autonomy, its own general secretariat and appropriate funding, all of which have enabled it to exercise its supervisory functions more effectively.Its powers are,however,limited to the issue of public reprimands.Licences can only be withdrawn by the Government.

DAB

**For additional analytical, business and investment opportunities information, please contact Global Investment & Business Center, USA at (202) 546-2103. Fax: (202) 546-3275. E-mail: rusric@erols.com**

In 2001, the Luxembourg Government asked the Parliament to discuss an amendment of the media legislation to enable the issue of operating licences for digital radio (DAB). Almost all of the country's radio stations have joined forces to form a DAB association to promote the introduction of this technology in Luxembourg. The country has already been allocated two frequency blocks of six frequencies each under international treaties.

Licences to use the DAB frequencies are expected to go primarily to the national and regional stations in the forthcoming public tender,and the service will probably be introduced during 2002. A number of private telecommunications network operators have also expressed an interest in DAB.

In November 2000, the Government signed a memorandum of understanding with the company "Global Radio", under which it pledged to grant the company a broadcasting licence if it succeeds in its plans to broadcast digital radio programmes for Europe via satellite.

SES

The Société européenne des satellites (SES) operates a broadband communication network via satellite from Luxembourg which seamlessly spans four continents

and has been used for some time now for the transmission of both radio signals and multimedia data. The company's own Astra fleet is the leading satellite system for direct reception in Europe. Astra currently transmits over 1,000 TV and radio programmes as well as multimedia and internet services to over 87 million households in Europe by both analogue and digital transmission (as of June 2001).

Following a string of strategic investments in AsiaSat

(34.10 per cent), NSAB in Scandinavia (50 per cent) and Star One in South America (19.99 per cent), the Luxembourg company announced, on 28 March 2001, its intention to complete a 100 per cent takeover of the US satellite operator GEAmericom and received approval for this undertaking from the regulatory authorities concerned. All the participating interests of the SES Group are now held by the new management company SES Global.

SES Global, which has its headquarters in Betzdorf/Luxembourg in a castle which is a former residence of the grand ducal family, is quickly becoming the world's leading satellite service provider, with a fleet of 29 satellites of its own (12 Astra and 17 Americom) and 13 additional satellites from its participating interests. Additional satellites are already under construction and are scheduled to go into operation in 2002. ASTRA launches take place alternately from Kourou in French Guyana and Baikonour in Kazakhstan. Having secured a third orbital position through an agreement with Deutsche Telekom, one of its shareholders, SES now plans to deploy a satellite for multimedia services, ASTRA 3A, at 23.5 degrees East.

SES employs an international team of experts and, at the end of 2000, had 435 employees from 20 countries, of which 330 were based in Betzdorf.The start of the company's long success story came in December 1988 with the launch of its first broadcast satellite,ASTRA 1A.

Under a licence agreement with the Government, the joint-stock company, which numbers the state itself among its shareholders, has been granted exclusivity on the Luxembourg orbital positions 19.2 degrees East and 28.2 degrees East until 2015.

RTL Group

The "L" in the name of the leading European radio concern RTL Group stands for Luxembourg, and the abbreviation RTL is synonymous with a remarkable success story. In 1929, in what subsequently proved to be a far-sighted measure, the Luxembourg Parliament passed an initial, extremely liberal, radio law.With this law, the politicians laid the foundations of a successful media location policy.

Back in 1931, a small private enterprise called "Compagnie luxembourgeoise de radiodiffusion" started work on the broadcast of radio services for France, followed by services for Germany and Great Britain.Thanks to a clever niche policy and up-to-date formats, its medium and short wave programmes enjoyed fast-growing popularity. In the 1950s, it followed this success with a second pioneering achievement when Europe's first private television station went on air in Luxembourg. With the liberalization of broadcasting in the neighbouring countries in the 1980s, the way was finally clear for the company operating under the brand name "Radio Télévision Luxembourg" (RTL).

In 1996,the Kirchberg-based media group merged with the German Bertelsmann subsidiary Ufa.This was followed in 2000 by a second merger with Britain's Pear-son Television (PTV) to give the company increased access to programme content. PTV produces up to 200 television formats in 35 countries worldwide, primarily game shows, drama series and light entertainment programmes, which together account for over 10,000 programme hours a year.

Under the new name RTL Group and with the German company Bertelsmann as its principal shareholder, a media empire came into being which is now number one in Europe,with interests in 24 TV and 17 radio stations, dozens of production companies and extensive rights catalogues.The group also provides digital TV, telecommunications and internet services through its subsidiary Broadcasting Center Europe (BCE).

Although today the group conducts most of its operations through subsidiaries and associated companies abroad, Luxembourg continues to play an important role as a location, and not just as the "L" in the company's name. Even in this age of TV satellites, Luxembourg still has valuable assets to offer in the form of terrestrial frequencies. It provides the licences for seven RTL TV channels which broadcast to Belgium,the Netherlands, Poland and France, and several radio stations for the broadcast of programmes abroad.

Audiovisual production

Until the 1990s, the cinematic arts played only a minor role in the Grand Duchy's history, which goes back just over 150 years.There were only two full-time professional Luxembourgish film producers, René Leclère (active 1930 to 1953) and Philippe Schneider (active 1945 to 1979), who mostly made advertising films for industry and state documentaries.

They were followed with greater success by a number of enthusiastic amateur filmmakers with higher artistic standards, who produced short films on super eight cameras. The most talented of this group was Andy Bausch, whose comedy thriller "Troublemaker", shot in 1987 in co-production with Saarländischer Rundfunk, is today regarded as a cult film. Both Bausch and his leading actor at that time,Thierry van Werveke, became established figures on the film scene in the German-speaking countries.

1988 brought a turning point for the audiovisual industry with the introduction of financial concessions for audiovisual productions.The main beneficiary at whom this media policy initiative might have been directed, the RTL group, surprisingly showed no interest in producing home-grown soap operas and sitcoms. However, their lack of interest was offset by a sudden increase in enthusiasm for Luxembourg on the part of foreign producers.The massive influx of film teams,

**For additional analytical, business and investment opportunities information, please contact Global Investment & Business Center, USA at (202) 546-2103. Fax: (202) 546-3275. E-mail: rusric@erols.com**

many from the United States of America, led to a fundamental rethink in 1993.Financial support would no longer be provided for any number of separate works but for projects that would help to build Luxembourg's film industry into a strong pillar of the media sector.This was largely achieved through co-productions with foreign companies, due to the lack of a national television corporation to act as a project partner for the domestic film sector.

Filming

In the early summer of 2001, a team of 200 people from joiners to plasterers worked to create a film set on a former mining site in the south of Luxembourg which would provide a historically accurate recreation of Venice in the year 1492.These costly and laborious preparations for filming of the 18 million euro European costume drama "Secret Passage" were a first for the Grand Duchy.

Centre national de l'audiovisuel

The Fund is also responsible for representing Luxembourg in European initiatives, such as Eurimages in Strasbourg, and works closely with the "Centre national de l'audiovisuel" (CNA) in Düdelingen to promote Luxembourg audiovisual works at home and abroad. Since 1989, the CNA has maintained a national photographic, picture and sound archive. It participates in the production and distribution of Luxembourg films,where activities have included the video series "Films made in Luxembourg", arranges screenings of films produced in the Grand Duchy at international festivals and organizes training courses.

MEDIA Desk Luxembourg

MEDIA Plus (2001-2005) is the European Union's third five-year programme for the promotion of audiovisual works.With a total budget of 400 million euros, it supports:

1. vocational and continued training for the industry

2. development, distribution, promotion and pilot projects, especially in the digital field.

Information bureaux in the Member States called MEDIA Desk or Antenna disseminate important information and provide assistance to applicants for aid from Brussels. Luxembourg also has one of these information bureaux and, in addition, is the location for the government and MEDIA sponsored "Strategics" initiative, which offers marketing training and advice to the film sector.

Portrait: Dan Wiroth, filmmaker

The young Luxembourgish producer and object animator Dan Wiroth received considerable international acclaim for his short film "Erè mèla mèla" (2001), which has won several awards.The film met with an enthusiastic response from both public and jury at the Berlinale film festival. In June 2001, the Arte channel showed it with six other short films as part of its "One Dance, One Song" cycle. Wiroth sees his art as a "medium for critical comment"."Erè mèla mèla", which consists of a song, two men and articles of clothing that walk, is a touching plea for the acceptance of homosexuality. By using special animation effects and different camera speeds and playing with perspective,Wiroth gives his film a charming, easy quality.

Object animation is a medium which suits this graduate of the Brussels "La Cambre" academy of arts well.In his graduation film "Crucy Fiction" (1996), he brought kitchen cutlery to life without the use of computer effects.To achieve this, he had to bend 2,000 forks, which were then filmed

**For additional analytical, business and investment opportunities information, please contact Global Investment & Business Center, USA at (202) 546-2103. Fax: (202) 546-3275. E-mail: rusric@erols.com**

before being bent again. In 1998, he made "Fragile", the witty tale of a beer glass and a wine glass who both fall passionately in love with a champagne glass. This talented newcomer is currently working on his first full-length film.

Animators,

" made in Luxembourg"

The Luxembourg "Lycée technique des arts et métiers" offers a special two-year degree course in animation.The course is run in close co-operation with the "Centre de formation technologique des Gobelins" in Paris and is supervised by CARTOON,the animation branch of the European MEDIA Programme. Subjects on the syllabus include anatomy, life drawing, caricature, applied perspective, background design, history of the cinema and technical English.The course also comprises a compulsory six-week work placement at a cartoon studio. Each year, applications are received from up to 40 applicants, of whom only 15 will be successful. Places are allocated on the basis of a selection procedure.The basic admission requirements are secondary school qualifications, artistic talent and a good general education.

The languages of instruction are German and French. The course leads to the state-approved "Brevet de technicien supérieur en dessin d'animation" diploma. A number of Luxembourg graduates have already gained employment in Hollywood studios.

## TELECOMMUNICATIONS

The consumer is no longer charged for the duration of the call but the amount of data sent and received.

The award of the four UMTS licences at the end of 2001 will not be carried out by auction but in accordance with the "beauty contest" principle.This means that the winners will not be the companies offering the most in terms of quantity but those with the most attractive bids.The rules are being drawn up by the regulatory authority, the ILR (Institut luxembourgeois de regulation), which will place a particularly high premium on certain requirements.The needs of the consumer, who must have access to reliable, attractive services offering value for money, must always come first

– bearing in mind that the potential value of UMTS for the consumer is still an unknown quantity.Another key criterion is the shared use of infrastructure, such as transmission masts, by the candidates. The emissions produced by UMTS must be kept to a minimum at all times.

The companies who eventually win the four licences will pay a yearly fee of 0.2 per cent of annual turnover.This revenue will not be paid to the state but to the regulatory authority, which will use it to fund its supervisory activities.

Institut luxembourgeois de régulation

The Institut luxembourgeois de régulation (ILR), established on 21 March 1997 in the wake of the liberalization of the telecommunications sector,is responsible for co-ordinating and controlling the frequency spectrum, processing licence applications, and ensuring access to universal services at fair prices for all citizens. Since August 2000, it has had the additional responsibility of monitoring competition in the national gas and electricity markets.

Internet

According to a study conducted by the Chamber of Commerce in March 2001, 80 per cent of the 97 per cent of enterprises using information technology are connected to the internet and use e-mail for business correspondence. The majority of companies still use their websites primarily for the purpose of image promotion. However, approximately every tenth Luxembourg company is actively engaged in preparing for the advent of electronic commerce, and this trend is rising. With the provision of the statutory basis for e-commerce – the "electronic signature" – in 2000, Parliament has already put in place the most important condition for this new way of doing business.The next stage is the reform of the 1979 Data Protection Law.

In October 2001, the Luxembourg opinion research institute ILRes reported that 45 per cent of all households had access to the internet. At the final count, approximately 49 per cent of the population were experienced in using the internet. According to the ILRes figures, surfing at home accounts for the highest percentage of internet use (83 per cent), with the office in second place and schools and universities lying third.Twenty-nine per cent of internet users surf between one and two hours per week and 16 per cent surf between six and ten hours per week.

Prime Minister Jean-Claude Juncker spelled out the objective for the education sector in 1998 with the words "A PC for every pupil". Since then, the Government has steadily increased budgetary resources for information technology each year. A campaign called "PC driving licence for schoolchildren" is currently underway in the classroom, the "eLëtzebuerg" programme includes a broad-based information campaign aimed at the general population, and a group of local authorities have set up the first community internet chat rooms.

The Henri Tudor public research centre has had a multimedia department since 1992, now called the "New Media Group" (NMG). The Group analyses development in the new technologies, publishes specialised literature and organizes conferences and training courses. The NMG is based at the state-sponsored "Technoport Schlassgoart" in Esch/Alzette.

This "incubator" for high-tech entrepreneurs provides accommodation for start-up companies until they are in a position to set up their own offices. Its floor space was increased in October 2001, and it now has room for up to 30 companies.

In Bonnevoie, an urban district in Luxembourg, a private enterprise is currently conducting trials of internet via the power socket. This service will be marketed in 2003 under the name Powerline.

Restena

In 1989, an agency of the Ministry of Education known by the acronym Restena (Réseau Téléinformatique de l'Education Nationale et de la Recherche) started a project to create an electronic network that will link all the institutions and agents involved in the education and research fields in Luxembourg. Restena officially launched the first internet connection in March 1992.

Since 2000, the agency has operated independently from the state in the form of a trust. Its main responsibilities include control of the domain name system and allocation of the country suffix .lu for Luxembourg web-sites. At the beginning of 2001, the register contained over 14,500 names, of which 9,000 were in active use.

Useful addresses

Service information et presse    MEDIA Desk Luxembourg

3, place du St Esprit    5, rue Large

L-1475 Luxembourg L-1917 Luxembourg Tel.: + 352 478-2181 Tel.: + 352 478-2170 Fax: + 352 47 02 85 Fax: + 352 46 74 95 info@sip.etat.lu mail@mediadesk.etat.lu www.gouvernement.lu www.mediadesk.lu

Service des médias et des communications Restena 5, rue Large (Maison de Cassal) 6, rue Coudenhove-Kalergi L-1917 Luxembourg L-1359 Luxembourg Tel.: + 352 478-2167 Tel.: + 352 42 44 09 Fax: + 352 47 56 62 Fax: + 352 42 24 73 www.etat.lu/SMA/ admin@restena.lu www.restena.lu

Fonds national de soutien à la production audiovisuelle

5, rue Large Conseil de presse L-1917 Luxembourg 24, rue du Marché-aux-Herbes Tel.: + 352 478-2065 L-1728 Luxembourg Fax: + 352 22 09 63 Tel.: + 352 22 23 11 info@filmfund.etat.lu Fax: + 352 22 23 40 www.filmfund.lu www. press.lu

Centre national de l'audiovisuel (CNA) Conseil national des programmes 5, rue Zouffgen 5, rue Guillaume Kroll L-3598 Dudelange L-1882 Luxembourg Tel.: + 352 52 24 24-1 Tel.: + 352 478 20 66 Fax: + 352 52 06 55 Fax: + 352 478 20 73 info@cna.etat.lu carole.kickert@cnp.etat.lu www.cna.lu (under construction)

Lycée technique des arts et métiers Institut luxembourgeois de régulation 19, rue Guillaume Schneider 45a, avenue Monterey L-2522 Luxemburg L-2922 Luxembourg Tel.: + 352 46 76 16-1 Tel.: + 352 45 88 45-1 Fax: + 352 47 29 91 Fax: + 352 45 88 45-88 ilt@ilt.etat.lu www.ilr.lu

## POLICY DIRECTIONS

Entitled "A policy of solidarity with those most in need", the coalition agreement entered into by the government resulting from the 1999 elections adopted the following policy guidelines for its development cooperation policy.

"It is imperative that we help reduce the dangerous divide which has been widening continuously between industrialised countries and developing countries, particularly due to globalisation. As the main instrument of Luxembourg's foreign policy, development cooperation should enable our country to raise its profile on the international stage.

With regard to public development aid, the government will reach the objective of 0.7% in terms of GDP in 2000, and will then increase that aid with a view to nearing 1% at the end of the new legislature.

The construction of a nursery school on the Isle São Nicolau (Cape Verde) was financed in part through Luxembourg cooperation

"... if all the rich countries in OECD were to live up to their responsibilities by devoting 0.7% of their Gross National Income to public development assistance, poverty could be eradicated by 2015"

Extract from the statement on development Cooperation and Humanitarian Action to, policy by Mr Charles Goerens, Minister for Cooperation and Humanitarian Action, to the Chamber of Deputies on 12 February 2003

**For additional analytical, business and investment opportunities information, please contact Global Investment & Business Center, USA at (202) 546-2103. Fax: (202) 546-3275. E-mail: rusric@erols.com**

The fight against poverty and support for sustainable development constitute the major objectives of the development cooperation policy. This will be carried on in a spirit of partnership and participatory development. It will focus its action on the social sectors, particularly education and health, and for the benefit of a limited number of target countries which are among the poorest on the planet.The government will pay particular attention to women and their key role in the society of developing countries.

A policy of evaluation of cooperation will have to be developed and the policy of cooperation will be given the necessary qualified personnel. In the target countries, starting with West Africa, a regional presence needs to be provided in order to reinforce the effectiveness and visibility of our action.

Development cooperation policy will be based on respect for democratic principles, human rights, the constitutional state, and good governance, ensuring the coherence of policies, particularly at European level.

In Niger, as in a great many target countries, almost everything is still to be done. In close collaboration with the governments of those countries, Luxembourg cooperation puts programmes in place which combine several vital aspects of development: constructing schools, drilling wells, supplying drinking water and implementing hygiene and health programmes

The government will place particular emphasis on cooperation with non-governmental organisations by pursuing continuing dialogue and a system for cofinancing their projects. At the same time, it will offer them the means to enable them to improve their operation and the quality of their action.

Promoting a development education policy and increasing the awareness of public opinion, particularly among young people, is most important."

## DEVELOPMENT COOPERATION

Inter-ministerial Committee for Development Cooperation

The Ministry of Foreign Affairs is also assisted by an "Inter-Ministerial Committee for Development Cooperation", consisting of representatives of various ministries. This committee performs an essentially consultative function, and issues opinions on the main lines of development policy and particularly on matters relating to technical assistance. More recently, the committee started to examine issues connected with the coherence of policies, in particular on the subject of the Common Agricultural Policy (CAP).

### VOLUME OF LUXEMBOURGPUBLIC AID

Since the end of the 1980s, Luxembourg public development aid (PDA) has increased regularly and substantially. The year 2000 marked a new stage in this trend. That was the year when, in accordance with the commitments given at the Earth Summit in 1972, Luxembourg reached and even exceeded 0.7% of its GNI devoted to public development aid.

In 2002, Luxembourg reached fourth place worldwide among the countries with the greatest commitment in this field, with 0,78% of GNI. Behind Denmark (0.96%), Norway (0.89%) and the Netherlands (0.82%), Luxembourg ranked higher than Sweden (0.74%) as well as all the other OECD countries belonging to the Development Assistance Committee (DAC).This major change corresponds to the government's target of Public Development Aid reaching 1% of GNI by 2005.

**For additional analytical, business and investment opportunities information, please contact Global Investment & Business Center, USA at (202) 546-2103. Fax: (202) 546-3275. E-mail: rusric@erols.com**

All the political parties supported this policy of solidarity. Reaching this target was probably facilitated by the strong economic growth experienced by Luxembourg over many years, even though there has been an economic slowdown more recently. Nevertheless, Luxembourg is noted for a rather pronounced "social culture", as demonstrated by the relatively low levels of poverty and inequality in the country.

## COOPERATION TARGET PROGRAMS

To give Luxembourg development cooperation a more strategic dimension, with a sharper long-term focus, Luxembourg decided to switch from a project approach to a programme approach.

To this end,Cooperation Target Programmes (Programmes indicatifs de coopération) have been devised and signed with four target countries (Cape Verde, Senegal, Vietnam and El Salvador) since the beginning of 2002. In the medium term, these documents of a political nature should also be signed with Laos.

Cooperation Target Programmes last for 4 to 5 years in principle, and are designed as an instrument for steering development cooperation.The government of the partner country is invited to submit its national development strategy as well as national policies for the priority sectors chosen.The CTP guarantees greater transparency and predictability in Luxembourg development cooperation activities, and gives them a strategic nature. Its aim is also to improve and facilitate the management of the cooperation.

The explicitly recognised objective is to reduce poverty. The CTP identifies the priority sectors for cooperation. Usually this concerns social sectors such as education and the training of human resources, health, water and integrated rural development.

The CTP opens up an area of political dialogue relating to issues of mutual importance. Within this context, the two parties undertake to promote the respect of democratic principles, human rights, the constitutional state, good governance and the fight against poverty. Other issues such as regional integration, globalisation, social cohesion and the reduction of inequalities may also be raised.Through the CTP,the two governments are committed to taking account of gender, environment, good governance and transfer of know-how.

With the signature of the CTP, Luxembourg also institutionalised its development cooperation relations with its partners, by setting up a partnership commission with each of them. These Commissions enable the respective ministers in charge of cooperation from each country to meet each year, review their development cooperation relations and give the necessary impetus for future activities.

The opening of the cooperation mission in Dakar (Senegal) in January 2001, with regional powers and responsibilities for Senegal, Mali and Burkina Faso, initiated a major movement to bring Luxembourg's development cooperation closer to work in the field, in order to reinforce its effectiveness and visibility.The ministry has expressed the wish to continue this trend towards greater decentralisation in years to come.

The same year, a cooperation coordination office was opened in Praia (Cape Verde). A similar office had been opened in Pristina in Kosovo in 1999. The organisation of a regional presence in Vietnam and in Central America should soon come to a successful conclusion.

It should also be pointed out that development cooperation policy alone cannot solve the problems of poverty and development.The coherence of policies is a fundamental aspect of

**For additional analytical, business and investment opportunities information, please contact Global Investment & Business Center, USA at (202) 546-2103. Fax: (202) 546-3275. E-mail: rusric@erols.com**

Luxembourg development cooperation policy. It is a necessary condition to ensure progress in North-South relations and to provide a social and human dimension to globalisation.

about.... development cooperation / Press and Information Service of the Luxembourg governement / www.gouvernement.lu

## THE AGRICULTURAL ISSUE

Therefore, Luxembourg is supporting the efforts of

peasant organisations in West Africa, aiming to streng-In 2001 and 2002, Luxembourg organised several then their organisational capacity, and cooperate with workshops, seminars and special days devoted to the their governments in setting up a common agricultural agricultural issue in cooperation with consultants policy at the level of the West African Economic and from the FAO, thus showing their special interest in Monetary Union. this issue.

This process and quest are also justified by the major The analyses presented on these occasions showed objective of Luxembourg's development cooperation that the operation of the world agricultural economy, policy: the fight against poverty. The majority of the which concerns 1.2 billion people, or half the active population of most developing countries - and particularly population of the planet, has led to an explosion of the target countries - is a rural population. It is in this the productivity gap between farmers in the North population that we find the poorest people. In Niger, and South. This situation inevitably led to a fall in for example, 85% of the population live in rural areas. prices and thereby a continuous impoverishment of the rural populations of the South. The regional integration of developing countries,

which is also recommended by the Convention of The effects of the Common Agricultural Policy (CAP) Cotonou, will certainly have beneficial effects on their were analysed within the same context. Without opportunities to develop trading and economic relawishing to underestimate the complexity of the issues, tions between themselves, and to increase their the question arises as to whether it would make more access to world markets.This appears very important, sense to advocate the creation of regional agricultural particularly for the least advanced countries (LACs). markets in the South, grouping together agricultural They have experienced population growth rates over producers with comparable productivity, enabling the last decade that are 2 to 3 times higher than those them to obtain fairer prices and protection from the of the economy.These countries are becoming increacompetition of the North. singly poorer. The inability to get the economies of

these countries off the ground poses a constant chal-This will be the price of maintaining and developing lenge for development cooperation policies. subsistence farming capable of feeding these populations.

about.... development cooperation / Press and Information Service of the Luxembourg governement / www.gouvernement.lu

## BILATERAL COOPERATION

This term designates projects generally referred to as "government to government". It therefore concerns the aid that Luxembourg grants directly to a programme managed in partnership between Luxembourg and the authorities of the developing country.

Target countries

To reinforce the effectiveness of its policy and make it easier to manage, the ministry focuses most of its action on 10 target countries. Some 57% of the funds committed to bilateral cooperation are invested in these 10 countries. The remaining 43% are spread among fewer than 20 other countries.

the 10 target countries were in:

› Asia (Vietnam and Laos);

› Central America (Nicaragua and El Salvador);

› Africa (Niger, Namibia, Cape Verde Islands, Senegal, Mali and Burkina Faso).

The Palestinian occupied territories benefit from the same advantages as those prevailing in the target countries.

The choice of target countries is essentially based on the political decision by the government to make the fight against poverty the key to its development cooperation policy.While poverty is widespread in all these countries, the Luxembourg government is aware of the inequalities that exist within the society of these countries. Luxembourg's cooperation authorities took care to select, as far as possible, the poorest and most disadvantaged regions of those countries for its programmes and projects.

The basic criterion for this choice is the UN's human development index, established on the basis of a number of criteria, three of which are essentials in human development, i.e. longevity, education and living conditions, refined by two other indicators: the gender development index and the human poverty index. All the target countries of the Luxembourg cooperation are in the second half of the rankings of the human development index and five of them are among the least advanced.

Other countries such as Tunisia, Mauritius and Ecuador have become, over the years,"countries with a transitional regime". There, Luxembourg's development cooperation was reduced over time, in view of the performance recorded in the human development indicators of the country.

Luxembourg's bilateral cooperation is not limited, however, to the target countries and countries with a transitional regime.To a lesser extent it also supports specific programmes in what are referred to as "project countries". For this type of cooperation, Luxembourg concentrates its action on a limited number of projects with traditional partners such as Rwanda, Burundi, Morocco, and with more recent partners, including South Africa, India, Chile or China.

Since 1999, Luxembourg has been working in a new geographical area: the western Balkans, and particularly the State of Serbia-Montenegro (including Kosovo) and Albania. The objective of this intervention is to make a bilateral contribution to the efforts of the international community, which aims to create greater stability in this part of Europe.

This cooperation took account of the specific situation of this region, which has been marked in particular by a difficult transition to a market economy and a high level of unemployment. Particular emphasis is being placed on job creation, restructuring the economy, development of agriculture and microfinance.

**For additional analytical, business and investment opportunities information, please contact Global Investment & Business Center, USA at (202) 546-2103. Fax: (202) 546-3275. E-mail: rusric@erols.com**

## PRIORITY SECTORS

Luxembourg is concentrating its development cooperation activities on the main social sectors of education and the training of human resources, health, water and integrated development.

In 2002, 19.21% of cooperation was reserved for education, 29.50% for health and 9.64% for water; 10.18% went to the production sectors of agriculture, forestry, fishing, trade and tourism; 1.63% went to environmental conservation.

In education, Luxembourg tends to align its action in two directions: technical training and vocational training, including the infrastructure, equipment and training of teaching staff.

In the field of health, the Grand Duchy attaches particular importance to the dimension of sustainability. Its intervention combines the aspects of infrastructure, equipment and education of nursing staff by setting up workshops and maintenance policies and methods. A new form of intervention, developed in Rwanda, aims at introducing therapeutic treatment via the supply of anti-retroviral drugs by setting up twinning between hospitals in Luxembourg and Rwanda for the purpose of transfer of know-how.This action is carried out as part of the "ESTHER" initiative which involves four other European countries. In addition, there is close cooperation with WHO, UNAIDS and the World Fund to combat AIDS, tuberculosis and malaria.

Projects to provide safe drinking water have been implemented in El Salvador, Nicaragua, Senegal, Mali, Morocco and the Cape Verde Islands. Other actions, which may or may not be combined with the former, relate to sanitation.These interventions,carried out in cooperation with the relevant authorities, often include awareness and reforestation campaigns.

Integrated rural development also plays a key role in several target countries.This is a multidirectional approach covering the aspects of irrigation, agriculture, health and education.

As far as gender is concerned, the government supports projects that, by their nature, particularly benefit women. Cooperation carried out with UNFPA in several countries enables women to find out about progress in reproductive health.

The environment is another important sector, given that the projects in the field of water sanitation also have a direct impact on the environment.

about.... development cooperation / Press and Information Service of the Luxembourg governement / www.gouvernement.lu

Luxembourg is endeavouring to promote good governance by various means:

› in all the new general agreements on development cooperation, the two governments undertake to respect democratic principles, human rights, the constitutional state and good governance;

› these various subjects are also mentioned, in a specific way, within the context of the political dialogue foreseen by the Cooperation Target Programmes;

› some projects have been implemented in this field, such as the aid management support project at Luxembourg's Ministry of Foreign Affairs.

The private sector in the countries of the South is encouraged particularly through craft projects in Niger and Burkina Faso, with special emphasis on training, organisation of management

**For additional analytical, business and investment opportunities information, please contact Global Investment & Business Center, USA at (202) 546-2103. Fax: (202) 546-3275. E-mail: rusric@erols.com**

structures and micro-finance. Development of hotel and tourism colleges support the development of tourism in Vietnam or Nicaragua.

ESTHER for the fight against AIDS. It is via this therapeutic solidarity among networked hospitals that health care The ESTHER initiative (Ensemble pour une solidarité professionals in the North will help their colleagues in thérapeutique hospitalière en réseau contre le sida – the South fight the disease that now affects 40 million Network for Therapeutic Solidarity in Hospitals people worldwide. against AIDS) was launched officially in Rome on 9 April 2002 by Luxembourg, France, Spain and Italy.This Hundreds of European hospitals have expressed their acronym is the name of a completely new network of wish to take part in this initiative, including the hospital solidarity between countries of the North Centre hospitalier de Luxembourg (CHL) and the and South. Centre hospitalier du Nord (CHN) in Ettelbrück in the

Grand Duchy.These hospitals have launched their acti-The ESTHER initiative is a cooperation programme vities in Africa. With the benefit of the experience intended to fight against the AIDS epidemic, which is acquired in implementing projects to fight AIDS in particularly deadly in African countries, and to facilitate Rwanda, the Luxembourg Ministry of Foreign Affairs access to treatment, particularly to tri therapies. The decided to focus on this country that is so seriously lack of drugs, inadequate staff training and dys-affected by this curse. functional health care structures are the main shortcomings of African countries.To remedy this situation, According to Charles Goerens,"Luxembourg is thus hospitals in industrialised countries will be twinned among the first to engage in a process aimed at put-with those from developing countries to enable ting into practice the principle according to which exchanges of know-how.They will also supply logistical AIDS sufferers in developing countries also have the support to the establishments concerned. right to be treated, and also have the right to hope,

just like sufferers who have the good fortune to live in According to Mr Charles Goerens, Luxembourg's the rich countries on our planet" Minister of Cooperation and Humanitarian Action, this type of initiative is a prerequisite for the correct Statement on development cooperation policy to the allocation of the resources that will be made available Chamber of Deputies on 12 February 2003

## MULTILATERAL COOPERATION

Working with multilateral organisations remains an important component of Luxembourg's development cooperation. This type of cooperation is born out of the determination to benefit from the infrastructures and skills of large international organisations. It involves financing or co-financing a project that will be executed by an international agency. Generally, the ministry will choose programmes that are complementary to its bilateral cooperation.

In this field, the main partners are, inter alia, the World Health Organisation (WHO), the United Nations Development Programme (UNDP), the United Nations Population Fund (UNPF) and the United Nations Relief and Works Agency for Palestine Refugees in the Near East (UNRWA).

## COOPERATION WITHNON-GOVERNMENTALORGANISATIONS

Luxembourg is engaged in cooperation with more than 77 non-governmental organisations.

The commitment of the permanent staff and volunteers of these NGOs, their direct contact with the populations concerned, the diversity of their actions and the relations they have with the South constitute a valuable and indeed vital contribution to Luxembourg's work to help the poor.

Relations with NGOs are the subject of consultations within the working group that meets at regular intervals with representatives of the Ministry of Foreign Affairs and the Circle of NGOs.This group enables discussions to be held on the various aspects of the government's development cooperation policy. The minister in charge of this cooperation also has the opportunity to meet once a year with the representatives of all the NGOs participating in their assembly.

› organise and run collective theoretical training sessions and training/coaching sessions for the management of the project cycle, particularly the setting up and use of the logical framework. So, in 2000, training on managing the project cycle was provided to a hundred members of NGOs;

› supply NGOs, upon request, with information on and explanations of the criteria, frameworks and administrative and financial procedures for submitting projects and framework agreements to the ministry;

› set up a database of experts from the North and South.

**PUBLIC OPINION**

Luxembourg attaches great importance to increasing awareness and informing public opinion on issues of development cooperation.

At the beginning of 2002, the Ministry of Foreign Affairs decided to launch a perennial campaign to increase public awareness in the Grand Duchy, with the backing of the Chamber of Deputies.This campaign aims to:

› inform public opinion about the development cooperation policy implemented by the government;

› encourage acceptance of this policy;

› foster greater knowledge and understanding of the realities of developing countries, and the relations between industrialised and developing countries;

› encourage tolerance as well as a spirit of solidarity with regard to disadvantaged populations in developing countries.

This action complements a series of actions carried out on a regular basis, including press conferences; publication and wide dissemination of the annual report on development cooperation; presentation to the press of the UNDP report on human development and the UNFPA report on the development of the world population; participation in the Consolidated Appeal Process (CAP); organisation of cultural weeks on one or other of the target countries; participation in debates in schools, etc.

In 2000, a North-south Education Service (Service d'Education Nord-Sud known as SENS) was set up within the Circle of NGOs, under the authority of a steering committee with the financial support of the Ministry of Foreign Affairs. This service organises and runs development education activities of various kinds throughout the year with the involvement of many partners (Ministry of Education, National Youth Service, secondary schools, NGOs, etc.) in the Grand Duchy, including courses, workshops in secondary schools, education for teachers and members of NGOs, cooperation with Youth Centres in towns, and so on.

**For additional analytical, business and investment opportunities information, please contact Global Investment & Business Center, USA at (202) 546-2103. Fax: (202) 546-3275. E-mail: rusric@erols.com**

Finally, the ministry is also developing relations with Luxembourg local authorities, in a bid to encourage them to engage in development cooperation.

about.... development cooperation / Press and Information Service of the Luxembourg governement / www.gouvernement.lu

Evaluation and audit

Greater importance is now being attached by the cooperation in evaluating its activities. This is reflected by the establishment of an "evaluation and audit" unit within the ministry.

This strategy of evaluation will lead, first and foremost, to the assessment of results of projects and actions by external assessors, verifying whether and to what extent the objectives have been met. It must also enable the lessons learned from the past to be incorporated into future actions. Carrying out this exercise in partnership with the government of the country concerned is another principle that governs this strategy. Operations to evaluate bilateral and multilateral projects as well as projects co-financed with NGOs are also carried out in growing numbers, and serve to optimise the aid granted by Luxembourg to poor countries.

Contribution of the Ministry of Finance to Development Assistance

Through its responsibility for international financial institutions, the Ministry of Finance has a complementary role in Luxembourg's development assistance strategy. The Bretton Woods organisations, i.e. the World Bank and the International Monetary Fund (IMF), are in fact among the most important sources of finance for developing countries. The Ministry of Finance, in collaboration with the Luxembourg Central Bank, is represented on the board of directors of these organizations and is thus able (within the limits of its relative capital share) to influence the policies of both institutions. Most of the assistance provided by Luxembourg is directed towards the "soft loan windows" of the World Bank and IMF, which are used to extend credits on preferential terms as well as grants for social projects and programmes in the poorest developing countries. In addition to the World Bank and the IMF, the Ministry of Finance also provides funding to the International Fund for Agricultural Development (IFAD), the Global Environment Facility (GEF), as well as for development projects in various countries of operation of the European Bank for Reconstruction and Development (EBRD). Since September 2003 Luxembourg is also a member of the Asian Development Bank (AsDB), focused on poverty reduction in the most heavily populated continent in the world.

In recent years the expenditures by the Ministry of Finance on official development assistance (ODA) have amounted to between EUR 8 million and EUR 10 million a year, which corresponds to approximately 6% of Luxembourg's total ODA budget. However of more importance than the scale of the expenditures are the specific areas targeted, which complement the development assistance provided by the Ministry of Foreign Affairs. Thus, the Ministry of Finance focuses on:

› Debt relief assistance for the poorest countries in order to free up domestic budgetary resources for priority programmes like education or health care (although Luxembourg itself is not a creditor country);

› Improving the investment climate in developing countries so as to encourage domestic savings and check the flight of capital on the one hand, and to attract urgently needed foreign capital and know-how on the other;

› Support for the banking sector to ensure the availability of finance to the real economy (mainly for small and medium-sized enterprises which form the backbone of a healthy economy; particular attention is also paid to microfinance in this regard);

› Investment opportunities in the environmental area as offered to developing countries under the Kyoto Protocol: these mechanisms permit to tackle global environmental problems more cost-efficiently than through implementing exclusively national measures in the industrialized countries;

› The use of modern communications and information technologies – ICT to promote the interests of developing countries (Internet portals for the procurement and exchange of knowledge and experiences, for enhancing democratic decision-making processes, etc.);

› The financing of research, especially in the area of agriculture and with a three-pronged focus: securing adequate food supplies in the light of a continuing demographic explosion, preserving the genetic resources of plants, as well as promoting the use of biological pesticides that do not damage the environment.

about.... development cooperation / Press and Information Service of the Luxembourg governement / www.gouvernement.lu

Useful Addresses

Ministry of Foreign Affairs, Foreign Trade, Cooperation and Defence Direction de la Coopération au développement 6, rue de la Congrégation L-1352 Luxembourg Tel. : +352 47 82 35 1 Fax: +352 22 20 48 E-mail: information@mae.etat.lu www.mae.lu Lux-Development S.A. 10, rue de la Grève B.P. 2273 L-1022 Luxembourg Tel.: +352 29 58 58 1 Fax: +352 29 58 58 200 E-mail: ask@lux-development.lu www.lux-development.lu

Bureau d'Assistance technique aux ONG (BAT) 13, avenue Gaston Diederich L-1420 Luxembourg Tel.: +352 26 02 09 21 / 22 Fax: +352 26 02 09 26 E-mail: bat@cercle.lu Centre d'Information Tiers Monde (CITIM) 55, av. de la Liberté L-1931 Luxembourg Tel.: +352 40 04 27 1 Fax: +352 40 04 27 27 E-mail: education@astm.lu www.astm.lu

Imprint Publisher Press and Information Service Publishing Unit Published in cooperation with the Direction de la Coopération au développement Layout BIZART Impression xxx Photos Direction de la Coopération au développement Photothèque SIP ISBN 2-87999-097-1 January 2004

## LANGUAGES IN LUXEMBOURG

### LUXEMBOURG: A LINGUISTIC PUZZLE.

The linguistic situation in Luxembourg is characterised by the fact that several languages are spoken and written at the same time in the same place. Names of streets, shops, travel tickets, hotel registries and menus are mostly in French (some street and place names are also added in Lëtzebuergesch). Newspapers printed in the Grand Duchy are mostly in German, but some cultural articles, many advertisements and social announcements are in French. In other countries too, several languages are spoken, but they almost always are limited to specific regions, to the exclusion of other tongues. In Luxembourg, the various languages are superimposed in an almost hierarchical manner. There is, however, a certain logic to the puzzle.

On all levels of society, only one language is used in oral communication: **"Lëtzebuergesch"**. This is the everyday spoken language of the people, and the symbol of the Luxembourgers national identity. Although of Germanic origin (around the 4th Century), 'Lëtzebuergesch' has sufficiently differentiated itself from its parent language, so as no longer to be readily understood by many a German. German native speakers might well recognise this or that word or construction used in Lëtzebuergesch -in the same way that a German from one region can 'understand' a dialect from another German region- but are often caught out by 'non-Germanic' words or turns of phrase.

'Lëtzebuergesch' is taught in schools and in language courses mostly addressed to the resident foreigners. Whilst it is an extremely practical and useful means of everyday conversation, it is a poor culture-bearer. As soon as a conversation reaches out into the higher levels of abstraction or refined sentiment, the limits of the vocabulary and grammatical constructions available are all too apparent and it becomes necessary to borrow from other languages.

This switch-over to foreign languages, namely French and German is a necessity in written communication. A number of attempts have been made to establish Lëtzebuergesch as a written language. The first real orthography for use in schools was set up in 1914 by the Education Minister Nicolas Welter, because this was when Lëtzebuergesch was for the first time taught as a school subject (Education Law of 1912). This system never became official, though a generation of Luxembourg schoolchildren became familiar with it, and the system was used by the Resistance in the second World War for the publication of their leaflets and later the newspaper *D'Uni'on*, which for about three years after 1945 was published entirely in Lëtzebuergesch. This became unmanageable, and they had to revert to standard German. At the same time as this was going on, the Education Minister Nicolas Margue commissioned Jean Feltes, a phonetician, to invent a new orthography for Lëtzebuergesch.

This was, however, so far away from German that no guidance could be got from that language, and the new *Lëzebuurjer Ortografi* as it was called, even though it was made official under an Arreté ministériel of 5 June 1946, never became popular in schools, in spite of the fact that textbooks were prepared in which it was used, i.e. *Lëzebuurjer Gedichter a Proosashteker fiir ons Schoulen*. In 1950, a new dictionary of the Luxembourg language was commissioned under Joseph Tockert, Helene Palgen, and Robert Bruch. First they had to invent an orthography that was more transparent than that of Feltes, and closer to the German. Bruch did this, and it was used for all the volumes of the Luxemburger Wörterbuch, in a publication period which lasted from 1950 to 1978. When Bruch died in a road-crash in 1959, the work of the Dictionary publication was taken over by Henri Rinnen, who later became influential in the *Actioun Lëtzebuergesch* (1972ff).

He of course wanted the dictionary spelling to be made official. This was done in 1976, when Feltes' system was officially dropped. From that time, Actioun Lëtzebuergesch actively promoted the new official spelling in its own publication *Eis Sprooch*, and elsewhere, wherever it could. Since the language law of 1984, this influence has grown, and now all signs, notices, etc appearing in Lëtzebuergesch have to be in this official orthography. If civil servants don't know it, there are courses to teach them. It is no longer possible to write Lëtzebuergesch (for publication at any rate) in any old system invented by yourself. And this is what many Luxembourgers find annoying, that for the first time they can be found guilty of misspelling their own language, a burden other nations have suffered from for centuries.

As the above brief historical overview shows, neither the artificial creation of an official orthography, nor the efforts of the linguists have been able to displace German, which - thanks to its close relationship to the vernacular - is favoured by the popular classes, or French which by virtue of its evident quality and long tradition has been the means of expression of those who see themselves as the intellectual élite. This situation is reflected whenever the use of languages

**For additional analytical, business and investment opportunities information, please contact Global Investment & Business Center, USA at (202) 546-2103. Fax: (202) 546-3275. E-mail: rusric@erols.com**

exceeds the requirement of daily conversation. French is used as much as possible; German where it is indispensable, in fact, whenever the less educated public has to be reached. That is certainly not to imply that a German speaker is less well educated, but many of those folk who grew up in Luxembourg during and immediately after the second World War somehow lost out on a French education, as only German was allowed during the War, and afterwards, well, there was a country to rebuild, and perhaps not so much importance was placed on learning foreign languages.

In this way French is the official language of the authorities. Parliamentary documents, proposed bills, procedures in court, administrative and judicial acts, are held and written in French, but the synoptic accounts of parliamentary debates (themselves carried out in Lëtzebuergesch or in French) are printed in German (Analytischer Kammerbericht) because they are distributed to all households in the country. Speeches at political rallies and other public occasions are in Lëtzebuergesch. Certain texts are multilingual, depending on the need to make sure that information is brought to all levels of the population. Thus for example, when a new law relating to rents (the equivalent of the British "Landlord & Tenant Act") was brought into force, the texts of the new law were printed in the newspapers in 5 different languages, a page each. (Lëtzebuergesch, French, German, Portuguese and Spanish). The latter two were included, since many immigrants from these countries live and work in Luxembourg (some 36% of the country's population, and a staggering 48% of the country's workforce hold a foreign passport).

Historic tradition, economic necessity, and above all a genuine desire to counteract any linguistic (or other) imperialism on the part of the powerful neighbours have brought about this peculiar situation. Whilst this places a heavy burden on the educational system, it does however give the students a unique opportunity to learn many languages and thus gives access to many cultures.

From the second year of primary school onwards, French is added as a discipline to the general program of education which, at this stage is still taught in German. Over the years, however, and particularly in secondary education, French gets an ever bigger share until it completely replaces German as the language of instruction, German being limited to the specialised courses in German language and literature. English too, it should be added, is required as a compulsory language throughout most of secondary education, and students choosing language studies also have the option to add Latin and/or ancient Greek. (see also  Luxembourg Schools)

It appears therefore that the Luxembourg intellectual is mainly orientated towards French cultural values through his education, the more so since he will most probably attend University either in Belgium or in France (attendance at German Universities is statistically in third place).

Tradition, natural sympathy and education all concur to put the Luxembourg élite within the French cultural orbit: French books and publications are widely read, written communication is mostly in French. Most of the Luxembourg periodicals aimed at the intellectual are almost entirely written in French, and so are the literary reviews and student magazines. The knowledge and understanding of German and the root relationship existing between German and the local dialect however, add a dimension of wealth and objectivity which make for a unique situation indeed.

Luxembourg is thus prepared to be widely open to foreign culture, especially because the small size of the country (999 square miles) and its population (399 239 inhabitants) hardly allow for a rich national cultural life of high standard.
An open-minded attitude to foreign culture permits Luxembourg to escape the narrowness of provincial thought and life. In fact, the intensity and diversity of cultural life in Luxembourg is surprising. The theatre season regularly brings to Luxembourg outstanding performances by the best companies of France, Germany and Belgium.

The more popular cinemas play throughout the year the whole range of the international film productions in their original language. A favourable geographic location brings into the Luxembourg homes radio and television programs from France, Germany and Belgium in addition to the Luxembourg national ones. Satellite television with its worldwide network is very popular. The ASTRA ground control station is situated in the Grand Duchy.

The possibility to use several languages of high civilisation as cultural instruments is certainly an advantage, but there are also drawbacks. Lacking its own spiritual roots, the Luxembourg writer is almost doomed to a certain creative sterility because he can very seldom manage to really make his own a tongue that he learned at school and has only occasionally spoken. Critical consciousness of a foreign language is thus more common than partaking in its proper and peculiar imagination and sentiment.

It would seem that only the mother tongue, which one thinks and speaks, is really an instrument of original creation. And in fact, within the evident limitations imposed by the relative poverty of the local dialect, Luxembourg writers are creative, especially in lyrical poetry and local theatre which more often are spoken rather than written media. (See also: Edition Phi, the main publisher in Luxembourg for books on Lëtzebuergesch Literature and Theatre). Luxembourg writers in German are dealing with an instrument close to their mother tongue and familiar to all readers. Certainly "Luxembourg" high German seldom achieves the purity and exactness of genuine German, but the "Luxembourgisms" lend their works a local flavour which makes them somehow true and genuine. In that respect, the Luxembourger writing in French is less favoured. He faces the refinements and intricacies of a completely foreign language learned and cultivated in Germanic territory. He seldom reaches the higher realms of creativity, unless he expatriates himself into completely French surroundings. And the public moreover is likely to prefer the Paris literary production to his own. He is at his best as an often brilliant critic, essayist or scientific writer, where he can take full advantage of his unique participation in two cultural worlds of equally high standard.

As with all questions of languages, borders are not so easily drawn. Hence it should come as no surprise that the political boundaries of the Grand Duchy do not sharply delimit the situation depicted above. Indeed, in the surrounding areas of Luxembourg, many people have grown up with a variant of our Luxembourgish lingua: the "platt" of Alsace-Lorraine is similarly connected to middle-high German, yet the area (nowadays) is part of France; many inhabitants of the so-called "Areler Land" just inside Belgium also grew up speaking Lëzebuergesch, yet they are imbued with French all around them; ... Since a lot of these adjacent regions are similarly - though perhaps not to quite the same extent - shaped by both German and French culture, the whole area around Luxembourg can truly be called a Franco-German Cultural Melting Pot.

## PUBLICATIONS ON "LËTZEBUERGESCH"

Readers may be interested to hear that there are a number of books available on the language of Luxembourg. Here's a list of some of the more interesting publications available.

Some of the information below is taken from Jul Christophory's book: "A Short History of Literature in Luxembourgish" (1994 Bibliothèque Nationale - ISBN2-87980-011-0)

## ABOUT LËTZEBUERGESCH

### LUXEMBOURG & LËTZEBUERGESCH, LANGUAGE AND COMMUNICATION AT THE CROSSROADS OF EUROPE[2]

The Grand Duchy of Luxembourg sits at the heart of the European Union, yet it forms a very private and close-knit community. This book addresses that apparent paradox, and shows how it is reflected in and sustained by the linguistic practices of the people who live there, both native and foreign. Lëtzebuergesch, the country's national language, is most closely related to the German dialects of the western Rhineland and the Moselle river valley, but the country's historical and cultural links with Belgium, the Netherlands, and France are much closer than with Germany. Since the demise of Latin in the late Middle Ages as the language of administration, that role has been filled at various times by the standard varieties of French and German.

Since 1945, French and Lëtzebuergesch have come to predominate and the use of German has once again receded. It is the unwritten social code governing the use of these languages (and latterly also of English) which gives this volume of specially commissioned papers its focus: the purpose is to provide an insider's view of the community, and of its little-known language. The book contains the most detailed linguistic description of Lëtzebuergesch so far available in English."

**Who's afraid of Luxembourgish? Lëtzebuergesch? Qui a peur du Luxembourgeois? Bilingual guide to Luxembourgish conversation**

Jul Christophory. Luxembourg. Imprimerie Bourg-Bourger, 1979, 120 p.
About a third of Luxembourg's population consists of foreigners. This Luxembourg phrase-book with English and French translation was compiled for all English- and French-speaking people living in Luxembourg. By presenting them with dialogues and vocabulary for about thirty everyday situations, it sets out to give an insight into Luxembourgish as spoken by the average inhabitant

### GERMAN DIALECTS: PHONOLOGY AND MORPHOLOGY WITH SELECTED TEXTS

R.E.Keller. Manchester, England: Manchester University Press, 1961. 369 p. map. bibliog.
This book affords the student of German a descriptive phonological and grammatical survey of certain dialects. Keller devotes chapters to Schwyzerdütsch, Alsatian, Darmstadt dialect, Upper Austrian, Lëtzebuergesch, Westphalian and North Saxon (lower Elbe). The chapter on Lëtzebuergesch (p.248-99) is subdivided into phonology, morphology, an extract from Michel Rodange's *De Renert*, notes and glossary. It offers a very proficient and systematic survey of the area, status and general characteristics of Luxembourgish. The whole book constitutes a unique comparative study and stimulating starting-point for further research.

**Luxembourgeois, Qui êtes-vous? Echos et chuchotements** by Jul Christophory

(Ed. Guy Binsfeld) An interesting essay to characterize the Lëtzebuerger

### DICTIONARIES

**Luxemburger Wörterbuch (5 Volumes)**

[2] by Dr Gerald Newton, Director of the Centre for Luxembourg Studies at the University of Sheffield Oxford University Press (21st March 1996) ISBN 0-19-824016-3 Cost: 2320 Flux

For additional analytical, business and investment opportunities information,
please contact Global Investment & Business Center, USA
at (202) 546-2103. Fax: (202) 546-3275. E-mail: rusric@erols.com

Ed. Paul Linden 1950/54; reprint 1978 Joseph Beffort
Members of the original Dictionary commission: J. Tockert, R. Bruch, R. Palgen, I Comes, J. Hess, E. Ludovicy, J. Meyers, J.P. Zanen.
Members of the 1976 Dictionary commission: H. Rinnen, A. Atten, H. Palgen, G. Reuland, T. Schroeder, P.Schumacher, E. Steinmetzer, M. Werdel, P. Jost, H. Klees, E. Leytem, F. Lorang, C. Meder, V. Rasqu, J.Scheer, O. Scholer.
This book has been defined by some as the "ultimate" Luxembourg dictionary. It lists Lëtzebuergesch words and defines them in standard German, along with examples of their use (eg idioms). It was published in instalments, between 1950 and 1978, the last volume (5) being a supplement of what they had forgotten to include. A new Commission for a new Dictionary was set up in 1994, but since the government didn't grant any money towards compiling the dictionary, and they couldn't find anybody willing to do the compiling anyway, the whole thing was abandoned, and a decision taken instead to reprint the 5 volumes unchanged, except for being compressed into 2 volumes. This came out in 1995/96, distributed by Librairie Krauss. It costs about 160 UK pound.

**English-Lëtzebuergesch Dictionary** by Jules Christophory

(New edition, 1996) consisting of 35 000 words
ISBN 2-87 953-015-6
Editions Schortgen
Jean-Paul Schortgen
121 rue de l'Alzette
L-4011 Esch-sur-Alzette
Tel: (+352) 54 64 87
Fax: (+352) 53 05 34
Cost: 748 FLUX

### 6000 Wierder

(6000 essential Luxembourgish words are translated from Lëtzebuergesch into French, German, English, Spanish and Portuguese by Jacqui Zimmer)
Editions: Imprimerie St Paul ISBN 2 879 631 777
2 rue Christophe Plantin
Z.I. Luxembourg-Gasperich
L-2988 Luxembourg
Cost: 585 Flux

## LEARNING LËTZEBUERGESCH

**"Parler Luxembourgeois / Esou Schwaetze mir / Living Luxembourgish"** by Gilbert Sondag, Josiane Kartheiser, Henry Wickens

Editions Le Phare, Esch-sur-Alzette, 1996, pp. 347.

### "Lwei Lëtzebuergesch. Lëtzebuergesch fir all Dag"

Book and Cassette made by the "Centre de Langues Luxembourg".
Luxembourg Ministry of Education. Provisional Edition 1993."

**Mir schwätze Lëtzebuergesch. Nous parlons luxembourgeois. Abécédaire luxembourgeois. Guide bilingue de grammaire et de lecture.**

(We speak Luxembourgish. Luxembourgish primer. Bilingual guide to grammar and reading.)
Jul Christophory. Luxembourg: Imprimerie Saint-Paul, 1974. 167p.
This textbook was written for the English- and French-speaking communities living in Luxembourg. It is a complement to the phrase-book: *Who's afraid of Luxembourgish?* Part I provides essential data on Luxembourgish; Part II is a closer study of the main grammatical features; Part III gives a survey of the literary scene and quotes extracts from the most popular authors (with English and French translations).

### DA LASS - MIR LÉIERE LËTZEBUERGESCH

Video cassette (240 minutes) + Two books (Vol1: 160 pages / 600 colour illustrations; Vol2: 262 pages / 700 colour illustrations)
Learn the Luxembourg language in 20 interesting lessons, complete with grammatical, phonetic and lexicographic elements, as well as (solved) exercises.
[cost: 1475 Flux = 26.56 Euros]

- A most interesting site on **learning Lëtzebuergesch** (and the spelling thereof) is at: http://w3.restena.lu/al/interact/index.htm. This interactive site also includes sound files, but requires Netscape 3 to operate at it's best.
- Several organisations in Luxembourg can assist with learning Lëtzebuergesch, in day-time and/or evening **Courses**:

### MINISTÈRE DE L'EDUCATION NATIONALE

Lycée Technique du Centre
106 Avenue Pasteur
L-2309 Luxembourg
Tel: (+352) 478 5153

**Centre de Langues et de Culture**

80, Boulevard General Patton
L-2316 Luxembourg
Tel: (+352) - 40 39 41

### INTERNATIONAL LANGUAGE CENTRE / PROLINGUA

140 Rue Adolphe Fischer
L-1521 Luxembourg
Tel: (+352) 40 39 91 / 40 39 92

### LUXEMBOURG - ACCUEIL - INFORMATION

10 Bisserwé
L-1238 Luxembourg
Tel: (+352) 24 17 17 (9 - 12 a.m.)

### ECOLE PRIVÉE GRANDJEAN

7 Rue Adolphe Fischer
L-1521 Luxembourg
Tel: (+352) 49 17 92

**CELAC - CENTRE EUROPÉEN DES LANGUES ET DE LA COMMUNICATION**

2 Circuit de la Foire Internationale
L-1347 Luxembourg
Tel: (+352) 42 62 30 312

**ASTI** - a.s.b.l. - **Association de Soutien aux Travailleurs Immigrés**

10 Rue Auguste Laval
L-1922 Luxembourg
Tel: (+352) 43 83 33

**SERVICE INTERNATIONAL DE FORMATION LANGUES - INLINGUA**

72 Rue du Cimetière
L-1338 Luxembourg
Tel: (+352) 40 35 47
Fax: (+352) 40 35 48

**INFO-ACCUEIL**

9 Rue Chimay
Tel: (+352) 47 96 27 51
Fax: (+352) 46 06 35

## FURTHER INFORMATION ABOUT LËTZEBUERGESCH

You can find some texts and .wav files of Luxembourg songs at http://www.restena.lu/lmr/luxbg/ltzbgsch.html

The Institut Grand-Ducal, Section de Linguistique, de Folklore et de Toponymie, who have contributed to the Luxemburger Wörterbuch, is now available via email. The Secretary is Henri Klees at henri.klees@ci.rech.lu and Ralph Fichtner, who is currently employed to put the archive on computer, is at ralph.fichtner@ci.educ.lu

At http://www.igd-leo.lu/igd-leo/onomastics/villages/villages.html is a most useful gazetteer of villages and towns, explaining Luxembourg Place names.

Jean ENSCH (email: jean.ensch@ci.rech.lu), the creator of the above page(s), writes: "Due to its particular situation on the French-German language frontier, Luxembourg place names have the peculiarity of having sometimes 3 differents versions according to the French, German or Luxembourgish languages used. Therefore the alphabetical lists of place names are presented in three different language series, each giving the corresponding version in the two other languages. Moreover, the name of the municipality these villages administratively belong to is also supplied. A clickable map, indicating the municipal boundaries is also availabe at this site."

An interesting discussion on the economic weight of the Luxembourg language (De l'importance économique du luxembourgeois) followed by an article on the French language use in Luxembourg "Parlez français, s.v.p.!" is at: http://www.igd-leo.lu/igd-leo/linguistics/baleine/igdbaleine.html

A more indepth discussion on the use of languages in Luxembourg is presented at:http://www.restena.lu/asti/cdaic/baleine/Baleine1.html

Literary Life in Luxembourg

Centre National de Littérature

Luxembourg and its Languages SHAPE Community Life 19 March 1998

Mercator-Education European network for information, documentation and research into regional or minority languages in education.

The "Lëtzebuerger Mailing List" at www.prophecy.lu is held mostly in the Lëtzebuergesch language, although other languages too (French, German, English) are acceptable. Enquire within, if you have any questions to which the mailing-list members (some 50 at the time of writing [aug '98]) might perhaps have an answer. Most members are based in Luxembourg.

... eis Sprooch To help keep our language -the symbol of our national identity- alive, this site by the "Lycée Michel Rodange" gives some texts of Luxembourg poems, and also has a number of audio files available for download

We hope that this brief synopsis on the Luxembourg language situation is of use, and would be pleased to assist further. We are continuously trying to improve this (and our other) page(s), so please do get in touch, if you have any comments.
You can reach us by: phone: +44 (0) 207 434 2800 fax: +44 (0) 207 734 1205

# ECONOMY AND FINANCE

The economic performance of the Grand Duchy was among The media, communication and the audio-visual industry

Luxembourg owes its wealth to the discovery of iron ore in the southern area of the country called the "Minett". Today, the vibrant expansion of the financial centre, the emergence of new service activities and the leading-edge industrial companies characterize Luxembourg's economy. This economy is also distinguished by a calm and peaceful social climate.

## AGRICULTURE

The importance of agriculture, wine growing and forestry for the Grand Duchy's economy has steadily declined over the years. Today's official Statec figures for 2003 show Luxembourg's agriculture accounting for just 0.5% of the total value added at market prices, while it amounted to around 4 % a quarter of a century ago. Nevertheless, the output of this sector has almost tripled in the past 25 years. Moreover, this phenomenon is not peculiar to Luxembourg's agriculture, but can also be observed in the European Union as a whole. The shrinking role played by agriculture in Luxembourg's GDP is mainly due to the expansion of the service sector and, in particular, banking, telecommunications, air-transport and audiovisual services. Today's agriculture is more aware of environmental issues and contributes to protecting the natural habitat.

## INDUSTRY

The early stages of Luxembourg's industrial development were dominated by the steel industry in the mid-19th century. This domination continued until the 1974-75 oil crisis, which transformed Luxembourg's industrial habits and encouraged a service economy. The emergence of the service sector was accelerated by the trend towards "outsourcing", which involves shifting certain services to specialist sector companies. Lastly, industrial diversification seems to be establishing itself as a permanent objective of economic policy. It has encouraged the emergence of a second industrial pole that includes the chemical industry, rubber and plastics. Today, the first steel-industry in the world, stemming from the merging of Arbed, Usinor and Aceralia in February 2001, has its head-quarters in Luxembourg.

As a multilingual country located at the crossroads of the French-and German-speaking cultures, Luxembourg plays a special role on the European media scene. The Grand Duchy is the home of two giants in the world of audio-visual communication, the European television and radio broadcaster RTL Group, and the satellite company Société Européenne des Satellites (SES), which operates the Astra satellites. On March 28, 2001 SES merged with GE Americom to create SES Global, the biggest satellite company in the world. Many SMEs active in the converging fields of multimedia and telecommunications have been set up in Luxembourg around these two pillars of audio-visual communication, forming a network of skills that is driving future economic development. Besides the SMEs, some multinational companies of the New Economy, like AOL and iTunes Music Store established their offices in Luxembourg during 2004. The Luxembourg government is pursuing an active policy of developing audio-visual and communication services underthe banner of the Luxembourg Mediaport. To this end, the potential offered by the movement towards liberalizing the European telecommunications market and the progress of technology are lending support. As part of this proactive policy, Luxembourg adopted a number of public support schemes in the early 1990s to encourage the development of audio-visual production.

Ministère des Classes moyennes, du Tourisme et du Logement (Ministry of Middle classes, Tourism and Housing)

6, avenue Emile Reuter, L-2420 Luxembourg Tel.: (+352) 478 47 06, Fax: (+352) 478 47 40 www.mcm.public.lu

**A FINANCIAL CENTRE**

The establishment of the Luxembourg Stock Exchange and the 1929 laws on holding companies marked the beginning of international development in the financial sector. The Eurobond market of the 1960s contributed to the emergence of real banking know-how in Luxembourg. The country's current cash and asset management activities testify to Luxembourg's adaptable approach to its development as a financial centre. The real expansion of Luxembourg's collective investment undertakings (organismes de placement collectif OPC) dates from 1983, with the first law regarding unit trust companies (sociétés d'investissement à capital variable - Sicav). The net assets of collective investment undertakings rose from 2 billion euro in 1970 to 1,037.3 billion euro as at April 2004 (Source: CSSF), taking Luxembourg to the first place in Europe for unit trust asset management.

Useful addresses :

STATEC (Central Statistics and Economic Studies Service)

13, rue Erasme, bâtiment Pierre Werner,

B.P. 304, L-2013 Luxembourg Tel.: (+352) 478 42 52, Fax: (+352) 46 42 89 www.statec.lu info@statec.etat.lu

Ministère de l'Economie (Ministry of Economy)

6, boulevard Royal, L-2449 Luxembourg Tel.: (+352) 478 6712, Fax: (+352) 46 04 48
www.eco.public.lu

Ministère des Finances (Ministry of Finance)

3, rue de la Congrégation, L-1352 Luxembourg Tel.: (+352) 478 26 17, Fax: (+352) 47 52 41
www.fi.etat.lu

Ministère de l'Agriculture, de la Viticulture et du Développement rural (Ministry of Agriculture, Viticulture and Rural Development)

1, rue de la Congrégation, L-1352 Luxembourg Tel.: (+352) 478 25 00, Fax: (+352) 46 40 27

# FOREIGN POLICY AND INTERNATIONAL RELATIONS

## FOREIGN RELATIONS

Luxembourg has long been a prominent supporter of European political and economic integration. In efforts foreshadowing European integration, Luxembourg and Belgium in 1921 formed the Belgium-Luxembourg Economic Union (BLEU) to create an inter-exchangeable currency and a common customs regime. Luxembourg is a member of the Benelux Economic Union and was one of the founding members of the European Economic Community (now the European Union). It also participates in the Schengen Group, whose goal is the free movement of citizens among member states. At the same time, Luxembourgers have consistently recognized that European unity makes sense only in the context of a dynamic, transatlantic relationship and have traditionally pursued a pro-NATO, pro-U.S. foreign policy.

Luxembourg is the site of the European Court of Justice, the European Court of Auditors, and other vital EU organs. The Secretariat of the European Parliament is located in Luxembourg, but the Parliament usually meets in nearby Strasbourg.

## DEFENSE

The Luxembourg army is under civilian control. Responsibility for defense matters is vested in the Minister of Cooperation, Humanitarian Action and Defense, Charles Goerens, under the Ministry of Foreign Affairs, Trade, Cooperation and Defense.

Luxembourg has no navy or air force. A 1967 law made the army an all-volunteer force with current strength of approximatel 450 professional soldiers, about 340 enlisted recruits and 100 civilians, and a total budget of $120 million. Luxembourg has participated in the European Corps (EUROCORPS) since 1994, has contributed troops to the UNPROFOR and IFOR missions in former Yugoslavia, and participates with a small contingent in the current NATO SFOR mission in Bosnia. The Luxembourg army is integrated into the Multinational Beluga Force under Belgian command. Luxembourg has financially supported international peacekeeping missions during the 1991 Gulf war, in Rwanda and, more recently, Albania. The army also has participated in humanitarian relief missions such as setting up refugee camps for Kurds and providing emergency supplies to Albania.

Luxembourg's foreign policy is determined by its dual concern for its security and its integration in a large geographical economic area. It is more than 150 years since Luxembourg first recognized the necessity of integration in an economic union and joined the Prussian Customs Union in 1842. After World War I it freed itself of its economic ties with Germany and in 1922 entered an economic union with Belgium that is still in place today. In 1948, Luxembourg was a co-founder of the BENELUX economic union and a few years later a founding member of the European Coal and Steel Community (ECSC), the European Economic Community (EEC) and the European Atomic Energy Community (EURATOM). Luxembourg foreign policy currently focuses on cooperation with the western partners, bilaterally and within the EU and NATO, in the awareness that this is the best way to guarantee the independence of Luxembourg as an equal state. Luxembourg is an active contributor to EU policy and a firm believer in ensuring that the smaller EU member states can participate fairly in the reform and further development of the EU institutions.

Luxembourg attaches particular importance to maintaining relations with the countries of Central and Eastern Europe, in particular Romania, which is even today home to many descendants of

Luxembourg emigrants from the 12th and 18th centuries. It moreover sees itself as an advocate for the EU candidate countries. Luxembourg makes a notable contribution in the field of humanitarian assistance and development aid. In 2003 it spent 0.8% of its GDP on development cooperation, thereby exceeding the UN and OECD target of 0.7%; it plans to increase funding to 1% by the year 2005.

The close and friendly relations with its neighbouring states are fostered through regional cooperation (Saar-Lor-Lux-Trier/Westphalia/Wallonia), for which a legal framework was established with the four-party Karlsruhe Agreement of 23 January 1996 between Germany, France, Switzerland and Luxembourg.

In those countries in which it does not maintain its own embassy or consulate, Luxembourg is represented in diplomatic matters by the Netherlands and in consular matters by Belgium.

## SECURITY POLICY

According to the Treaty of London of 1867, Luxembourg was to be neutral and raise no army of its own. As a result of its experiences in World Wars I and II, when it was occupied by German forces notwithstanding its status of perpetual neutrality, Luxembourg formally abandoned this policy in 1948 with the parliamentary confirmation of the Grand-Ducal decree of 30 November 1944 that ended neutrality and introduced general conscription. Conscription was abolished in 1967.

The Luxembourg army is integrated into NATO and well organized and trained to meet its constitutional functions. It consists of some 800 officers, non-commissioned officers and privates. Military service is voluntary, but it does facilitate entry to a career in the civil service (e.g. in the police, post office, customs, law enforcement). The defence budget was equal to 1% of GDP in 2001. An increase in defence spending is expected over the coming years. Luxembourg participates in international peace missions (e.g. the NATO peace mission KFOR in Kosovo and the EU mission in Macedonia).

## U.S. RELATIONS

Bilateral relations between the United States and Luxembourg are excellent, both historically and through common membership in the Organization for Cooperation and Economic Development (OECD), OSCE, and NATO. More than 5,000 American soldiers, including Gen. George S. Patton, are buried at the American Military Cemetery near the capital.

**For additional analytical, business and investment opportunities information, please contact Global Investment & Business Center, USA at (202) 546-2103. Fax: (202) 546-3275. E-mail: rusric@erols.com**

# LUXEMBOURG CONSTITUTION[3]

## BASIC INFORMATION

The **Constitution of Luxembourg** is the supreme law of the Grand Duchy of Luxembourg. The modern constitution was adopted on 17 October 1868.

Whilst the constitution of 1868 marked a radical change in Luxembourg's constitutional settlement, it was technically an amendment of the original constitution. That original constitution was promulgated on 12 October 1841, came into effect on 1 January 1842, and was acutely amended on 20 March 1848, and again on 27 November 1856

## CHAPTER I THE STATE, ITS TERRITORY, AND THE GRAND DUKE

**Article 1 [Independent State]**
The Grand Duchy of Luxembourg is a democratic, free, independent, and indivisible State.

**Article 2 [Boundaries]**
The boundaries and chief towns of judicial or administrative districts and of cantons and communes may only be changed pursuant to a law.

**Article 3 [Hereditary Crown]**
The Crown of the Grand Duchy is hereditary in the Nassau family in accordance with the Pact of 30 June 1783, Article 71 of the Treaty of Vienna of 9 June 1815, and Article 1 of the Treaty of London of 11 May 1867.

**Article 4 [Grand Duke]**
The person of the Grand Duke is inviolable.

**Article 5 [Majority and Oath of the Grand Duke]**

(1) The Grand Duke of Luxembourg attains his majority on the completion of eighteen years of age. On assuming the reins of government, he shall take the following oath as soon as possible, in the presence of the Chamber of Deputies or of a deputation appointed by it:
(2) *"I swear to observe the Constitution and the laws of the Grand Duchy of Luxembourg, to maintain the national independence and integrity of the territory, as well as public and individual liberties."*

**Article 6 [Succession of Minors]**
If on the death of the Grand Duke his successor is a minor the regency shall be exercised in accordance with the Family Pact.

**Article 7 [Inability]**

[3] { Adopted on: 17 Oct 1868 } { ICL Document Status: 5 Nov 1998 } { **Editor's Note:** The original ICL-edition has been amended up to and including the amendments of 12 July 1996 and 12 Jan 1998. The 1998 amendment changed Articles 33, 73, 80, 83bis, 95bis, 95ter, and 115. The integrity of this consolidated edition was last checked by Mr. Stephane Jacoby on the Status Date above.}

**For additional analytical, business and investment opportunities information, please contact Global Investment & Business Center, USA at (202) 546-2103. Fax: (202) 546-3275. E-mail: rusric@erols.com**

(1) If the Grand Duke finds he is unable to reign, the regency shall be ensured as in the case of minority.
(2) Should the Throne become vacant, the Chamber shall make temporary arrangements for the regency. A new Chamber, to be summoned with double the customary number of members within thirty days, shall take the final steps to fill the vacancy.

**Article 8 [Oath of the Regent]**

(1) On taking up his functions the Regent shall take the following oath:
(2) *"I swear to be faithful to the Grand Duke; I swear to observe the Constitution and the laws of the country."*

## CHAPTER II LUXEMBOURGERS AND THEIR RIGHTS

**Article 9 [Citizenship, Political Rights]**

(1) The status of Luxembourger shall be acquired, retained, and lost in accordance with the rules determined by civil law.
(2) The Constitution and the other laws relating to political rights determine what conditions in addition to this status are necessary for the exercise of these rights.
(3) By way of derogation from the preceding paragraph, the law may confer the exercise of political rights to non-Luxembourgers.

**Article 10 [Naturalization]**

(1) Naturalization is granted by the legislature.
(2) The law determines the effects of naturalization.

**Article 11 [Basic Rights]**

(1) There is no distinction of orders in the State.
(2) Luxembourgers are equal☐ before the law; they alone are eligible for civil and military service, save as the law may in particular cases otherwise provide.
(3) The State guarantees the natural rights of the individual and of the family.
(4) The law guarantees the right to work and assure to every citizen the exercise of this right.
(5) The law organizes the social security, health protection, and rest of workers and guarantee the freedom of trade unions.
(6) The law guarantees freedom of trade and industry, the exercise of the professions and of agricultural labor, subject to any restrictions that may be imposed by the legislature.

**Article 12 [Individual Freedom]**
Individual freedom shall be guaranteed. No one may be prosecuted except for the cases and according to the procedure laid down by the law. Except in *flagrante delicto*, no one may be arrested without the reasoned order of the judge served at the time of arrest or within twenty four hours at the latest.

**Article 13 [Legal Judge]**
No one may be deprived, against his will, of the Judge assigned to him by the law.

**Article 14 [*Nulla Poena Sine Lege*]**
No penalty may be fixed or applied except in pursuance of the law.

**Article 15 [Home]**
The home is inviolable. No domiciliary visit may be made except in cases and according to the procedure laid down by the law.

**Article 16 [Property, Compensation]**
No one may be deprived of his property except on grounds of public interest in cases and in the manner laid down by the law and in consideration of prior and just compensation.

**Article 17 [No Confiscation]**
Confiscation of property as a penalty may not be instituted.

**Article 18 [Abolished Penalties]**
The death penalty on political grounds and civil death and branding are hereby abolished.

**Article 19 [Freedom of Religion]**
Freedom of religion and of public worship as well as freedom to express one's religious opinions are guaranteed, subject to the repression of offenses committed in the exercise of such freedoms.

**Article 20 [No Forced Religion]**
No one may be forced to take part in any way whatsoever in the acts and ceremonies of a religion or to observe its days of rest.

**Article 21 [Civil Marriage]**
Civil marriage must always precede the nuptial benediction.

**Article 22 [State and Church]**
The State's intervention in the appointment and installation of heads of religions, the mode of appointing and dismissing other ministers of religion, the right of any of them to correspond with their superiors and to publish their acts and decisions, as well as the Church's relations with the State shall be made the subject of conventions to be submitted to the Chamber of Deputies for the provisions governing its intervention.

**Article 23 [Education, Health]**

(1) The State ensures that every Luxembourger receives primary education which is compulsory and provided free of charge. Medical and social assistance is regulated by the law.
(2) The State sets up secondary educational establishments and the necessary courses of higher education. It also establishes free vocational training courses.
(3) The law determines the means of supporting State education and the conditions under which it is to be supervised by the Government and the communes; it also regulates all educational matters and creates a fund for the exceptionally gifted.
(4) Every Luxembourger is free to pursue his studies in the Grand Duchy or abroad and to attend universities of his own choosing, subject to the provisions of the law concerning admission to employment and the exercise of certain callings.

**Article 24 [Expression]**
Freedom of speech in all matters and freedom of the press is guaranteed, subject to the repression of offenses committed in the exercise of these freedoms. No censorship may ever be introduced. Security may not be demanded of writers, publishers, or printers. Stamp duty on native journals and periodicals is hereby abolished. No publisher, printer, or distributor may be prosecuted if the author is known, if he is a Luxembourger, and resident in the Grand Duchy.

**For additional analytical, business and investment opportunities information, please contact Global Investment & Business Center, USA at (202) 546-2103. Fax: (202) 546-3275. E-mail: rusric@erols.com**

**Article 25 [Assembly]**
Luxembourgers have the right to assemble peaceably and unarmed in compliance with the laws governing the exercise of this right which may not require prior authorization. This provision does not apply to open-air political, religious, or other meetings which are fully governed by laws and police regulations.

**Article 26 [Association]**
Luxembourgers enjoy freedom of association. This right shall not be made subject to any prior authorization.

**Article 27 [Petition]**
Everyone has the right to address petitions signed by one or more persons to the public authorities. Only constituted authorities have the right to address petitions collectively.

**Article 28 [Correspondence]**

(1) The secrecy of correspondence is inviolable. The law determines the agents responsible for the violation of the secrecy of correspondence entrusted to the postal services.
(2) The law determines the guarantee to be afforded to the secrecy of telegrams.

**Article 29 [Language]**
The law shall regulate the use of languages in administrative and judicial matters.

**Article 30 [Proceedings Against Public Officials]**
No prior authorization is required for instituting proceedings against public officials for their administrative acts, except as provided for in respect of members of the Government.

**Article 31 [Punishment of Public Officials]**
Public officials, to whatever order they may belong, members of the Government excepted, may be deprived of their office, honors, and pensions only in the manner laid down by law.

**Chapter III Sovereign Power**

**[Section 0 General Provision]**

**Article 32 [Sovereign Power]**

(1) The sovereign power resides in the Nation.
(2) The Grand Duke□ exercises it in compliance with this Constitution and the laws of the country.
(3) He shall has no powers other than those formally vested in him by the Constitution and the special laws passed pursuant to the Constitution, without prejudice to Article 3.

**Section 1 The Grand Duke's Prerogative**

**Article 33 [Executive Power]**
The Grand Duke is the head of the State, the symbol of its unity and the guarantee of national independence. He exercises the executive power in conformity with the Constitution and the laws of the country.

**Article 34 [Sanctioning and Promulgation of Laws]**
The Grand Duke sanctions and promulgates the laws. He makes his resolve known within three months of the vote in the Chamber.

**Article 35 [Appointments]**

(1) The Grand Duke appoints to civil and military posts, in compliance with and subject to any exceptions made by the law.
(2) No office remunerated by the State may be created other than in pursuance of a legislative provision.

**Article 36 [Regulations and Orders]**
The Grand Duke enacts the regulations and orders necessary for carrying laws into effect, but he may never suspend the laws themselves or dispense with their enforcement.

**Article 37 [Treaties]**

(1) The Grand Duke concludes treaties. These do not come into effect until they have been sanctioned by law and published in the manner laid down for the publication of laws.
(2) The treaties referred to in Chapter III, Section 4, Article 49a, are sanctioned by a law voted under the conditions laid down in Article 114 (5).
(3) Secret treaties are abolished.
(4) The Grand Duke enacts the regulations and orders necessary for carrying the treaties into effect in accordance with the procedure governing measures for the execution of laws and with the effects attaching to such measures, without prejudice to matters reserved to the law by the Constitution.
(5) No cession, exchange, or adjunction of territory is effected except pursuant to a law.
(6) The Grand Duke commands the armed force; he declares war and the cessation of hostilities after having been authorized by a vote in the Chamber taken under the conditions laid down in Article 114 (5).

**Article 38 [Pardon]**
The Grand Duke has the right to remit or reduce penalties awarded by the judges, except as provided for in respect of members of the Government.

**Article 39 [Minting Money]**
The Grand Duke has the right to mint money in pursuance of the law.

**Article 40 [Awarding Titles and Nobility]**
The Grand Duke has the right to bestow titles of nobility without being able to attach any privilege to them.

**Article 41 [Awarding Orders]**
The Grand Duke confers civil and military orders, while complying with the provisions of the law.

**Article 42 [Prince]**

(1) The Grand Duke may have Himself represented by a Prince of the blood, who shall bear the title of Lieutenant of the Grand Duke and reside in the Grand Duchy.
(2) This representative shall take an oath to observe the Constitution before entering upon the exercise of his powers.

For additional analytical, business and investment opportunities information,
please contact Global Investment & Business Center, USA
at (202) 546-2103. Fax: (202) 546-3275. E-mail: rusric@erols.com

**Article 43 [Remuneration]**

(1) The Civil List is fixed at three hundred thousand gold francs a year.
(2) It may be changed by law at the beginning of each reign. The budget law may allocate each year to the Sovereign Household the sums needed to cover representation expenses.

**Article 44 [Residence]**
The Grand Ducal Palace in Luxembourg and the Chateau de Berg are reserved for the residence of the Grand Duke.

**Article 45 [Countersignature]**
All provisions of the Grand Duke require the countersignature of a responsible member of the Government.

**Section 2 Legislature**

**Article 46 [Chamber of Deputies]**
Each law requires the assent of the Chamber of Deputies.

**Article 47 [Proposing Bills]**

(1) The Grand Duke addresses to the Chamber the proposals or bills of law he wishes to submit for adoption.
(2) The Chamber has the right to propose Government Bills to the Grand Duke.

**Article 48 [Authoritative Interpretation]**
The interpretation of laws by way of authority may only be effected through the law.

## CHAPTER 3 JUDICIARY

**Article 49 [Judgments]**

(1) Justice is rendered in the name of the Grand Duke by the courts and the tribunals.
(2) Judgments and decisions are enforced in the name of the Grand Duke.

**Article 49bis [International Institutions]**
The exercise of the powers reserved by the Constitution to the legislature, executive, and judiciary may be temporarily vested by treaty in institutions governed by international law.

## CHAPTER IV CHAMBER OF DEPUTIES

**Article 50 [Representation]**
The Chamber of Deputies represents the country. Deputies vote without referring to their constituents and may have in view only the general interests of the Grand Duchy.

**Article 51 [Parliamentary Democracy, Election, Referendum]**

(1) The Grand Duchy of Luxembourg is ruled by a system of parliamentary democracy.
(2) The organization of the Chamber is regulated by law.
(3) The Chamber is composed of 60 deputies. A law passed under the provisions of Article 114 (5) sets the number of deputies to be elected in each of the constituencies.

**For additional analytical, business and investment opportunities information, please contact Global Investment & Business Center, USA at (202) 546-2103. Fax: (202) 546-3275. E-mail: rusric@erols.com**

(4) The election is direct.
(5) Deputies are elected by straightforward universal suffrage on the party-list system, in accordance with the rules of proportional representation, the principle of the smallest electoral quota, and the rules to be determined by the law.
(6) The country is divided into four electoral districts: the South (Esch/Alzette and Capellen), the Center (Luxembourg and Mersch), the North (Diekirch, Redange, Wiltz, Clervaux and Vianden) and the East (Grevenmacher, Remich and Echternach).
(7) The electors may be requested to pronounce themselves by way of a referendumin cases and under conditions to be determined by law.

**Article 52 [Qualifications]**

(1) To qualify as an elector it is necessary:
1. to be a Luxembourger, man or woman;
2. to enjoy civil and political rights;
3. to have completed 18 years of age.
(2) To these three qualifications shall be added those determined by the law. No tax qualification may be imposed.
(3) To be eligible it is necessary:
1. to be a Luxembourger, man or woman;
2. to enjoy civil and political rights;
3. to have completed 21 years of age;
4. to be resident in the Grand Duchy.
(4) No other condition of eligibility may be imposed.

**Article 53 [Non-Qualification]**

(1) The following may not be electors nor eligible:
1. persons sentenced to criminal punishment;
2. persons sentenced for minor offenses depriving them of the right to vote;
3. persons of full age under guardianship.
(2) No other exclusion clause may be foreseen.
(3) The right to vote may be restored to persons sentenced by penal courts by the way of reprieve.

**Article 54 [Incompatibilities]**

(1) The deputy's mandate is incompatible with:
1. the duties of member of the Government;
2. those of member of the Council of State;
3. those of member of the judiciary;
4. those of member of the Audit Chamber;
5. those of district commissioner;
6. those of State collector or accounting officer;
7. those of career soldier on active service.
(2) Officials involved in a case of incompatibility have the right to choose between the mandate confided to them and their duties.
(3) A deputy called upon to perform the duties of member of the Government and who relinquishes these duties is automatically reinstated as first substitute on the list on which he was elected. The same applies to the substitute deputy who, called upon to perform the duties of member of the Government, renounces the deputy's mandate devolving upon him in the course of these duties. In the event of a contest between two or more rightful claimants, reinstatement shall follow the order of the number of votes polled in the elections.

**For additional analytical, business and investment opportunities information, please contact Global Investment & Business Center, USA at (202) 546-2103. Fax: (202) 546-3275. E-mail: rusric@erols.com**

**Article 55 [Other Incompatibilities]**
The incompatibilities referred to in the preceding article do not preclude the law from stipulating others in the future.

**Article 56 [Term]**
Deputies are elected for a term of five years.

**Article 57 [Oath of Deputies]**

(1) The Chamber verifies the credentials of its members and settles any disputes arising on the subject.
(2) On taking up office, deputies shall take the following oath:
*"I swear to be faithful to the Grand Duke and to obey the Constitution and the laws of the State."*
(3) This oath is to be taken at a public sitting before the President of the Chamber.

**Article 58 [Government Incompatibility]**
A deputy appointed by the Government to a salaried post which he accepts immediately ceases to sit in the Chamber and does not resume his functions except by virtue of a new election.

**Article 59 [Two Votes]**
All Bills are submitted to a second vote unless the Chamber, in agreement with the Council of State, otherwise decides at a public sitting. There shall be an interval of a least three months between the two votes.

**Article 60 [President of the Chamber]**
At each session, the Chamber appoints its president and vice-presidents and sets up its Bureau.

**Article 61 [Publicity]**
Sittings of the Chamber are held in public, except where otherwise provided in the rules of procedure.

**Article 62 [Majority]**

(1) Resolutions require an absolute majority of votes. Should the votes be equally divided, the measure under discussion is rejected.
(2) The Chamber may not pass a resolution unless the majority of its members are present.

**Article 63 [Voting by Role Call]**
Voting on Bills as a whole always takes place by roll call.

**Article 64 [Right of Inquiry]**
The Chamber has the right of inquiry. The exercise of this right is regulated by the law.

**Article 65 [Article by Article Voting]**
A Bill may be passed by the Chamber only after it has been voted article by article.

**Article 66 [Amendments]**
The Chamber has the right to amend and divide the articles and amendments proposed.

**Article 67 [Petitions]**

**For additional analytical, business and investment opportunities information, please contact Global Investment & Business Center, USA at (202) 546-2103. Fax: (202) 546-3275. E-mail: rusric@erols.com**

(1) Petitions to the Chamber may not be presented in person.
(2) The Chamber has the right to refer to members of the Government any petitions addressed to it. Members of the Government shall provide explanations of their contents whenever the Chamber so requests.
(3) The Chamber does not concern itself with any petition that has private interests in view, unless it is aimed at redressing grievances stemming from unlawful acts of the Government or the authorities, or unless the decision to intervene lies within the competence of the Chamber.

**Article 68 [Indemnity]**
No deputy may be prosecuted or investigated on account of opinions expressed or votes cast by him in the course of his duties.

**Article 69 [Immunity]**
No deputy can be prosecuted or arrested in a repressive matter in the course of a session, without the Chamber's authorization, unless caught in the act of committing a serious offence. None of its members may be imprisoned for debt during the session without the same authorization. The detention or prosecution of a deputy is suspended during and throughout the session if the Chamber so demands.

**Article 70 [Rules of Procedure]**
The Chamber determines in its rules of procedure the manner in which it exercises its powers.

**Article 71 [Place of Sittings]**
The sittings of the Chamber are held in the place of residence of the administration of the Grand Duchy.

**Article 72 [Sessions]**

(1) The Chamber meets each year in ordinary session at the time specified in the rules of procedure.
(2) The Grand Duke may summon the Chamber to an extraordinary session; he is required to do this if a third of the deputies so request.
(3) Every session is opened and closed by the Grand Duke in person, or in his name by an authorized representative appointed for the purpose.

**Article 73 [...]**
*{ Abolished on 12 Jan 1998. The old provision read: "The Grand Duke may adjourn the Chamber. Such adjournment, however, may not exceed a period of one month nor be repeated during the same session without the Chamber's consent." }*

**Article 74 [Dissolution]**
The Grand Duke may dissolve the Chamber. New elections are held at the latest within three months of the dissolution.

**Article 75**
Members of the Chamber of Deputies receive, in addition to their travelling expenses, an allowance of which the law determines the amount and conditions.

**For additional analytical, business and investment opportunities information, please contact Global Investment & Business Center, USA at (202) 546-2103. Fax: (202) 546-3275. E-mail: rusric@erols.com**

# CHAPTER V GOVERNMENT OF THE GRAND DUCHY

**Article 76 [Organization of Government]**
The Grand Duke regulates the organization of his Government, which shall consist of at least three members.

**Article 77 [Ministers]**
The Grand Duke appoints and dismisses the members of Government.

**Article 78 [Responsibility]**
Members of the Government are responsible.

**Article 79 [No Intermediate Authority]**
There is no intermediate authority between the members of Government and the Grand Duke.

**Article 80 [Government and Parliament]**

(1) Members of the Government have access to the Chamber and must be heard at their request.
(2) The Chamber may require their presence.

**Article 81 [No Relief of Responsibility]**
In no case shall an oral or written order of the Grand Duke relieve a member of the Government of responsibility.

**Article 82 [Accusation]**
The Chamber has the right to accuse members of the Government. A law shall determine the cases of responsibility, the penalties to be inflicted, and the procedure to be followed as regards either the accusation admitted by the Chamber or the action brought by the injured parties.

**Article 83 [No Pardon for Ministers]**
The Grand Duke my not pardon a condemned member of the Government except at the request of the Chamber.

**Chapter Vbis Council of State**

**Article 83bis [Council of State, Litigation Committee]**

(1) The Council of State is called to express its views on bills and proposition of law and amendments that might be proposed thereto, as well as on all other matters deferred to it by the Government or by the laws. On articles voted on by the Chamber pursuant to Article 65, it gives its opinion within the time limits set by the law.
(2) The organization of the Council of State as well as the way its prerogatives are carried out, are regulated by law.

# CHAPTER VI JUDICIARY

**Article 84 [Civil Rights Jurisdiction]**
Disputes over civil rights lie exclusively within the jurisdiction of the courts.

**For additional analytical, business and investment opportunities information, please contact Global Investment & Business Center, USA at (202) 546-2103. Fax: (202) 546-3275. E-mail: rusric@erols.com**

**Article 85 [Political Rights Jurisdiction]**
Disputes over political rights lie within the jurisdiction of the courts except as otherwise provided by law.

**Article 86 [No Extraordinary Jurisdiction]**
No court or jurisdiction in contentious matters may be set up, except by virtue of a law. No extraordinary commissions or courts may be set up, under whatever name.

**Article 87 [Superior Court of Justice]**
The organization of a Superior Court of Justice is provided for by law.

**Article 88 [Publicity]**
Hearings in court shall be public unless such publicity is a threat to good order and morality, in which case the court so declares by ruling.

**Article 89 [Judgments]**
All judgments shall be reasoned. They are pronounced in public court session.

**Article 90 [Appointment of Judges]**
Justices of the Peace and judges of the courts are appointed directly by the Grand Duke. Members of the Superior Court of Justice and presidents and vice-presidents of the district courts are appointed by the Grand Duke on the advice of the Superior Court of Justice.

**Article 91 [Term, Sanctions]**

(1) Justices of the peace, district court judges, and members of the Superior Court of Justice are appointed for life. None of them may be deprived of his post or suspended save by a judicial decision. None of these judges may be transferred except by way of a new appointment and with his consent.
(2) In the event of infirmity or misconduct, however, he may be suspended, dismissed, or transferred, under the conditions laid down by the law.

**Article 92 [Salaries]**
The salaries of members of the judiciary are fixed by law.

**Article 93 [Incompatibility]**
Except where otherwise provided by law, no judge is allowed to accept salaried functions from the Government unless he performs them free of charge, without prejudice, however, to cases of incompatibility determined by law.

**Article 94 [Military Tribunals, Labor and Social Security Jurisdiction]**

(1) Special laws regulate the organization of military tribunals, their duties, and the rights, obligations, and terms of office of their members.
(2) The law also regulates the organization of the jurisdictions pertaining to labor and social security matters, their duties, the mode of appointment, and the terms of office of their members.

**Article 95 [General and Local Decisions]**
Courts and tribunals may apply general and local decisions and regulations only in so far as these comply with the laws. The Superior Court of Justice settles disputes as to competence, in accordance with the procedure laid down by the law.

**Article 95bis [Administrative courts]**

(1) Jurisdiction in administrative matters belongs to the Administrative Tribunal and the Administrative Court. These courts also have jurisdiction in tax matters in the cases and under the conditions determined by the law.
(2) The law may create other administrative jurisdictions.
(3) The Administrative Court constitutes the supreme court of the administrative order.
(4) The attributions and the organisation of the administrative courts are regulated by the law.
(5) The magistrates of the Administrative Court and the Administrative Tribunal are nominated by the Grand-Duke. The nomination of the members of the Administrative Court as well as of the president and the vice-presidents of the Administrative Tribunal are made, except concerning the initial nominations, upon the opinion of the Administrative Court.
(6) The provisions of Articles 91, 92, and 93 are applicable to the members of the Administrative Court and of the Administrative Tribunal.

**Article 95ter [Constitutional Court]**

(1) The Constitutional Court decides, by way of arrêt, on the conformity of the laws with the Constitution.
(2) The Constitutional Court is seized, in a prejudicial manner, pursuant to the modalities to be determined by the law, by any court to decide on the conformity of the laws, save the laws approving treaties, to the Constitution.
(3) The Constitutional Court is composed of the President of the Superior Court of Justice, the President of the Administrative Court, two counselors of the Cour de Cassation and five magistrates nominated by the Grand Duke, upon the joint opinion of the Superior Court of Justice and Administrative Court. The provisions of Articles 91, 92, and 93 apply to them. The Constitutional Court comprehends a chamber sitting with five magistrates.
(4) The organsiation of the Consitutional Court and the manner in which it exercises its attributions are regulated by the law.

## CHAPTER VII PUBLIC FORCE

**Article 96 [Armed Forces]**
All matters connected with the armed forces are regulated by the law.

**Article 97 [Gendarmerie]**
The organization and the powers of the forces in charge of public order are settled by law.

**Article 98 [Civil Guard]**
A civil guard, whose organization is regulated by the law, may be formed.

**Chapter VIII Finances**

**Article 99 [Taxation]**
No tax may be imposed for the benefit of the State except pursuant to a law. No loan to be borne by the State may be contracted without the consent of the Chamber. No real property of the State may be alienated, unless such alienation is authorized by a special law. However, a general law may fix a limit up to which no special authorization is requested. Every purchase by the State of significant real property, every significant commitment of funds in large infrastructure or important building plans, must be authorized by a special law. A general law sets the thresholds from which this authorization is requested. No commitment may burden the State budget further than one fiscal year, except by a special law. No communal charge or tax may be introduced except with

the consent of the communal council. A law determines the exceptions shown by experience to be necessary as regards communal taxes.

**Article 100 [Renewing Taxation]**
Taxes for the benefit of the State are voted annually. Legislation introducing them remains in force for only one year unless renewed.

**Article 101 [No Privilege or Exemption]**
No privilege may be introduced in the matter of taxation. No exemption or abatement may be established except by law.

**Article 102 [No Other Duties]**
Save in cases formally excepted by law, no recompense may be demanded of citizens or public establishments except in the form of taxes for the benefit of the State or of the commune.

**Article 103 [Pension, Half-Pay, Gratuity]**
No pension, half-pay, or gratuity charged to the Treasury may be granted except by law.

**Article 104 [Accounts, Budget]**
Each year, the Chamber passes the Accounts Bill and votes the budget. All revenue and expenditure of the State is shown in the budget and in the accounts.

**Article 105 [Audit Chamber]**

(1) An Audit Chamber is required to audit and settle the accounts of the general administration and of all accountable to the Public Treasury.
(2) The law regulates its organization, the exercise of its powers, and the method of appointing its members.
(3) The Audit Chamber ensures that no budget item of expenditure is exceeded.
(4) No transfer may be made from one section of the budget to another except by law.
(5) Members of the Government may, however, within their own departments, transfer surpluses of one item to another item in the same section, provided that they justify their action before the Chamber of Deputies.
(6) The Audit Chamber draws up the accounts of the different administrations of the State and is required to collect for this purpose all the information and vouchers necessary. The general account of the State shall be submitted to the Chamber of Deputies together with the Audit Chamber's comments.

**Article 106 [Salaries of Priests]**
The salaries and pensions of ministers of religion shall be borne by the State and regulated by the law.

## CHAPTER IX COMMUNES

**Article 107 [Local Authorities]**

(1) Communes form autonomous authorities, on a territorial basis, possessing legal personality and administrating their patrimony and own interests.
(2) In each commune there is a communal council directly elected by the inhabitants; the conditions to be elector or eligible will be fixed by law.
(3) The council draws up a yearly budget and closes the accounts. It issues communal regulations, except in case of emergency. It may impose taxes, with the Grand Duke's approval.

**For additional analytical, business and investment opportunities information, please contact Global Investment & Business Center, USA at (202) 546-2103. Fax: (202) 546-3275. E-mail: rusric@erols.com**

The Grand Duke may dissolve the council.
(4) The commune is administered under the authority of the corporate body of the major and the aldermen who must be chosen among the communal councilors. The conditions of nationality to be fulfilled by the members of the corporate body of major and aldermen will be determined in a law passed under the provisions of Article 114 (5).
(5) Supervision of the communal administration is ruled by law. Certain decisions of communal authorities have to be authorized by the supervision authority or may be cancelled or suspended should they be illegal or contrary to the public interests, without prejudice to the powers of the law courts or administrative tribunals.

**Article 108 [Registration Authority]**
The preparation of birth, marriage, and death certificates and the keeping of the registers shall lie exclusively within the competence of the communal authorities.

## CHAPTER X GENERAL PROVISIONS

**Article 109 [Capital, Seat of Government]**
The city of Luxembourg is the capital of the Grand Duchy and the seat of the Government. The seat of the Government may be moved only temporarily and then only for serious reasons.

**Article 110 [Oath]**

(1) No oath may be imposed, except pursuant to the law, which determines in what form it is to be taken.
(2) All civil public officials, before entering upon their duties, take the following oath:
*"I swear allegiance to the Grand Duke and obedience to the Constitution and the laws of the State. I promise to fulfill my duties with integrity, exactitude, and impartiality."*

**Article 111 [Rights of Foreigners]**
Every foreigner on the territory of the Grand Duchy shall enjoy the protection afforded to persons and property, except as otherwise provided by the law.

**Article 112 [Promulgation of Laws]**
No law or general or communal administrative decision or regulation shall come into force until it has been published in the form determined by the law.

**Article 113 [No Suspension]**
No provision of the Constitution may be suspended.

**Article 114 [Constitutional Amendment]**

(1) The legislature has the right to declare the need to amend any constitutional provision it specifies.
(2) Following such declaration, the Chamber automatically dissolves.
(3) A new Chamber convenes in accordance with Article 74.
(4) This Chamber decides, by common consent with the Grand Duke, on the points to be amended.
(5) In such a case, the Chamber shall not proceed to the vote unless at least three-quarters of its members are present, and no amendment may be adopted unless it is backed by at least two-thirds of the votes.

**For additional analytical, business and investment opportunities information, please contact Global Investment & Business Center, USA at (202) 546-2103. Fax: (202) 546-3275. E-mail: rusric@erols.com**

**Article 115 [No Amendment During Regency]**
During a regency, no amendment can be made to the Constitution concerning the constitutional prerogatives of the Grand Duke, his status as well as the order of succession.

## CHAPTER XI TRANSITORY AND ADDITIONAL PROVISIONS

**Article 116 [Accusation of Ministers]**
Until provided for by a law, the Chamber of Deputies has discretionary power to accuse a member of the Government, and the Superior Court shall try him in general assembly, specifying the offence and determining the penalty. The penalty may not, however, exceed that of confinement, without prejudice to cases expressly provided for by the penal laws.

**Article 117 [Conflicting Old Law]**
From the day the Constitution enters into force, all laws, decrees, decisions, regulations, and other acts in conflict with it are abolished.

**Article 118 [Conversion of Death Penalty]**
The death penalty, abolished in political matters, shall be replaced by the penalty immediately below it, until such time as this matter has been covered by the new law.

**Article 119 [Provisions Concerning Religions]**
Pending the conclusion of the conventions referred to in Article 22, the current provisions concerning religions shall remain in force.

**Article 120 [Old Law]**
Until the laws and regulations provided for by the Constitution have been promulgated, the laws and regulations at present in force continue to be applied.

**Article 121 [...]**
*{Abolished on 31 March 1989}*

**For additional analytical, business and investment opportunities information, please contact Global Investment & Business Center, USA at (202) 546-2103. Fax: (202) 546-3275. E-mail: rusric@erols.com**

# CITIZENSHIP AND RESIDENCE IN LUXEMBOURG

## LUXEMBOURGIAN NATIONALITY LAW

### BASIC INFORMATION

**Luxembourgian nationality law** is ruled by the Constitution of Luxembourg.

The Grand Duchy of Luxembourg is a member state of the European Union and, as such, its citizens are also EU citizens.

Since 1 January 2009, Luxembourg has allowed dual citizenship.[1] Since then, many Belgians have made use of the new law to adopt Belgian-Luxembourgish citizenship, especially Belgians living in Arelerland, a part of the Belgian province of Luxembourg at the border with the Grand Duchy

One may request Luxembourgian nationality through naturalisation under several conditions:

being at least eighteen years old
living there for four consecutive years
passing an exam testing knowledge of the Luxembourgish language
taking courses of "civic instruction" (about Luxembourgian institutions, law, etc.)

It is also possible to "recover" Luxembourg nationality if one can prove he had an ancestor who was Luxembourgish as at 1 January 1900. The Luxembourg diaspora at the time moved to France, Belgium and the US. As at end of 2013, thousands of people recovered the nationality of their Luxembourgish ancestor.

Luxembourgian citizens are also citizens of the European Union and thus enjoy rights of free movementand have the right to vote in elections for the European Parliament.

### REFORM OF THE LAW ON LUXEMBOURG NATIONALITY

In September 2012, the Minister of Justice François Biltgen launched a public debate on the reform of the law of 23 October 2008 on Luxembourg nationality. Interested persons were invited to submit their comments and suggestions on the basis of an evaluation report prepared by the Ministry of Justice.

The purpose of the Act of 23 October 2008 on Luxembourg nationality is to adapt the nationality law to changes in Luxembourg society in recent decades and contribute to consolidate the integration of foreigners residing in Luxembourg.
Alongside the economic development of the country and the European dimension of the capital of the Grand Duchy of Luxembourg, the number of non-Luxembourg nationals in our country has risen sharply to over 40% of the total population.

While many of these foreigners stay only a few years in our country, others have decided to settle there permanently and want, through the acquisition of Luxembourg nationality, demonstrate their commitment to our country and their willingness to integration of our national community, while wishing to keep, through their national origin, a link with the homeland and culture of their ancestors. This is especially today's children and grandchildren of migrant workers who came to work in our country during the second half of the 20th century.

. The proposed reform of the law of Luxembourg nationality is enshrined in the government's program In August 2004 the government statement, the Prime Minister said: "Integration and cohesion: this double requirement is especially evident in our shared life with those not Luxembourgers. There should be no gap between them and us. The integration of non-Luxembourgers is an offer Luxembourgers to do. Non-Luxembourgers have to accept this offer. (...) So, we want to establish dual citizenship. It brings us closer, encourages community life without the one who gets a Luxembourg passport must abandon the non-Luxembourg part of his life. Thus, we will offer more courses Luxembourg. Many non-Luxembourgers would love to learn our language (...) to better integrate: supply integration goes hand in hand with the provision of the Luxembourgish language. "

Dated 13 October 2006, the Minister of Justice introduced Bill Luxembourg nationality in the House of Representatives (Parliamentary Document No. 5620). This text was passed by the House of Representatives October 15, 2008 The law of 23 October 2008 on Luxembourg nationality (Mémorial A - N ° 158 of 27 October 2008). Came into force on 1 January 2009.

## LUXEMBOURG NATIONALITY BY ORIGIN

### A. LUXEMBOURG NATIONALITY BY BIRTH (ARTICLE 1)

. 1 Birth of a Luxembourg author

child born, even in foreign countries, a Luxembourg author is Luxembourg, where the following conditions are met:

the parentage must be established before he reached the age of 18 years;

the author must be a Luxembourg when this relationship is established.

When the adjudication of parentage is made after the death of the father or the mother, the child is when the author Luxembourg Luxembourg nationality on the day of his death.

2 Double birth. Luxembourg

Parliament has provided a new case for obtaining the quality of Luxembourgish origin is based on jus soli.

The child, born in the Grand Duchy of Luxembourg non-parents, one of whose parents (father or mother) was born in the Grand Duchy of Luxembourg nationality has.

This provision applies not only to the child born from the entry into force of the Act of 23 October 2008 on Luxembourg nationality (1 January 2009), but also one that has not yet reached the . age of 18 years at the time of entry into force of this Act In summary, only child, born from 1 January 1991, benefiting from the Luxembourg nationality, provided that:

that the child was born in Luxembourg and

at least one of its non-Luxembourg parents also born in Luxembourg.

3 Simple birth in Luxembourg

**For additional analytical, business and investment opportunities information, please contact Global Investment & Business Center, USA at (202) 546-2103. Fax: (202) 546-3275. E-mail: rusric@erols.com**

In three cases, a child gets Luxembourg nationality by mere birth in the Grand Duchy:

child born in the Grand Duchy of parents lawfully unknown: the child found in the Grand Duchy is presumed, until the contrary is proved, be born on the territory of Luxembourg;

child born in the Grand Duchy that has no nationality due to the fact that his or author (s) are stateless;

child born in the Grand Duchy of foreign parents which foreign nationality laws do not in any way that is way pass citizenship of either of his parents: Parents must provide proof that their national legislation in no way allows the transmission of nationality to children.

### B. Luxembourg nationality as a result of adoption (Article 2, paragraph 1)

A minor who is the subject of an adoption by a Luxembourger, gets the Luxembourg nationality.

The novelty lies in the fact that the text no longer make a distinction between the type of adoption. In other words, the full adoption and simple adoption are placed on an equal footing in terms of transmission of Luxembourg nationality adopted children.

### C. Luxembourg nationality by changing the nationality of the perpetrator or the adopter (Article 2, paragraph 2)

Gets Luxembourg nationality:

minor whose author or adopting for which affiliation is established acquires or recovers Luxembourg nationality; and

minor whose author or adopting for which affiliation is established obtained Luxembourg nationality in accordance with point 1).

### D. Retroactivity (Article 32)

Articles 1 and 2 apply even to persons born before the entry into force of the Act, that is to say, before 1 January 2009, if they have not yet at that time, reached 18.

Both sections apply even if the facts and acts which result in the acquisition of Luxembourg nationality occurred prior to January 1, 2009.

However, this application does not affect the validity of contracts by the person or rights acquired by third parties on the basis of previous legislation acts. The interested party may not invoke the rights arising from the Luxembourg nationality as from 1 January 2009.

### E. Establishment of the quality of origin (Articles 3 and 4) Luxembourg

Quality Original Luxembourg is established by:

by birth in Luxembourg before 1 January 1920; or

by the evidence of the possession of the state of Luxembourg in person that the authors of the claimant whose nationality is the condition of his. Evidence to the contrary is right. The state of Luxembourg possession is acquired by the exercise of the rights such capacity confers.

## III. LUXEMBOURG NATIONALITY BY VOLUNTARY ACQUISITION

A. Naturalization

quality Luxembourgish is acquired by naturalization. Naturalization conferred abroad all civil and political rights attached to the status of Luxembourg. This only has effect for the future.

### 1. Major new

Law of 23 October 2008 on Luxembourg nationality is an important reform of the naturalization level eligibility, the applicable procedure and remedies. The main new features can be summarized as follows:

under the principle of dual nationality, the person who wishes to acquire Luxembourg nationality is no longer obliged to renounce his nationality of origin;

extending the minimum period of compulsory residence in the land of 5 to 7 years, which is an appropriate time to ensure that the applicant is sufficiently integrated into Luxembourg society;

precision of the language requirement:

requirement to pass an assessment test in Luxembourg spoken language, which is a more neutral more objective method of assessment, and egalitarian in respect of all applicants for naturalization;

setting a level of competence to be achieved in Luxembourgish (listening comprehension and oral expression), which ensures that the applicant for naturalization is able to participate in social and political life of Luxembourg;

State reimbursement of registration fees Luxembourg language courses and evaluation of spoken language of Luxembourg, pursuant to the terms laid down by Grand-Ducal test;

obligation to take civics courses, which allow applicants to gain knowledge on Luxembourg institutions and human rights;

precision-repute:

setting objective criteria that assess whether the applicant has sufficient guarantees of good repute;

power to suspend the issue of naturalization in case of criminal judicial proceedings;

creating an administrative procedure that will simplify and expedite the processing of applications for naturalization:

creation of a single procedure for voluntary acquisition of Luxembourg nationality, so that the process of acquisition of nationality by option is no longer applicable;

transmission, directly and without delay, the record of naturalization by the municipalities to the Ministry of Justice, without passing through the district police;

lack of referral for review of municipal councils and the Council of State;

administrative investigation carried out at the Department of Justice (Department of the rights of citizenship);

obligation to make a decision within 8 months from the declaration of naturalization;

effectiveness of naturalization from the date of the decision and absence of publication thereof in the Memorial;

transfer decision-making power of the House of Deputies to the Minister of Justice, who may grant or refuse the Luxembourg nationality;

creating remedies against the refusal of naturalization before the Administrative Tribunal, with the possibility of appeal to the Administrative Court.

### 2. Principle of dual or multiple nationality

Act of 23 October 2008 on Luxembourg nationality does not include the condition of loss or renunciation of nationality of origin in the head of the foreigner who wishes to acquire Luxembourg nationality , contained in Article 7, paragraph 2, of the Law of 22 February 1968 on Luxembourg nationality law. From 1 January 2009, to be eligible for naturalization abroad therefore no longer need prove by certificates or attestations, he lost his original nationality or he loses the right following the acquisition of another nationality. However, this does not necessarily mean that abroad, which has made a declaration of naturalization, will have dual citizenship after acquisition of Luxembourg nationality. Whether the acquisition of Luxembourg nationality can be combined with the maintenance of foreign nationality must also consider foreign law. As all states have not adhered to the principle of plurinationality, it could be that the stranger who wishes to acquire the nationality or native to a State whose law does not permit dual or multiple nationality.

The applicant is responsible to the Luxembourg national who wishes to retain his nationality of origin, perform the following steps before: The candidate must ask the competent authorities of his country of origin, such as the embassy or consulate, if he can continue to keep his nationality of origin in case of acquisition of Luxembourg nationality.

When foreign authorities agree, a person with two foreign nationals may also, after the acquisition of Luxembourg nationality, have three nationalities.

Subject to international conventions and laws of the Grand Duchy, anyone with addition Luxembourg nationality, one or more other nationalities, is considered by the authorities of the Grand Duchy of Luxembourg as exclusively.

### 3. Conditions of naturalization (Sections 6 and 7)

The requirements for Luxembourg nationality by naturalization, are enacted in order to ensure social cohesion of all those who want to be part of the Luxembourg community and ensure their integration. Consequently, the applicant for naturalization must demonstrate sufficient integration in the country. The condition of sufficient integration is the essence of the device naturalization.

**For additional analytical, business and investment opportunities information, please contact Global Investment & Business Center, USA at (202) 546-2103. Fax: (202) 546-3275. E-mail: rusric@erols.com**

Parliament has provided several criteria to determine whether the condition of sufficient integration is fulfilled or not.

Age

Applicants must have attained the age of 18 years on the date of submission of the application for naturalization. The age requirement shall be met at the time of submission of the application. Therefore, the minor may not make an application for naturalization.

Residence

The minimum residence requirement in the country to acquire Luxembourg nationality is 7 years. More specifically, the applicant for naturalization must reside in the country for at least 7 years must be consecutive and immediately precede the application. On the other hand, the residence must be:

effective: the applicant must actually reside in the country;

Notice: The applicant must have a residence permit in Luxembourg.

For recognized refugees according to the Geneva Convention of 28 July 1951 relating to the Status of Refugees, the period between the date of filing of the asylum application and the date of recognition of refugee status by the competent minister is treated as a allowed the country. stay The residence requirement must be completed at the time of submission of the application.

Language skills

The applicant for naturalization must demonstrate a sufficient active and passive knowledge of at least one of the languages permitted by the law of 24 February 1984 on the language regime and pass a test to assess the Luxembourgish spoken. shall be exempt from the success of an evaluation test of spoken Luxembourgish language:

those who have completed at least 7 years of schooling in Luxembourg under Luxembourg public education or private education applying Luxembourg public education programs;

those who disposed of a residence permit in Luxembourg before 31 December 1984 and since that date at least resident in Luxembourg.

The level of competence to be achieved in Luxembourg spoken language is that of level B1 of the Common European Framework of Reference for Languages for oral comprehension and A2 the same framework for oral expression. This level implies, firstly, that the alien is able to follow a program on radio or television in Luxembourg and secondly, that it is able to speak in general on his daily life, his work, his family life and leisure. In summary, the applicant for naturalization must be able to participate in social and political life of Luxembourg. Luxembourg The Language Centre is responsible for the verification and certification of skills in Luxembourgish language for admission to naturalization. It organizes the evaluation test several times a year. The test for inclusion in the evaluation fee is reimbursed by the State applying for naturalization, pursuant to the terms laid down by Grand-Ducal. A candidate who withdraws without cause or do not appear at the time of testing is not reimbursed and must re-register. Participation in Luxembourg language courses is purely optional. If prior to the evaluation of spoken Luxembourgish language test, the candidate has attended courses at the Language Centre Luxembourg Luxembourg, registration fees relating thereto shall be reimbursed by the State. If courses were taken outside of the Language Centre Luxembourg, the registration fee will be reimbursed on production of a receipt and to a height equivalent to the registration fee Language Center Luxembourg. The claim for inclusion in the assessment and / or Letzeburgesh fresh proof is submitted to the Ministry of Justice (Department of the rights of citizenship).

Civics

The applicant for naturalization must take at least 3 civics. It must necessarily follow a course in Luxembourg institutions and a course on human rights. A third course must be chosen from a topic on the history, communities, the economy, labor law, social security and the media. shall be exempt from participation in civics, the same categories of people who are not subject to the obligation of passing the test for assessing the spoken language of Luxembourg. civics courses are organized in a decentralized manner by the Ministry of Education and Training Professional Service (adult education). These courses are taught in several schools established in different regions of the country. The schools are appointed annually by the Minister of National Education and Vocational Training. Course registration civics is free. These courses are offered in multiple languages. The duration of a course is 2 hours. The courses are organized in the evening or on Saturday morning aware. There is no exam at the end of the course. A certificate of attendance is established based on an attendance list.

Repute

applicant for naturalization must demonstrate sufficient repute guarantees. The Act of 23 October 2008 on Luxembourg nationality gives the Minister of Justice the power to suspend the issue of naturalization and / or refuse naturalization. 's naturalization record may be suspended when the applicant for naturalization been . judicial proceedings in criminal matters Naturalization is refused:

where the applicant has been, either in the country or abroad, a conviction for a felony or a conviction to imprisonment for a term of one year or more; and

the facts underlying the conviction by a foreign court also constitute a criminal offense under Luxembourg law; and

that, where appropriate and without the benefit of a pardon, the penalty has been finally executed less than 15 years before the introduction of the application for naturalization.

## 4. Naturalization procedure

Submission of the application (Article 10, paragraph 1)

When the age and residence requirements are met, the alien may submit in writing to the municipality of residence for naturalization, which must be signed by the applicant and to the Minister of Justice. The application must be submitted personally by the applicant, together with the file. This application is naturalization statement.

Documents to be attached to the application (Article 10, paragraph 2)

The applicant must attach to the application for naturalization the following parts:

the birth certificate of the applicant and, if applicable, the birth of his children;

a biography written with accuracy: The applicant must complete a questionnaire;

a certificate stating the period of compulsory residence issued by the municipalities in which the alien has stayed during the time of his compulsory residence in the country;

a certified copy of the passport of the applicant, the applicant respectively for copy, Luxembourg recognized as a refugee within the meaning of the Geneva Convention of 28 July 1951 relating to the Status of Refugees, a certificate of such quality and issued by the competent authority;

an extract from the judicial record Luxembourg and a similar document issued by the competent authorities of the country of origin and country of previous residences in which the applicant has resided from the age of 18 years during the 15 years preceding the introduction the application;

a certificate of completion of the evaluation test of spoken Luxembourgish;

a certificate of attendance of Luxembourg civics.

Are exempted from the production of parts sub f) and g), people who are not subject to the requirement of a successful evaluation of the spoken language and Luxembourg participation event at civics. The application for naturalization statement is that if all the required documents and exhibits were attached to the application. All documents must be translated, either in French or in German by a certified translator. The municipality of residence of the applicant shall apply for naturalization, together with the record, directly and without delay, the Ministry of Justice (Department of the rights of citizenship).

Decision authority (Articles 5 and 11)

Naturalisation is granted or denied by order of the Minister of Justice. The refusal of naturalization must be substantiated. Minister of Justice must make a decision within eight months from the date on which the application for naturalization as a declaration of naturalization. However, this period shall not apply:

during the suspension procedure naturalization record if criminal justice process; and

for applications for naturalization or option that has been made before 1 January 2009.

Naturalization takes effect on the day of the ministerial decision. The Minister of Justice shall notify the person the order granting or denying citizenship to serve as its title. Mention of the Ministerial Order is made by the municipality or in a special register kept in duplicate, either in the register of birth. The order is not subject to publication in the Mémorial.

Special procedure (Articles 8 and 9)

Under a special procedure, which is intended to apply only very rarely, the naturalization decision is taken by the Chamber of Deputies in exceptional circumstances. When the legal conditions are not met, naturalization may be granted in exceptional circumstances, the major foreign makes or has rendered outstanding services to the state. Naturalization may even in the absence of a request, be given by the Government. 's naturalization application or proposal is submitted to the Chamber of Deputies, which decides whether to adopt or not adopt this request or proposal. The

Act conferring naturalization is inserted extracted Memorial. The Minister of Justice shall issue to the applicant a certified duplicate of the law conferring naturalization to be his title.

Remedies (Article 26)

Under the influence of the law of 22 February 1968 on Luxembourg nationality (Articles 13 and 14) Act, the Chamber of Deputies has exclusive jurisdiction to grant or deny naturalization. Naturalisation is granted by law. The refusal of naturalization by the Chamber of Deputies may not be subject to appeal by the applicant dismissed. Act of 23 October 2008 on Luxembourg nationality by creating innovative ways of use, and more particularly to a dual degree jurisdiction. This is a strengthening of the rights of citizens wishing to acquire Luxembourg nationality. Given that the Ministerial Order to refuse naturalization is an administrative decision, the jurisdiction is given to the administrative courts. At trial, the Administrative Tribunal is competent to decide on appeals against ministerial orders refusing applications for naturalization. The appeal is brought before the Administrative Court. However, no appeal is possible when the Chamber of Deputies refused naturalization under the above special procedure (Articles 8 and 9). For further information, reference is made in section VII. Litigation Luxembourg nationality .

Entry into force and transitional provisions (Article IV)

The entry into force of the Act of 23 October 2008 on Luxembourg nationality was set at 1 January 2009. This Act applies to applications for naturalization or collection introduced from January 1, 2009. Applications for naturalization, option or recovery, worth statement and commenced before 1 January 2009:

remain subject to the conditions as substantive provisions of the law of 22 February 1968 on Luxembourg nationality law;

are subject, depending on the procedure and possible appeals, the provisions of the Act of 23 October 2008 on Luxembourg nationality.

### B. Recovery

In general, the law of 23 October 2008 on Luxembourg nationality relaxes the conditions for recovery of Luxembourg nationality and simplifies the procedure by which a person may recover that nationality.

By applying the principle of dual or multiple nationality, the recovery of Luxembourg nationality is no longer subject to the loss of foreign nationality.

The text provides three scenarios in which a person may recover Luxembourg nationality.

#### 1. Cases of Luxembourg origin (Article 14)

From the age of 18, the original Luxembourgers, who lost his capacity as Luxembourg, Luxembourg nationality may recover.

It can keep the foreigners, where the foreign law relevant permits.

Whoever wishes to recover Luxembourg nationality must meet the same conditions of age and respectability that the applicant for naturalization. It should produce the same parts as the candidate for naturalization, except certificates of residence in the country, the success of the Luxembourgish language spoken and participation in Luxembourg during civics.

At the procedural level, the applicant must sign a declaration to the recovery officer Vital last place of residence in the Grand Duchy, and in the absence of such a residence before the officer of civil status of the city of Luxembourg.

The declaration of recovery is submitted for decision to the Minister of Justice, which grants or denies recovery by ministerial decree. The refusal must be justified.

The Minister of Justice shall notify the person the order granting or denying recovery to be his title. Mention of the Ministerial Order is made in the margin of the declaration of recovery.

The decision to refuse collection may be appealed to the Administrative Tribunal. The appeal is brought before the Administrative Court. Is made in section VII. Litigation nationality.

2. Case daughter having a grandfather who owned the Luxembourg nationality by origin (Article 29)

The Act of 23 October 2008 on Luxembourg nationality introduced a new recovery cases whose application is limited in time.

Daughter in direct paternal or maternal line, even foreign-born, a grandfather Luxembourg at the date of 1 January 1900 and that it respectively one of his descendants lost Luxembourg nationality on the basis of legal provisions earlier, may recover Luxembourg nationality by declaration. Such a declaration recovery can be made until 31 December 2018.

The requirements, the required documents, the procedure and the remedies are the same as those for the case of the aforementioned recovery.

An additional document is required, namely a certificate issued by the Ministry of Justice (Service right of citizenship) stating that the applicant has an ancestor of Luxembourg nationality on the date of January 1, 1900, he is the direct descendant .

### 3. Cases of women who have lost Luxembourg nationality without committing an act of will (Article 31)

Luxembourg woman who has lost the status of Luxembourg to have acquired as a result of her marriage, or because of the acquisition by her husband of a foreign nationality, without any voluntary on his part, the foreign nationality of her husband, may recover Luxembourg nationality by a declaration to the officer before the registrar.

The state registrar shall, within eight days of the declaration, a duly certified copy of it to the Minister of Justice shipping.

## IV. LOSS OF LUXEMBOURG NATIONALITY

The Act of 23 October 2008 on Luxembourg nationality reduced the number of loss of Luxembourg nationality.

By applying the principle of dual or multiple nationality, the voluntary acquisition of a foreign nationality is no longer a loss of Luxembourg nationality.

**For additional analytical, business and investment opportunities information, please contact Global Investment & Business Center, USA at (202) 546-2103. Fax: (202) 546-3275. E-mail: rusric@erols.com**

### A. Loss of Luxembourg nationality waiver (Article 13, paragraphs 1 and 2)

Conditions of cancellation Loses quality Luxembourgers, who renounces the Luxembourg nationality. Whoever wishes to waive the Luxembourg nationality must meet the following conditions:

have reached the age of 18 years;

make a disclaimer before the registrar of civil status;

adduce evidence or to possess a foreign nationality or to acquire or recover a foreign nationality automatically, by virtue of the declaration.

The state registrar shall, within eight days of the declaration, a duly certified copy of it to the Minister of Justice shipping.

Effects of the waiver on the minor waiver has the following consequences for the minor child: Loses Luxembourg nationality, children under 18 years of age, whose parentage is established in respect of a single author or adopting, when it loses the Luxembourg nationality by virtue of the waiver, provided that the foreign nationality of the perpetrator or the adopter is imparted to the child or that it already has. When filiation is established in respect of his parents or two adoptive parents, children under 18 years of age does not lose the Luxembourg nationality as one of them still has the. He loses when this adopting or author himself comes to losing, provided that the child acquires the nationality of one of its authors or ouadoptants he already possesses.

### B. Loss of Luxembourg nationality by parentage cessation (Article 13, paragraph 3)

Lose Luxembourg nationality, the child whose parentage against a Luxembourg author ceases to be established before it reaches the age of 18 years, unless another author has the quality of Luxembourg or the child becomes stateless.

A person is stateless if he has no nationality.

## V. FORFEITURE OF LUXEMBOURGERS

Forfeiture is to remove the Luxembourg nationality, when it was obtained by unfair methods.

### A. Conditions (Article 15)

The person who has acquired the status of Luxembourg, may be deprived of Luxembourg nationality, if she got the Luxembourg nationality:

or by false statements, by fraud or concealment of material facts;

is based on a false or use a false or based on impersonation and as it has been convicted of one of these offenses by a decision of casting justice res judicata.

Forfeiture is not possible, when it results in statelessness of the person concerned.

### B. Procedure (Article 16)

The Minister of Justice shall declare the forfeiture of Luxembourg nationality by reasoned order.

When the deprivation of nationality has become final, the ministerial decree ordering the revocation or the device of judicial decision confirming the ministerial decree of forfeiture is transcribed, or in a special register kept in duplicate, either in the register of deeds by birth, the officer of civil status of the domicile or residence of the person deprived of nationality or, in the absence of residence in the country, by the officer of civil status who received the document naturalization.

Mention is also made in the margin of the naturalness of the person deprived of nationality. Forfeiture takes effect on the day of transcription.

The ministerial decree ordering the forfeiture may be appealed to the Administrative Tribunal. The appeal is brought before the Administrative Court. Is made in section VII. Litigation nationality.

### C. Consequences (Articles 17 and 18)

The spouse and children of the fallen may waive Luxembourg Luxembourg nationality under the following conditions:

subscribe a declaration of renunciation before the registrar of civil status within three months from the date of the transcript of the decision to strip. With regard to minor children, the period is extended until the expiration of three months after their majority;

adduce evidence or to possess a foreign nationality or to acquire or recover a foreign nationality automatically, by virtue of the declaration.

In addition, the person declared forfeited quality Luxembourgers and their spouses and children, who have renounced the Luxembourg nationality, can not recover Luxembourg nationality or reapply acquisition of Luxembourg nationality by naturalization.

### D. Transitional provision (Article 30)

The device on the forfeiture may apply equally to all Luxembourgers not holding nationality of a Luxembourg author on the day of their birth and who have acquired the Luxembourg nationality before the entry into force of the Act of 23 October 2008 on Luxembourg nationality.

## VI. PROOF OF LUXEMBOURG NATIONALITY

Under the influence of the law of 22 February 1968 on Luxembourg nationality (Article 37) Act, a certificate of nationality (Heimatschein) is proof of Luxembourg nationality. It is especially required by state or local government (eg: for admission to the entrance examination to the public), by judicial authorities (eg: in case of adoption) and embassies and consulates (eg for a passport). The issuance of a certificate of citizenship involves many steps from the citizen is obliged to establish a record.

The Act of 23 October 2008 on Luxembourg nationality is an administrative simplification that will make life easier for citizens. Indeed, the Luxembourg nationality can be proved by other means that the certificate of nationality. A certificate of nationality is required only in exceptional circumstances.

### A. Passport or identity (Article 23) map

**For additional analytical, business and investment opportunities information, please contact Global Investment & Business Center, USA at (202) 546-2103. Fax: (202) 546-3275. E-mail: rusric@erols.com**

Luxembourg nationality of a person is established, until proven otherwise, by holding:

1) is a Luxembourg passport valid;

2) is a Luxembourg national identity card valid.

### B. Certificates of nationality (Articles 24 and 25)

In case of serious doubt or dispute Luxembourg nationality, a certificate of Luxembourg nationality may be issued to persons who prove they have Luxembourg nationality. A certificate of nationality may also be issued, if required by a foreign authority.

Nationality certificates are issued by the Minister of Justice, which determines the validity of certificates. Their validity may not exceed 5 years.

Certificates of nationality indicates that the person has the Luxembourg nationality and, at the request of the applicant, state the date from which he has acquired this quality.

They are prima facie evidence to the contrary. This same probative force attaches to licenses issued since September 10, 1944.

Certificates of nationality are liable to stamp duty amount to be determined by the Grand Ducal Regulation and can not exceed 30 euros.

## VII. LITIGATION LUXEMBOURG NATIONALITY

Under the influence of the law of 22 February 1968 on Luxembourg nationality (Article 40) law, litigation of nationality falls within the exclusive jurisdiction of civil courts.

The Act of 23 October 2008 on the Luxembourg nationality transfers litigation nationality to administrative courts, providing a higher court. Questions prior to the determination or acquisition of Luxembourg nationality remain the jurisdiction of civil courts.

A. Jurisdiction of administrative courts (Article 26)

are within the jurisdiction of the Administrative Tribunal, which decides on the bottom:

all actions or claim challenging the Luxembourg nationality;

appeals against ministerial orders refusing applications for naturalization or recovery and those exercised against the ministerial decrees declaring the disqualification as Luxembourg.

Against ministerial orders refusing applications for naturalization or recovery time to sue is 3 months from the notification of the decision. Against decisions imposing forfeiture, the time to sue is 3 months from the transcript of that decision.

The appeal is brought before the Administrative Court. The appeal period is 40 days from notification of the judgment of the Administrative Court by the Registry.

**For additional analytical, business and investment opportunities information, please contact Global Investment & Business Center, USA at (202) 546-2103. Fax: (202) 546-3275. E-mail: rusric@erols.com**

The proceedings before the Administrative Court and the appeal to the Administrative Court are formed by petition signed by a lawyer in court.

Communication to the person concerned of his rights of citizenship record is only possible in the context of an action.

### B. JURISDICTION OF CIVIL COURTS (ARTICLE 27)

The preliminary questions of civil law governing the granting of citizenship are governed by the applicable law under the general rule of conflict of laws. These issues are under the jurisdiction of civil courts.

If marital status is the result of a foreign judgment whose regularity is disputed, its recognition may be applied to the district court, which entered by application of attorney at law, statue in private, on conclusion of State Prosecutor.

## RECEPTION AND INTEGRATION OF FOREIGNERS IN THE GRAND DUCHY

Considering the decision of the House of Representatives on 11 November 2008 and the State Council of 9 December 2008 on there is no need to second vote;

Have ordered and order:

### CHAPTER 1. LUXEMBOURG OFFICE OF RECEPTION AND INTEGRATION

Art. 1 st .

This Act applies to all aliens legally resident in the Grand Duchy of Luxembourg.

Are not covered by paragraph 1 st applicants for international protection as defined by the Act of 5 May 2006 on the right of asylum and complementary forms of protection, with the exception of the provision in the Article 3, paragraph 2 on welfare.

Art. 2.

For the purposes of this Act, the term integration refers to a two-way process by which an alien expresses its willingness to participate in a sustainable way in the life of the host society, the social, economic, political and cultural takes him all the provisions to encourage and facilitate this process.

Integration is a task that the State, municipalities and civil society perform together.

For the purposes of this Act, means any person abroad who does not have Luxembourg nationality, whether it has exclusively another nationality or she has none.

By foreign newcomer, it is necessary to hear a person immigrated to Luxembourg for less than five years.

Art. 3.

**For additional analytical, business and investment opportunities information, please contact Global Investment & Business Center, USA at (202) 546-2103. Fax: (202) 546-3275. E-mail: rusric@erols.com**

It is established under the authority of the Minister with responsibility for Integration, hereinafter called "the Minister", a Luxembourg Office for the reception and integration, abbreviated "OLAI."

The OLAI's mission is to organize the reception of foreign newcomers, to facilitate the process of integration of foreigners in the implementation and coordination of the reception and integration policy, including the fight against the discrimination is an essential element, together with the municipalities and civil society, as well as organize social assistance to foreigners who do not qualify for existing aid allocations and persons seeking international protection as defined by Act of 5 May 2006 on the right of asylum and complementary forms of protection.

In fulfilling this mission, OLAI working with European and international bodies, as well as those of the country of origin of foreigners.

Art. 4.

The OLAI is authorized to:

- manage hosting structures reserved for the temporary accommodation of foreigners;

- collaborate with other organizations in the creation and management of accommodation facilities reserved for the temporary accommodation of foreigners;

- promote together with the competent authorities for the construction and development of housing reserved for foreign temporary accommodation centers.

Art. 5.

In exceptional and duly justified cases, the OLAI may grant a one-time support for foreigners who do not qualify for aid and existing allocations.

Art. 6.

The OLAI is responsible for establishing, in consultation with the Interdepartmental Committee on Integration project of national integration plan and multi-year fight against discrimination identifying key strategic areas of intervention and policy measures being and to implement.

The Minister shall submit the draft plan to the Government for approval.

The Government will present a comprehensive strategy and determine measures targeted integration and fight against discrimination.

Art. 7.

Every five years, the Minister address a national report on the reception and integration of foreigners, the fight against discrimination, social assistance to foreigners, as well as monitoring of migration in the Grand Duchy of Luxembourg the Chamber of Deputies.

The OLAI is entitled to appeal to the authorities of the State, municipal administrations, institutions and government agencies to lend him their assistance and provide all the necessary preparation of the report data.

**For additional analytical, business and investment opportunities information, please contact Global Investment & Business Center, USA at (202) 546-2103. Fax: (202) 546-3275. E-mail: rusric@erols.com**

## CHAPTER 2. AGREEMENT RECEPTION AND INTEGRATION

Art. 8.

A reception and integration contract is offered to foreigners legally residing in the territory of the Grand Duchy of Luxembourg and who wish to maintain a sustainable manner.

Art. 9.

The reception and integration contract contains reciprocal commitments to the state and abroad to organize and facilitate its integration.

It includes the part of the State's commitment to provide language training and civics and measures its social and economic integration.

Foreign undertakes to ensure, according to his abilities and possibilities, his livelihood by his own means, and to participate in social life.

The reception and integration contract is concluded for a period not exceeding two years.

Art. 10.

The conditions of application and implementation arrangements of the host contract and integration are laid down by Grand-Ducal.

Art. 11.

The OLAI is responsible for developing a standard contract of welcome and integration, to ensure its management and encourage foreigners to enter into such a contract with the state.

Art. 12.

Prior to the conclusion of a reception and integration with foreign contract OLAI shall, together with the Ministry of National Education and Vocational Training, an assessment of language skills.

Art. 13.

Foreigners who signed the host contract and integration are considered in priority measures and actions foreseen in the national integration plan.

The signature and the compliance with the provisions contained in the contract of welcome and integration from abroad are taken into account in assessing the degree of integration.

## CHAPTER 3. FINANCIAL AID

Art. 14.

The Government may grant based on available budgetary resources financial support to municipalities and agencies to carry out the tasks defined in Article 3 above.

**For additional analytical, business and investment opportunities information, please contact Global Investment & Business Center, USA at (202) 546-2103. Fax: (202) 546-3275. E-mail: rusric@erols.com**

Financial support may take the form of a grant or a financial contribution to operating costs.

The recipient of a financial contribution must sign an agreement with the State that determines:

a) deliverables by the beneficiary;

b) the type of financial participation by the State;

c) the means of information, control and sanction that the State has in relation to the duties of the beneficiary defined under a);

d) modalities of cooperation between the Contracting Parties without affecting the management is the responsibility of the recipient.

He agrees to keep proper accounts as required by the state.

The participation of the State shall be determined in the manner to be determined by agreement between the parties.

If the beneficiary is a legal entity of private law, it must be constituted either under a special legal provision, under the provisions of the Act of 28 April 1928 on associations and foundations, non-profit law, or accordance with the provisions of the amended law of 10 August 1915 on commercial companies.

Art. 15.

The state pays its participation in whole or in part in the form of monthly or bi advances. The beneficiary shall submit to the State an annual breakdown. Sums unduly affected shall be returned to the Treasury.

Art. 16.

The Government is authorized to participate in the construction or development of housing for applicants for international protection by municipalities or public agencies centers. Participation can achieve hundred percent is the cost of construction and original equipment or the cost of acquisition, development and original equipment.

## CHAPTER 4. INSTITUTIONAL STRUCTURES

Section 1. National Council for Foreigners

Art. 17.

There is established a National Council for foreigners, hereinafter called the Board.

Art. 18.

The Council is an advisory body to study, either on his own initiative or at the request of the Government issues concerning foreigners and integration. On all projects that the Government deems necessary to submit it gives its opinion within the time fixed by the Government. He has the right to submit to

**For additional analytical, business and investment opportunities information, please contact Global Investment & Business Center, USA at (202) 546-2103. Fax: (202) 546-3275. E-mail: rusric@erols.com**

Government any proposals it deems necessary to improve the situation of foreigners and their families. It will provide the Government, who make public an annual report on the integration of foreigners in Luxembourg.

Art. 19.

The board includes:

- twenty to two representatives of foreign;

- a representative of the refugees of the Geneva Convention of 28 July 1951 relating to the Status of Refugees;

- a representative of the multi-purpose municipal association of Luxembourg Towns and Municipalities for the promotion and safeguarding of general and common (SYVICOL) local interests;

- four representatives of employers' organizations;

- four representatives of the most representative trade union organizations;

- two representatives of the civil society.

Board members are appointed for a term of five years by the Minister on the proposal:

- Government regarding the representatives of refugees the Geneva Convention and representatives of civil society;

- employers' organizations in terms of their representatives;

- trade unions in terms of their representatives;

- foreign associations legally constituted and having a cultural or sports and associations working, primarily, for foreign social activity, registered with the OLAI regarding foreign representatives.

Grand-Ducal Regulation lays down rules for the designation of representatives of foreign and their breakdown by nationality on the basis of the proportional importance of the various nationalities in Luxembourg without the maximum number of representatives per nationality can be more than three. The proportional importance is evidenced by the last population census conducted by the Central Service for Statistics and Economic Studies (STATEC).

Seven representatives of countries that are not part of the European Union shall be members of the board.

Each board member is appointed an alternate. In case of death or resignation of a member of the Board, his deputy replaced until the renewal of the board. The individual mandate a representative of foreign ends except in the case of death or resignation, once it acquires Luxembourg nationality.

Art. 20.

**For additional analytical, business and investment opportunities information, please contact Global Investment & Business Center, USA at (202) 546-2103. Fax: (202) 546-3275. E-mail: rusric@erols.com**

The Chair and Vice-Chair are elected by a majority of members for a period of five years. Their mandates are renewable. They are appointed by the Minister.

The Board meets at least three times per year. The President shall convene the Board whenever the Minister or six members of the Board request.

The Minister and the Director of OLAI may attend board meetings.

Board meetings are not public. The reports of the Board with the Government and other public authorities are held through the Minister or the Director of OLAI.

An officer or employee of the OLAI assumes the role of secretary.

Board members are entitled to fees whose amount is set by the Government in Council.

The secretary of the board is entitled to compensation the amount of which is fixed by the Government in Council.

Board members are released from work to attend meetings of the Board with compensation for any loss of wages fixed by the Government in Council.

Art. 21.

The Board may appoint committees necessary to carry out its mission.

These committees may include persons not members of the Board appointed by the Minister on the proposal of the Board.

The Board may, in the exercise of his mission call in consultation with representatives of government and public and any person whose assistance, due to its jurisdiction or function, it appears relevant for the performance of its institutions mission.

Art. 22.

Operating procedures, deliberation and vote of the Board as well as the procedures for replacing members prevented from exercising their mandate will be determined by rules of procedure which will be submitted for approval to the Minister.

Section 2. Commissions Consultative integration

Art. 23.

In all municipalities, the municipal council shall constitute an advisory committee responsible for overall integration of living together of all residents of the town and especially the interests of residents of foreign nationality. Luxembourg residents and foreigners are included.

The organization and functioning of these committees are set by the Grand Ducal Regulation.

## CHAPTER 5. PERSONNEL OLAI

Art. 24.

**For additional analytical, business and investment opportunities information, please contact Global Investment & Business Center, USA at (202) 546-2103. Fax: (202) 546-3275. E-mail: rusric@erols.com**

Staff OLAI is placed under the authority of a director.

Art. 25.

Outside director, as part of staff OLAI includes the following functions and jobs:

1) In the upper quarry administration:

policy advisors first class

policy advisors

Advisors Assistant Management

Attached Government 1 st in a row

Attached Government

2) Average career of administration:

a) of social hygiene assistants

b) social workers

c) graduate nurses

d) Educators graduatese)

senior inspectors first in rank

senior inspectors

Inspectors

Heads of Office

Heads of Office Assistant

principal drafter

Editors

3) In the lower career of administration:

a) first chief clerks

main committed

clerks

For additional analytical, business and investment opportunities information,
please contact Global Investment & Business Center, USA
at (202) 546-2103. Fax: (202) 546-3275. E-mail: rusric@erols.com

Assistant Clerk

expeditionary

b) Nursing

c) Educators

d)

leaders artisans

first principal architects

the main architects

first artisans

artisans

e)

Senior Supervisors concierges

supervisors concierges

janitors.

The above framework can be completed by trainees. The OLAI may also obtain service employees and state workers.

Commitments pursuant to this section are to the needs of the OLAI and within the budget.

Art. 26.

Without prejudice to the general rules relating to the status of civil servants, the special admission to the course requirements, appointment and promotion are not fixed by this Act, shall be determined by the Grand Ducal Regulation .

Candidates for the office of Director of the Luxembourg Board reception and integration must satisfy the conditions of study for admission to the career of attached Government. They are exempted from examination competition, internship and final exam training provided for in Article 2 of the amended law of 16 April 1979 laying down the Staff Regulations of the State.

Art. 27.

The appointments to senior classified at grade 8 grades are made by the Grand Duke. Appointments to other functions are made by the Minister.

**For additional analytical, business and investment opportunities information, please contact Global Investment & Business Center, USA at (202) 546-2103. Fax: (202) 546-3275. E-mail: rusric@erols.com**

## CHAPTER 6. BUDGETARY AND FINANCIAL PROVISIONS

Art. 28.

By the limits laid down in the Act of 21 December 2007 on the budget of revenues and expenditures of the State for the year 2008, the Minister is authorized to make the commitment of two employees of the higher bracket (S) 5 officers and the average career (D).

The Article 14 of the aforementioned law on budget revenue and expenditure of the State and for the recruitment of employees of foreign nationality with government departments is completed to the corresponding paragraph in the Government Commission for Foreign by adding the following:

Employees career S - 2

Employees career D - 5.

## CHAPTER 7. AMENDING PROVISIONS

Art. 29.

The following changes and additions are made to the amended law of 22 June 1963 fixing the pay of civil servants:

a)

Appendix A Classification of Functions - Section I "General Administration" is amended and supplemented as follows:

in grade 17 the words "Government Commission for foreigners? Government Commissioner to strangers "is replaced by the term" Luxembourg Office for reception and integration? Director ".

b) Annex D? Determination? Section I "General Administration" is amended and supplemented as follows:

In the upper quarry administration:

grade 12 of the computation of the retirement bonus

in grade 17, in the list of Commissioners of the Government, the word "foreign" is deleted and replaced in the list of directors by the words "of the Luxembourg Office for the reception and integration."

At number 9 of Section IV of Article 22 the words "the Government Commissioner to strangers" is replaced by the term "the director of the Luxembourg Office for reception and integration."

Art. 30.

The Article 34, paragraph 1 of the amended law of 25 February 1979 concerning aid to housing is amended as follows:

**For additional analytical, business and investment opportunities information, please contact Global Investment & Business Center, USA at (202) 546-2103. Fax: (202) 546-3275. E-mail: rusric@erols.com**

Without prejudice to the powers and competences of medical inspectors and general and local police, municipal authorities and the Luxembourg Office for reception and integration (OLAI) are responsible for monitoring housing.

**CHAPTER 8. TRANSITIONAL**

Art. 31.

The National Council for Foreigners in its current composition will continue to function until the completion of his current term in 2010.

**CHAPTER 9. REPEALING**

Art. 32.

The amended law of 27 July 1993 concerning the integration of foreigners in the Grand Duchy of Luxembourg and social action in favor of foreigners is repealed.

**CHAPTER 10. ENFORCEMENT**

Art. 33.

This Act comes into force on the first day of the sixth month following its publication in the Memorial, with the exception of Article 28 which shall enter into force on the third day following its publication in the Mémorial.

We order and command that this Act be inserted Memorial to be performed and observed by all whom it may concern.

Palais de Luxembourg, 16 December 2008.
Henry
The Minister for Family and Integration,
Marie Josée Jacobs
Minister of National Education and Vocational Training,

Mady Delvaux-Stehres

**For additional analytical, business and investment opportunities information, please contact Global Investment & Business Center, USA at (202) 546-2103. Fax: (202) 546-3275. E-mail: rusric@erols.com**

# CITIZENSHIP OF THE EUROPEAN UNION

**Citizenship of the European Union** was introduced by the Maastricht Treaty, which was signed in 1992, and has been in force since 1993. European citizenship is supplementary to national citizenship and affords rights such as the right to vote in European elections, the right to free movement, settlement and employment across the EU, and the right to consular protection by other EU states' embassies when a person's country of citizenship does not maintain an embassy or consulate in the country they need protection in

EU citizenship as a distinct concept was first introduced by the Maastricht Treaty, and was extended by the Treaty of Amsterdam. Prior to the 1992 Maastricht Treaty, the European Communities treaties provided guarantees for the free movement of economically active persons, but not, generally, for others. The 1951 Treaty of Paris establishing the European Coal and Steel Community established a right to free movement for workers in these industries and the 1957 Treaty of Rome provided for the free movement of workers and services.

However, the Treaty provisions were interpreted by the European Court of Justice not as having a narrow economic purpose, but rather a wider social and economic purpose. In *Levin*, the Court found that the "freedom to take up employment was important, not just as a means towards the creation of a single market for the benefit of the Member State economies, but as a right for the worker to raise her or his standard of living".Under the ECJ caselaw, the rights of free movement of workers applies regardless of the worker's purpose in taking up employment abroad, to both part-time and full-time work, and whether or not the worker required additional financial assistance from the Member State into which he moves.

Since, the ECJ has held that a recipient of service has free movement rights under the treaty and this criterion is easily fulfilled, effectively every national of an EU country within another Member State, whether economically active or not, had a right under Article 12 of the European Community Treaty to non-discrimination even prior to the Maastricht Treaty.

In *Martinez Sala*, the European Court of Justice held that the citizenship provisions provided substantive free movement rights in addition to those already granted by Union law.

## STATED RIGHTS

Historically, the main benefit of being a citizen of an EU state has been that of free movement. The free movement also applies to the citizens of European Economic Area states and Switzerland. However with the creation of EU citizenship, certain political rights came into being. The Treaty on the Functioning of the European Union provides for citizens to be "*directly represented at Union level in the European Parliament*", and "*to participate in the democratic life of the Union*" (Treaty on the European Union, Title II, Article 10). Specifically, the following rights are afforded;

Political rights

**Voting in European elections**: a right to vote and stand in elections to the European Parliament, in any EU member state (Article 22)
**Voting in municipal elections**: a right to vote and stand in local elections in an EU state other than their own, under the same conditions as the nationals of that state (Article 22)
**Accessing European government documents**: a right to access to European Parliament, Council, and Commission documents (Article 15).

**For additional analytical, business and investment opportunities information, please contact Global Investment & Business Center, USA at (202) 546-2103. Fax: (202) 546-3275. E-mail: rusric@erols.com**

**Petitioning Parliament and the Ombudsman**: the right to petition the European Parliament and the right to apply to the European Ombudsman in order to bring to his attention any cases of poor administration by the EU institutions and bodies, with the exception of the legal bodies (Article 24)
**Linguistic rights**: the right to apply to the EU institutions in one of the official languages and to receive a reply in that same language (Article 24).

Rights of free movement

**Right to free movement and residence**: a right of free movement and residence throughout the Union and the right to work in any position (including national civil services with the exception of those posts in the public sector that involve the exercise of powers conferred by public law and the safeguard of general interests of the State or local authorities (Article 21) for which however there is no one single definition);
**Freedom from discrimination on nationality**: a right not to be discriminated against on grounds of nationality within the scope of application of the Treaty (Article 18);

Rights abroad

**Right to consular protection**: a right to protection by the diplomatic or consular authorities of other Member States when in a non-EU Member State, if there are no diplomatic or consular authorities from the citizen's own state (Article 23): this is due to the fact that not all member states maintain embassies in every country in the world (16 countries have only one embassy from an EU state)

## FREE MOVEMENT RIGHTS

Article 21 Freedom to move and reside

Article 21 (1) of the Treaty on the Functioning of the European Union states that

> Every citizen of the Union shall have the right to move and reside freely within the territory of the Member States, subject to the limitations and conditions laid down in this Treaty and by the measures adopted to give it effect.

The European Court of Justice has remarked that,

> EU Citizenship is destined to be the fundamental status of nationals of the Member States

The ECJ has held that this Article confers a directly effective right upon citizens to reside in another Member State. Before the case of *Baumbast*, it was widely assumed that non-economically active citizens had no rights to residence deriving directly from the EU Treaty, only from directives created under the Treaty. In *Baumbast*, however, the ECJ held that (the then) Article 18 of the EC Treaty granted a generally applicable right to residency, which is limited by secondary legislation, but *only* where that secondary legislation is proportionate. Member States can distinguish between nationals and Union citizens but only if the provisions satisfy the test of proportionality.

Migrant EU citizens have a "legitimate expectation of a limited degree of financial solidarity... having regard to their degree of integration into the host society" Length of time is a particularly important factor when considering the degree of integration.

**For additional analytical, business and investment opportunities information, please contact Global Investment & Business Center, USA at (202) 546-2103. Fax: (202) 546-3275. E-mail: rusric@erols.com**

The ECJ's case law on citizenship has been criticised for subjecting an increasing number of national rules to the proportionality assessment.

Article 45 Freedom of movement to work

Article 45 of the Treaty on the Functioning of the European Union states that

> 1. Freedom of movement for workers shall be secured within the Union.
> 2. Such freedom of movement shall entail the abolition of any discrimination based on nationality between workers of the Member States as regards employment, remuneration and other conditions of work and employment.

State employment reserved exclusively for nationals varies between member states. For example, training as a barrister in Britain and Ireland is not reserved for nationals, while the corresponding French course qualifies one as a 'juge' and hence can only be taken by French citizens. However, it is broadly limited to those roles that exercise a significant degree of public authority, such as judges, police, the military, diplomats, senior civil servants or politicians. Note that not all Member States choose to restrict all of these posts to nationals.

Much of the existing secondary legislation and case law was consolidated in the Citizens' Rights Directive 2004/38/EC on the right to move and reside freely within the EU.

Limitations

New member states may undergo transitional regimes, during which their nationals only enjoy restricted access to labour markets in other member states. EU member states are permitted to keep restrictions on citizens of the newly acceded countries for a maximum of seven years after accession. For the EFTA states (Iceland, Lichtenstein, Norway and Switzerland), the maximum is nine years.

Following the 2004 enlargement, three "old" member states—Ireland, Sweden and the United Kingdom—decided to allow unrestricted access to their labour markets. By December 2009, all but two member states—Austria and Germany—had completely dropped controls. These restrictions too expired on 1 May 2011.

Following the 2007 enlargement, all pre-2004 member states except Finland and Sweden imposed restrictions on Bulgarian and Romanian citizens, as did two member states that joined in 2004: Malta and Hungary. As of November 2012, all but 8 EU countries have dropped restrictions entirely. These restrictions too expired on 1 January 2014. Norway opened its labour market in June 2012, while Switzerland and Lichtenstein may keep restrictions in place until 2016.

Following the 2013 enlargement, it is expected that some countries will implement restrictions on Croatian nationals following the country's EU accession on 1 July 2013. As of July 2013, all but 13 EU countries have dropped restrictions entirely. The UK Home Office has announced a bill to this effect.

## ACQUISITION

There is no common EU policy on the acquisition of European citizenship as it is supplementary to national citizenship (one cannot be an EU citizen without being a national of a member state). Article 20 (1) of the Treaty on the Functioning of the European Union states that:

**For additional analytical, business and investment opportunities information, please contact Global Investment & Business Center, USA at (202) 546-2103. Fax: (202) 546-3275. E-mail: rusric@erols.com**

"Citizenship of the Union is hereby established. Every person holding the nationality of a Member State shall be a citizen of the Union. Citizenship of the Union shall be additional to and not replace national citizenship."

While nationals of Member States are citizens of the union, "It is for each Member State, having due regard to Union law, to lay down the conditions for the acquisition and loss of nationality." As a result, there is a great variety in rules and practices with regard to the acquisition and loss of citizenship in EU member states.

Thus in practice, a member state may withhold EU citizenship from certain groups of citizens — namely some in overseas territories of member states outside the EU. One example would be the Faroe Islands of Denmark which, though a part of Denmark, are outside the EU and do not have EU citizenship.

**SUMMARY OF MEMBER STATES' NATIONALITY LAWS**

This is a summary of nationality laws for each of the twenty-eight EU member states.

| Member State | Acquisition by birth | Acquisition by descent | Acquisition by marriage | Acquisition by naturalisation | Multiple nationality permitted |
|---|---|---|---|---|---|
| Austria | Persons born in Austria:<br>at least one of whose married parents is an Austrian citizen<br>out of wedlock and whose mother is Austrian citizen<br>who is foundling and is found out under the age of 6 months | Austrian nationality is acquired by descent under one of the following conditions:<br>Conditions | 6 years' residence if married for at least 5 years (and general citizenship conditions are met, including German language proficiency) | 6 years' residence if born in Austria, citizen of another EEC country, granted asylum, or "exceptionally integrated" depending on fulfillment of other conditions, up to 30 years' residence | Only allowed with special permission or if dual citizenship was obtained at birth (binational parents [one Austrian, one foreign] or birth in a jus-soli country such as USA and Canada) |
| Belgium | Persons born in Belgium who:<br>are stateless<br>are foundlings<br>lose any other nationality before 18<br>have a parent born in Belgium<br>have a birth or adopted parent resident in Belgium for at least 5 of the past 10 years | Belgian nationality is acquired by descent under one of the following conditions:<br>Belgian citizen father | Yes—after 3 years cohabitation in Belgium | 3 years' residence—can petition federal government<br>7 years' residence—automatic by request at city hall<br>2 years' residence (political refugees and stateless persons) | Yes |
| Bulgaria | Persons born in Bulgaria who:<br>are stateless<br>are foundlings | Bulgarian nationality is acquired by descent under one of the following conditions:<br>Conditions | The applicant should be at least 18 years old;<br>have permission for permanent or for long-term residence in Bulgaria since | The applicant should be at least 18 years old;<br>have permission for permanent or for long-term residence in Bulgaria since at least 5 years;<br>have not been investigated or | Yes - for Bulgarian citizens by birth;<br>Yes - for naturalized citizens of the EU and EEA countries, Switzerland |

| Member State | Acquisition by birth | Acquisition by descent | Acquisition by marriage | Acquisition by naturalisation | Multiple nationality permitted |
|---|---|---|---|---|---|
| | | | at least 3 years;<br>have not been investigated or sentenced by the Bulgarian authorities;<br>have income or occupation;<br>be able to speak and write in Bulgarian;<br>renounce previous citizenship (not applicable to citizens of the EU and EEA countries, Switzerland and countries with reciprocity agreement with Bulgaria; dual citizenship is allowed for them);<br>have marriage to Bulgarian citizen since at least 3 years and the marriage is actual. | sentenced by the Bulgarian authorities;<br>have income or occupation;<br>be able to speak and write in Bulgarian;<br>renounce previous citizenship (not applicable to citizens of the EU and EEA countries, Switzerland and countries with reciprocity agreement with Bulgaria; dual citizenship is allowed for them). | and countries with reciprocity agreement with Bulgaria |
| Croatia | Persons born in Croatia:<br>At least one parent is a Croatian citizen who is foundling (but such citizenship can be revoked if later established both parents were foreign citizens) | Croatian nationality is acquired by descent under one of the following conditions:<br>Conditions: born to Croatian parents born after March 1, 1991 and if parents are married at the time of birth, Croatian citizenship of mother the father is required should the parents happen to marry at some time after birth, citizenship is automatically granted to child retroactively. If the child is over 14 at that time, child's consent is needed. ? | 8 years' residence (can be shortened) | 8 years' residence sufficient knowledge of Croatian language | Yes, but persons seeking to become Croatian citizens by naturalisation are to renounce foreign citizenship unless applying by 'privileged naturalisation' (e.g. descendants of Croatian emigrants) |
| Cyprus | Persons born in | Cypriot nationality is | 3 years' | 7 years' residence | Yes |

| Member State | Acquisition by birth | Acquisition by descent | Acquisition by marriage | Acquisition by naturalisation | Multiple nationality permitted |
|---|---|---|---|---|---|
| | Cyprus who:<br>are stateless<br>are foundlings | acquired by descent under one of the following conditions:<br>Conditions | residence | | |
| Czech Republic | Persons born in the Czech Republic:<br>who are foundlings<br>whose parents are both stateless, and at least one of whom is a Czech permanent resident | | No | Holders of a Czech permanent residence permit for at least 5 years | No (unless the non-Czech citizenship is obtained by birth or by marriage) |
| Denmark | Persons born in Denmark who:<br>are foundlings | Danish nationality is acquired by descent under one of the following conditions:<br>The child's mother is a Danish citizen;<br>The child's father is a Danish citizen and the parents are married; | 6 years' residence if married for at least 3 years | 9 years' residence (holders of a permanent residence permit)<br>8 years' residence (refugees and stateless persons) | No |
| Estonia | Persons born in Estonia who:<br>are foundlings | Persons who have at least one parent with Estonian citizenship. | No (unless married to an Estonian citizen before 26 February 1992) | 8 years' residence | No (although Estonian citizens by descent cannot be deprived of their Estonian citizenship) |
| Finland | Persons born in Finland who:<br>are stateless, or<br>are foundlings | Finnish nationality is acquired by descent under one of the following conditions:<br>Conditions | Minimum residence requirement of four years of residence. | Five years of residence (or a total of seven years of residence since age 15) in Finland; and knowledge of at least one of Finnish, Swedish or Finnish sign language. Reductions apply under certain conditions. | Yes |
| France | At birth, persons born in France who:<br>are stateless, or<br>have a parent born in France<br>At 13, persons born in France upon the parent's request.<br>At 16, persons | French nationality is acquired by descent under one of the following conditions:<br>Through parentage (right of blood):<br>The child (legitimate or natural) is French if at least one parent is French. | 5 years' marriage; also, after 4 years outside France | Holders of a French permanent residence permit for at least 5 years' residence<br>No residence (former citizens with conditions) | Yes |

**For additional analytical, business and investment opportunities information, please contact Global Investment & Business Center, USA at (202) 546-2103. Fax: (202) 546-3275. E-mail: rusric@erols.com**

| Member State | Acquisition by birth | Acquisition by descent | Acquisition by marriage | Acquisition by naturalisation | Multiple nationality permitted |
|---|---|---|---|---|---|
| | born in France upon their own request.<br>At 18, persons born in France who:<br>have resided in France for at least 5 years since 11 | | | | |
| Germany | Persons born in Germany, if at least one parent has resided in Germany for at least 8 years and holds a permanent residence permit | German nationality is acquired by descent under one of the following conditions:<br>Member of recognized historical German community abroad (e.g. in the Balkans, Kazakhstan); Also granted to children/grandchildren of those deprived of citizenship by the Nuremberg Laws | 2 years of marriage and 3 years of continuous residence in Germany | 8 years' residence<br>7 years' residence (if an integration course has been completed)<br>6 years' residence (if especially well integrated and has a very high command of the German language, or a refugee or stateless person)<br>No residence (victims of Nazi persecution) | No, unless: Conditions |
| Greece | Persons born in Greece who:<br>have a parent born in Greece<br>are foundlings<br>are stateless | Greek nationality is acquired by descent under one of the following conditions:<br>Member of recognized historical Greek community abroad in countries of ex-USSR<br>Ethnic Greek of different citizenship accepted to military academies, or inscribes to serve to the army, or enlists as a volunteer in time of war | 3 years of continuous residence in Greece and has an offspring from the marriage | 10 years residence in the last 12 years<br>5 years residence in the last 12 years for refugees<br>Sufficient knowledge of Greek language, Greek history, and Greek culture in general<br>Athlete of an Olympic Sport, with 5 years residence in the last 12 years, who fulfills the conditions of being a member of the Greek National Team of that sport, as these are stated by the international laws for that sport | Yes |
| Hungary | Persons born in Hungary who:<br>are foundlings<br>are stateless | Hungarian nationality is acquired by descent under one of the following conditions:<br>At least one parent is a Hungarian citizen<br>Any person of Hungarian ethnicity, which has to be proven by sufficient level of | Yes After 3 years | After 8 years and meeting conditions of good character<br>After 5 years if born in Hungary<br>resided in Hungary in their pupillage<br>stateless<br>After 3 years if married to a Hungarian citizen<br>has a minor child that | Yes |

| Member State | Acquisition by birth | Acquisition by descent | Acquisition by marriage | Acquisition by naturalisation | Multiple nationality permitted |
|---|---|---|---|---|---|
| | | Hungarian language demonstrating at least one ancestor born in the Kingdom of Hungary (no limit on number of generations). | | is Hungarian citizen<br>adopted by a Hungarian citizen<br>refugee in Hungary | |
| Ireland | Persons born in Ireland:<br>are automatically an Irish citizen if he or she is not entitled to the citizenship of any other country.<br>entitled to be an Irish citizen if at least one parent is:<br>an Irish citizen (or someone entitled to be an Irish citizen).<br>a British citizen.<br>a resident of the island of Ireland who is entitled to reside in either the Republic or in Northern Ireland without any time limit on that residence.<br>a legal resident of the island of Ireland for three out of the 4 years preceding the child's birth. | Irish nationality is acquired by descent under one of the following conditions:<br>if at the time of birth, at least one parent was an Irish citizen.<br>if you have an Irish citizen grandparent born on the island of Ireland. The parent would have automatically been an Irish citizen. Grandchild can secure citizenship by registering themselves in the Foreign Births Register. Citizenship gained via the Foreign Births Register can only be passed on to children born after the parent themselves were registered. | 3 years of marriage or civil partnership to an Irish citizen | 5 years of residency in Ireland, of which 1 (one) year immediately before application | Yes |
| Italy | Persons born in Italy who:<br>have a parent born in Italy<br>are foundlings<br>are stateless | Italian nationality is acquired by descent under one of the following conditions:<br>Conditions | 2 years of legal residence in Italy (3 years if living abroad) through naturalisation | 10 years' residence, no criminal record and sufficient financial resources<br>7 years' residence for children adopted by Italian citizens<br>5 years' residence for refugees or stateless individuals<br>4 years' residence for EU member states nationals<br>3 years' residence for descendants of Italian grandparents and for foreigners born in Italy | Yes |
| Latvia | Persons born in | Latvian nationality is | | After 5 years of | Starting from |

| Member State | Acquisition by birth | Acquisition by descent | Acquisition by marriage | Acquisition by naturalisation | Multiple nationality permitted |
|---|---|---|---|---|---|
| | Latvia who: | acquired by descent under one of the following conditions: | | permanent residence | October the 1st, 2013 hereby listed persons are eligible to have dual citizenship with Latvia:<br>citizens of member countries of EU, NATO and EFTA (Iceland, Liechtenstein, Norway, Switzerland)<br>citizens of Australia, Venezuela, Brazil, New Zealand<br>citizens of the counties that have had mutual recognition of dual citizenship with Latvia<br>people who were granted the dual citizenship by the Cabinet of Ministers of Latvia<br>people of Latvian or Livonian ethnicity or exiles registering citizenship of Latvia<br>people who have applied for dual citizenship before the previous Latvian Citizenship law (1995). |
| Lithuania | Persons born in Lithuania who: are stateless. | Lithuanian nationality is acquired by descent under one of the following conditions:<br>at least one parent is a Lithuanian citizen | 7 years of permanent residence and demonstrating Lithuanian language ability | | No |

For additional analytical, business and investment opportunities information, please contact Global Investment & Business Center, USA at (202) 546-2103. Fax: (202) 546-3275. E-mail: rusric@erols.com

| Member State | Acquisition by birth | Acquisition by descent | Acquisition by marriage | Acquisition by naturalisation | Multiple nationality permitted |
|---|---|---|---|---|---|
| | | at least one direct ancestor was Lithuanian citizen during the period of 1918-1940. | | | |
| Luxembourg | Persons born in Luxembourg who: are stateless, or are foundlings, or have a parent born in Luxembourg | | No | 7 consecutive years' residence | Yes |
| Malta | Persons born in Malta between 21 September 1964 and 31 July 1989 Persons born outside Malta between 21 September 1964 and 31 July 1989 to a father with Maltese citizenship through birth in Malta, registration or naturalisation Persons born on or after 1 August 1989, inside or outside Malta, to at least one parent with Maltese citizenship through birth in Malta, registration or naturalisation | Maltese nationality is acquired by descent under one of the following conditions: | Yes 5 years of marriage to a Maltese citizen (if de jure or de facto separated, then still living together five years after the marriage) or a widow/widower of a Maltese citizen five years after the marriage | 5 years of residence | Yes |
| Netherlands | Persons born in Netherlands who: | Dutch nationality is acquired by descent under one of the following conditions: Persons with a Dutch parent | 3 years of residence and demonstrating Dutch language ability | After 5 years uninterrupted residence, with continuous registration in the municipal register | Under certain conditions: e.g. foreign citizenship may be kept in the event of naturalization via marriage. |
| Poland | Persons born in Poland. | Polish nationality is acquired by descent under one of the following conditions: Conditions | Yes | 3 years of residence with permanent residence permit card under the condition of speaking polish language 2 years of residence with permanent residence permit card under the condition of having polish ethnicity | Yes but in Poland, Polish identification must be used and the dual citizen is treated legally as only Polish |

| Member State | Acquisition by birth | Acquisition by descent | Acquisition by marriage | Acquisition by naturalisation | Multiple nationality permitted |
|---|---|---|---|---|---|
| Portugal | Persons born in Portugal who:<br>are stateless<br>are foundlings<br>have a birth parent resident in Portugal for at least 10 years on a valid residence permit<br>have a birth parent with citizenship of a Lusophone country and resident in Portugal for at least 6 years on a valid residence permit | Portuguese nationality is transmitted by descent under one of the following conditions:<br>Conditions | A person married to a Portuguese national for at least 3 years can apply to be registered as a Portuguese national as a matter of right, provided that the registration is applied for during the marriage (and not after its dissolution by death or divorce). Nationality takes effect upon registration and is not retroactive, and is not lost by the dissolution of the marriage. | Naturalisation conditions | Yes |
| Romania | Persons born in Romania who:<br>are foundlings<br>have Romanian parents | Romanian nationality is acquired by descent under one of the following conditions:<br>Conditions | 5 years' residence in Romania | 8 years' residence<br>4 years' residence (EU citizens) | Yes |
| Slovakia | Persons born in Slovakia who: | Slovak nationality is acquired by descent under one of the following conditions: | After 5 years' residence in Slovakia, and living in Slovakia without any immigration restrictions at the time of application | 6 years' residence (the last year of which without any immigration restrictions) | Dual citizenship is permitted to Slovak citizens who acquire a second citizenship by birth or through marriage; and to foreign nationals who apply for Slovak citizenship and meet the requirements of the Citizenship Act. |
| Slovenia | A child born in Slovenia is a | Slovenian nationality is acquired by | A person who is married to a | A total of 10 years residence in Slovenia, | Dual citizenship is |

| Member State | Acquisition by birth | Acquisition by descent | Acquisition by marriage | Acquisition by naturalisation | Multiple nationality permitted |
|---|---|---|---|---|---|
| | Slovenian citizen if either parent is a Slovenian citizen. Where the child is born outside Slovenia the child will be automatically Slovenian if: both parents are Slovenian citizens; or one parent is Slovenian and the other parent is unknown and/or of unknown citizenship the other is stateless. A person born outside Slovenia with one Slovenian parent who is not Slovenian automatically may acquire Slovenian citizenship through: an application for registration as a Slovenian citizen made at any time before age 36; or taking up permanent residence in Slovenia before age 18. Children adopted by Slovenian citizens may be granted Slovenian citizenship. | descent under one of the following conditions: A person of "Slovenian origin" up to the fourth generation in direct descent or a former Slovenian citizen may be naturalised without any residence requirements. | Slovenian citizen for at least two years may be naturalised after one year's residence in Slovenia | including 5 years continuous residence before the application | generally permitted in Slovenia, except for certain persons seeking to become Slovenian citizens by naturalisation they are to renounce any foreign citizenship (the requirement to renounce foreign citizenship may be waived upon special application). |
| Spain | Persons born in Spain who: are stateless, or are foundlings | Children of Spanish citizens | 1 year of marriage and residence in Spain | 10 years' residence 5 years' residence (refugees) 2 years' residence (for nationals of Iberoamerica, Andorra, Philippines, Equatorial Guinea, Portugal, or if the individual is a Sephardi Jew) 1 year's residence (persons born in Spain) | Yes (if a Spanish citizen by descent/origin); if naturalising in an Iberoamerican country, Spanish—and EU citizenship—is "dormant" until the return to Spain; see |

For additional analytical, business and investment opportunities information, please contact Global Investment & Business Center, USA at (202) 546-2103. Fax: (202) 546-3275. E-mail: rusric@erols.com

| Member State | Acquisition by birth | Acquisition by descent | Acquisition by marriage | Acquisition by naturalisation | Multiple nationality permitted |
|---|---|---|---|---|---|
| | | | | | Multiple citizenship. No (if a naturalised Spanish citizen, unless from Iberoamerica, Andorra, Philippines, Equatorial Guinea or Portugal) |
| Sweden | Persons born in Sweden who: are stateless, or are foundlings (canceled if parents found) | Swedish nationality is acquired by descent under one of the following conditions: Conditions | 3 years' marriage in case residing in Sweden, 10 years in case living abroad with a Swedish spouse and has 'strong ties' to Sweden, by family visits and such | 5 years normal residence permit(not the time limited residence/work permit/Study Permit) and must hold Swedish permanent residence permit at the time of applying or person with a visa intended for settlement in Sweden with 5 years residence in Sweden. 2 years if citizen of a Nordic country (i.e. Denmark, Finland, Iceland and Norway) | Yes |
| United Kingdom | Persons born in United Kingdom who: see: "British by birth" | British nationality is acquired by descent under one of the following conditions: see: "British by descent" | 6 years' residence (must be without any immigration restrictions on date of application) | 6 years' residence (the last year of which without any immigration restrictions) | Yes |

## DIRECTIVE 2004/38/EC ON THE RIGHT TO MOVE AND RESIDE FREELY

The ***Directive 2004/38/EC of the European Parliament and of the Council of 29 April 2004 on the right of citizens of the Union and their family members to move and reside freely within the territory of the Member States*** defines the right of free movement for citizens of the European Economic Area (EEA), which includes the European Union (EU) and the three European Free Trade Association (EFTA) members Iceland, Norway and Liechtenstein. Switzerland, which is a member of EFTA but not of the EEA, is not bound by the Directive but rather has a separate bilateral agreement on the free movement with the EU.

This directive is mostly a concentration of existing regulations and directives in one place, although it does also extend the rights of unmarried couples.

Whilst some of the formulations remain complex, the basic premise of the directive is simple: EEA citizens have the right of free movement and residence across the European Economic Area, as long as they are not an undue burden on the country of residence and have comprehensive health insurance. This right also extends to close family members that are not EEA citizens.

After five years, the right of residence becomes permanent, which means it does not depend on any precondition any longer. This permanent right of residence can be seen as a precursor to a true European Citizenship.

## APPLICABILITY

The directive applies to any EEA citizen that is moving to and living in an EEA state other than his own. (The exclusion is based on the principle of non-interference with purely national issues). However, it also applies when a European citizen is moving back to his home country after staying abroad, as defined in the case of Surinder Singh. For dual citizens with two EEA nationalities the directive can apply in any EEA state. Temporary limitations are in place for the new member states of the EU.
To be fully covered by the European right of free movement, the EEA citizen needs to exercise one of the four treaty rights:

working as an employee (this includes looking for work for a reasonable amount of time),
working as a self-employed person,
studying,
being self-sufficient or retired.

These rights are named after the Treaty of Rome, which defines the freedom of movement for workers. They have been extended over time, and are mainly of historical significance by now, since being self-sufficient has been added to the list. As long as a citizen has sufficient money or income not to rely on public funds and holds comprehensive health insurance, he/she exercises one or more treaty rights. If no treaty right is exercised, the right of free movement is limited to three months.
Family members are also covered by the right of free movement, but only as a dependent of the EEA citizen. The right is limited to the EEA state in which the EEA citizen is exercising treaty rights. In certain cases (e.g. divorce after at least 3 years of marriage where 1 year must have been spent in the host member state), the family member can retain the right of residence. A family member is defined as:

the spouse (unless in a marriage of convenience),
the registered same-sex partner (but only in a state where same-sex relationships are recognised),
a child under the age of 21, or
a dependent child or parent (of the EEA citizen or partner).

There is a second category of extended family members, which can be included at the discretion of national legislation. It covers dependent relatives (especially siblings), dependent household members and unmarried/unregistered partners in a "durable relationship".

## STATUS

The right of free movement is granted automatically when the requirements are fulfilled, and it is not subject to an administrative act. However, member states may require the EEA citizen and family members to register with the relevant authorities. The relevant documentations are:

an entry visa for the non-EEA family members if they are visa nationals and do not hold a residence card from another member state,
a residence certificate (for EEA citizens) or a residence card (for non-EEA family members), which may be valid for up to 5 years and confirms the right of residence,
a permanent residence certificate or a permanent residence card, which certifies the right of permanent residence.

Permanent residence is acquired automatically after exercising treaty rights for 5 years, with absences of normally less than 6 months a year, a single absences less than 12 months in certain circumstances (birth, severe sickness, etc.), or longer for military services. Permanent residence removes any restrictions that are in place concerning access to public funds (such as unemployment benefits, a state pension etc.), although some of these restrictions are already lifted after a period of 3 months. Permanent residence is only lost after an absence of 2 years. All applications covered by the directive are free, or require at most a moderate fee similar to comparable national documents.

**DISPUTED ISSUES AND CASE LAW**

While the directive is visionary and has far reaching implications, it is also the product both of a historical development and of conflicting interests. So it is not surprising that it contains unclear requirements and sometimes even contradictory statements, that require further interpretation. The main open questions are presented below.

Does the directive apply if a family member is currently outside of the EEA, or is illegally present in the EEA? The text of the directive seems to imply this, but there is also legal precedence to the contrary. The ECJ has passed a number of unclear judgements on this issue, which leaves a degree of discretion in the implementation. In the *Akrich* case, a remark limits the applicability to legal residence of the EEA. However, in the *MRAX* case, the unconditional right of family reunion is reiterated for spouses. In the *Metock* case, the ECJ has ruled that the non-community spouse of an EEA citizen can move and reside with that citizen in the Union without having previously been lawfully resident in a member state.

Does a residence card from one state serve as a visa for another? Again the text of the directive implies this, but it is not made explicit. Within the area of the Schengen Agreement this is not an issue, but the UK does not recognise cards issued by other member states. As of December 2008 five Member states have not transposed the Directive Article 5(2) correctly

Irish High Court Case Raducan & Anor -v- MJELR & Ors

The case is about the Moldovan wife of a Romanian citizen who was denied entry to Ireland and was detained for three days. She was not given entry on presenting her Residence Card as a family member of an EU citizen (Article 5(2) of the Directive 2004/38/EC), nor was her entry facilitated when she presented a marriage certificate proving her relationship to her EU husband The Irish Court Ruled It is a matter of profound regret that a perfectly innocent [family member of an EU citizen] who had every right to enter [Ireland] was instead refused entry and found herself obliged to spend the equivalent of almost three full days in custody.

What are the rights of a separated spouse before or during divorce? While the directive says that the family member is covered until the decree absolute is issued, the rights can be difficult to use. Without the cooperation of the EEA citizen, or if the EEA citizen leaves the country, the non-EEA spouse is left in a legal vacuum.

In which circumstances can the right of free movement apply to the home country of the EEA national? In the case of Surinder Singh, the ECJ rules that a worker can bring his spouse back to his home country after working in another EEA state for at least 6 months. However, this judgement was based on previous legislation, and it is unclear whether it also applies to more recent treaty rights.

The case of C-456/12 clarifies the directive. An EEA citzen can go to another state and exercise freedom of movement under Article 21(1) TFEU, the right to free movement, there is no requirement to be a worker or self employed. The EEA citizen and his non-EEA partner can return to his/her home state after a period of residence in a host state for longer than 3 months providing they have created or strengthened a family tie.

**IMPLEMENTATION**

As a Directive, this text is not directly applicable, but it has to be transposed into the national legislation.

It defines a basic right, while the member states can determine in which way this right is granted. The deadline for implementation was the 2006-04-30, although a number of member states have missed this deadline by a few months. The following presents an (incomplete) overview of the implementation. An implementation report by the European commission was published in December 2008 which concluded that "*Although national laws in some areas treat EU citizens and their families better than EU law requires, not one single Member State has transposed the Directive effectively and correctly in its entirety. Not one Article of the Directive has been transposed effectively and correctly by all Member States. The overall transposition of the Directive is rather disappointing.*" As announced in this report the European commission released guidance on how to better transpose and apply the Directive in July 2009.

**UK**

In the UK, the directive is transposed into the *Immigration (European Economic Area) Regulations 2006* amended by SI 2009/1117 and amended by SI 2011/1247. The implementation is reasonably complete and accurate although non-EEA family members require an entrance clearance (called EEA Family Permit) to enter the UK even if they are in possession of a 5-year residence card of *another* EEA member state, in breach of the Directive. The UK law recognises same-sex relationships, and it also has a clause for unmarried/unregistered partners. Applications are £55 and additional £55 per dependant.

**IRELAND**

In Ireland, the Directive is transposed into the *European Communities (Free Movement of Persons) (No. 2) Regulations 2006* amended by SI 310 of 2008 in reaction to the *Metock* case and amended by SI 146 of 2011 allowing visa free entrance with a residence card issued by another EEA member state.

The non-EEA family members of Irish citizens resident in Ireland are not normally issued EU Family Residency Cards (called Stamp 4 EU FAM) unless the Irish citizen and family members previously lived together in another EU state.

**AUSTRIA**

In Austria, the directive is transposed into national law mainly via the *Niederlassungs- und Aufenthaltsgesetz* (regarding residence) and the *Fremdenpolizeigesetz* (regarding entrance).

**For additional analytical, business and investment opportunities information, please contact Global Investment & Business Center, USA at (202) 546-2103. Fax: (202) 546-3275. E-mail: rusric@erols.com**

The applications are handled locally at the *Magistrat* or *Bezirkshauptmannschaft* (except in Styria where the *Landeshauptmann* takes direct responsibility). A credit card sized plastic card (costing about €57 in 2010) is issued to document one's right.

## GERMANY

In Germany, the directive is transposed into national law via the *Freizügigkeitsgesetz/EU*, which could be translated as freedom of movement law/EU. Wikipedia has a short German article on it. Not all mandatory sections of the Directive are included in the Freizügigkeitsgesetz/EU. The applications are handled locally, together with the mandatory registration of residence.

## ITALY

In Italy the directive has been implemented into Italian legislation with Legislative Decree n. 30 of February 6, 2007The applications are handled by the *"Questura"* of the province where the applicant takes his residence.

## THE NETHERLANDS

Applications are submitted locally at the municipality ("gemeente" in Dutch) together with the mandatory registration of residence, but they are processed centrally at the "Immigratie- en Naturalisatiedienst" (IND -- Immigration and Naturalisation Service). There is a charge (€42 in 2013) associated with the application.

The family members of Dutch citizens who are and have always been resident in the Netherlands are not permitted to hold EU Family Residency Cards, because EU nationals who have always lived in the country of their nationality are not exercising EU treaty rights and are therefore not considered EU citizens under Dutch law for the purposes of the Directive.

## SWEDEN

In Sweden the directive has been implemented through changes in several laws, like the Alien Act (SFS 2005:71), and the Aliens Decree (SFS 2006:97). Sweden does still (2013) not follow the directive fully, as the national identity card is not accepted when a Swedish citizen leaves Sweden for a non-Schengen EU member state, like the UK. The passport act (SFS 1978:302) requires a passport

# ECONOMY AND ECONOMIC DEVELOPMENTS

## ECONOMIC SUMMARY

Currency: euro Area: 2,586 sq.km Of which: 49% agricultural

Service information et presse du gouvernement 33, bd Roosevelt L-2450 Luxembourg Tel.: (+352) 478-2181 Fax: (+352) 47 02 85

The government, in the strict sense of the word, is the organ of executive power formed by the Grand Duke and the ministers in charge. In practical terms, the government means all ministers and secretaries of state who assist the Grand Duke in the exercise of his constitutional powers.

| Rank | 100th (PPP, est.) |
|---|---|
| Currency | 1 Euro = 100 eurocent |
| Fiscal year | Calendar year |
| Trade organisations | EU, WTO and OECD |
| | Statistics |
| GDP | ▲$42.19 billion (est.) |
| GDP growth | ▼1.0% (Real, est.) |
| GDP per capita | ▼$80,700 (PPP, est.) |
| GDP by sector | agriculture: 0.4%; industry: 13.6%; services: 86% (2007 est.) |
| Inflation (CPI) | ▼2.5% (CPI, est.) |
| Population below poverty line | NA% |
| Gini coefficient | 26 |
| Labour force | 368,400 of whom 154,900 are foreign cross-border workers commuting primarily from France, Belgium, and Germany (2011) |
| Labour force by occupation | agriculture: 2.2%; industry: 17.2%; services: 80.6% (est.) |
| Unemployment | ▲6.0% (est.) |
| Average gross salary | 4,051 € / 5,469 $, monthly |
| Average net salary | 2,693 € / 3,636 $, monthly |
| Main industries | banking and financial services, iron and steel, information technology, telecommunications, cargo transportation, food processing, chemicals, metal products, engineering, tires, glass, aluminum, tourism |
| Ease of Doing Business Rank | 56th |
| | External |
| Exports | ▼$15.5 billion (est.) |
| Export goods | machinery and equipment, steel products, chemicals, rubber products, glass |
| Main export partners | Germany 22.2%, France 15.6%, Belgium 13.2%, UK 7.3%, Italy 5.4%, Switzerland 4.3%, Netherlands |
| Imports | ▼$25.08 billion (est.) |
| Import goods | minerals, metals, foodstuffs, quality consumer goods |
| Main import partners | Belgium 30.3%, Germany 28.0%, France 10.8%, China 6.9%, Netherlands 5.8%, US 5.2% (2011) |
| FDI stock | $11.21 billion (est.) |
| Gross external debt | ▲$2.146 trillion (30 June 2011) |
| | Public finances |
| Public debt | ▲18.4% of GDP (est.) |
| Revenues | $23.05 billion (est.) |

**For additional analytical, business and investment opportunities information, please contact Global Investment & Business Center, USA at (202) 546-2103. Fax: (202) 546-3275. E-mail: rusric@erols.com**

| | |
|---|---|
| Expenses | $23.56 billion (est.) |
| Economic aid | donor: ODA, $235.59 million |
| Credit rating | Standard & Poor's:<br>AAA (Domestic)<br>AAA (Foreign)<br>AAA (T&C Assessment)<br>Outlook: Stable<br>Moody's:<br>Aaa<br>Outlook: Stable<br>Fitch:<br>AAA<br>Outlook: Positive |
| Foreign reserves | ▲$1.014 billion |

**The economy of Luxembourg** is largely dependent on the banking, steel, and industrial sectors. Luxembourgers enjoy the second highest per capita gross domestic product in the world (CIA 2007 est.), behind Qatar. Luxembourg is seen as a diversified industrialized nation, contrasting the oil boom in Qatar, the major monetary source of that nation.

Although Luxembourg in tourist literature is aptly called the "Green Heart of Europe", its pastoral land coexists with a highly industrialized and export-intensive economy. Luxembourg enjoys a degree of economic prosperity almost unique among industrialized democracies.

In 2009, a budget deficit of 5% resulted from government measures to stimulate the economy, especially the banking sector, as a result of the world economic crisis. This was however reduced to 1.4% in 2010

## HISTORICAL BACKGROUND

### ECONOMIC DEVELOPMENT (1839-1870)

In 1839, the Grand Duchy gained independence and assumed its present territorial form; pursuant to the Treaty of London (19 April 1839), Belgian Luxembourg was detached from the Grand Duchy, depriving the latter of two-thirds of its territory and half its population. The country was poor, with a pre-industrial type economic structure. Agriculture was by far the dominant economic sector; even in 1871, about 60% of the labour force was still working in this sector. The main industries were steel, textiles, tanning of leather, glove-making and ceramics; almost all these were family and craft businesses. The iron industry did not play a dominant role at that time. Based on alluvial deposits, it was located in the centre of the country along waterways and near forests which provided motive power and charcoal. In 1841, the country produced 7300 tonnes of iron.

The Grand Duchy had no significant navigable waterways, a situation which was not to change until 1964, the date of the inauguration of the canalised Moselle River. The road network was largely undeveloped and poorly maintained; this geographical isolation was hardly propitious to the economic development of the small State of 2586 km2, with its mere 170000 inhabitants.

### TRANSITION TO A MORE MODERN ECONOMY

#### MEMBERSHIP OF THE ZOLLVEREIN (CUSTOMS UNION)

In 1842, after long and arduous negotiations, Luxembourg entered the German customs union, the "Zollverein". Certain initial fears proved to be unfounded and in the long term this membership would contribute to the prosperity of the country.

#### EXTENSION OF THE COMMUNICATIONS ROUTES

From 1839 to 1870, public roads quadrupled in length from 176 km to 680 km, but it was above all the construction of the main railway lines (1859-1868) and their connection to those of the neighbouring countries which would release Luxembourg's economy from its isolation.

#### EXPLOITATION OF OOLITIC ORE (MINETTE)

The oolitic ore (minette), less rich in iron than the alluvial ore, had been abandoned, indeed even forgotten, since the times of antiquity and it was only at the start of the 1840s that it was rediscovered. The exploitation of these vast deposits, an extension of the Lorraine basin in Luxembourg territory, became of interest when a new method of production was adopted. The first coke-fired blast furnace was brought into service in 1858 and the last charcoal-fired blast furnace was extinguished in 1868.

## THE ECONOMIC TAKE-OFF (1870-1913):

A little on the late side, Luxembourg would make a success of its industrial revolution, which was not a sudden event, but the result of a long sequence of adaptations and good fortune. The steel industry would be the only driving force in the economic take-off.

### THE BOOM IN THE STEEL INDUSTRY

#### CREATION OF A NEW INDUSTRIAL SITE

From 1857 to 1868, the Grand Duchy increased its iron production more than sixfold; it nevertheless exported nearly two-thirds of its iron ore in its basic form. In order to improve its monitoring of the exploitation of the iron ore mines and to encourage companies to process the ore on site, the Government reorganised the mining system. A start was made on moving the blast furnaces to the ore field in 1870.

#### THE STEEL PHASE

In 1879, Sidney Gilchrist Thomas invented a process which, unlike the Bessemer process (1856), was able to handle the phosphoric iron obtained from minette; this would be of crucial importance for the Luxembourg steel industry.

Compared to the Bessemer process, this process gave a higher quality product at a lower cost price. The Luxembourg steel industry became competitive and started its real expansion from 1886.

#### A VAST CONCENTRATION MOVEMENT

The introduction of large-scale integrated industries required considerable financial resources and it was in this way that foreign capital, especially from Germany, acquired substantial holdings in the Grand Duchy's steel industry. Concentration took place by purchase or merger. On the eve of the First World War, nearly two-thirds of the Luxembourg steel industry was under German control. Arbed (Aciéries Réunies de Burbach, Eich et Dudelange), a company governed by Luxembourg law, controlled 31% of production in 1913.

**For additional analytical, business and investment opportunities information, please contact Global Investment & Business Center, USA at (202) 546-2103. Fax: (202) 546-3275. E-mail: rusric@erols.com**

At the time, Luxembourg produced 2500000 tons of iron and 1400000 tons of steel (3.2% and 1.7% respectively of world production). Over 40% of its iron was exported raw and over 40% of its rolled products were semi-finished. The explanation for this lies in the fact that its steel industry was strongly bound to that of Germany.

### Recourse to Foreign Labour

During the period from 1908 to 1913, foreigners accounted for nearly 60% of the total workforce employed in the steel and mining industries. In 1913, half the foreigners were Italian and a third German.

### A Dominant Position in the Industrial Structure

In 1907, about a third of the labour force of the industrial sector was working in the steel and mining industries and this share was growing.

During the period of the "Zollverein", the other industries developed to very varying extents and, like the steel industry, German capital infiltrated into them. The boom of the steel industry was at the heart of the development of certain industries, such as the cement factories, ironworks and machine shops.

## PROGRESS OF AGRICULTURE

It was from the 1870s that the yield from agriculture would rise substantially. Thomas dross, a by-product of the steel industry, was an excellent chemical fertiliser which was offered to farmers at a preferential price. However, at the beginning of the 20th century, the average farm size for farms of 2 hectares and over was only 8.9 hectares.

The area under vines, 840 hectares in 1839, increased constantly from 1870 to attain its historic peak in 1910 at 1640 hectares. Almost the entire production was sold to Germany, which used it to blend with its wines.

## THE MIGRATION FLOWS OF THE POPULATION

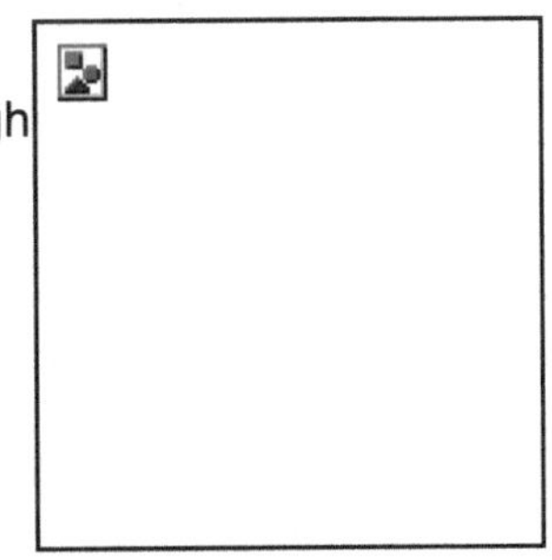

In view of the precarious living conditions of its inhabitants, there was high emigration from Luxembourg, especially from the 1850s. From 1840 to 1852, the population increased by 14%, whereas from 1852 to 1895 it grew by only 12%, despite a high fertility rate and the immigration flow.

### Emigration - Immigration

Some 80 000 Luxembourgers left the country definitively between 1840 and 1907, bound mainly for the United States and France.

Since Luxembourgers were not attracted by its activities, the steel industry hired a large number of foreigners. A substantial immigration movement is recorded from 1875, offsetting the vast emigration movement. The number of foreigners registered rose from 5900 in 1875 to 39700 in 1910.

### Concentration of the Population

From 1865 to 1910, the total population of the country rose by 27%. There were two focal points: the population of the Esch-sur-Alzette district (ore field) rose by 284% and that of the capital by 87%; in 1910 over 60% of the foreigners lived in the Esch district.

**For additional analytical, business and investment opportunities information, please contact Global Investment & Business Center, USA at (202) 546-2103. Fax: (202) 546-3275. E-mail: rusric@erols.com**

## THE INTER-WAR PERIOD: QUASI-STAGNATION (1919-1939)

Since Germany violated the neutrality of Luxembourg during the First World War, the Grand Duchy denounced its membership of the Zollverein in December 1918. Deprived from one day to the next of its former large protected internal market, the entire Luxembourg economy had to be reoriented.

### THE NEW ECONOMIC PARTNER: BELGIUM

The country could not live in economic isolation. In view of France's refusal to enter into an economic partnership with its small neighbour, Luxembourg signed the Belgo-Luxembourg Economic Union (BLEU) Treaty with Belgium, which entered into force in March 1922. The Treaty, concluded for a period of fifty years, was renewed for ten years in 1971, 1981 and 1991 respectively. The BLEU was consolidated by a monetary association with a common currency, the Belgian franc. The existence of a Luxembourg franc alongside the Belgian franc is above all a symbol of the sovereignty of the Grand Duchy (see chapter 7: Monetary status).

### REORIENTATION OF THE STEEL INDUSTRY

From 1920, Franco-Belgo-Luxembourg interests took over the country's German mining and steel companies. Luxembourg companies, and notably ARBED, acquired a large number of participating interests both upstream, to solve the problem of supply, and downstream, to ensure stable markets. The steel industry focused its manufacturing programme on the production of rolled finished products. Improving productivity henceforth took priority over the expansion policy. From 1920, the main Luxembourg companies set up a major world sales network.

The economic depression of the immediate post-war period was followed by a period of prosperity (1924-1929). In 1929, iron and steel production broke the world records of 1913 by 14% and 90% respectively. Employment in the steel and mining industries was some 50% higher than the 1913 level, with the foreign workforce equal once again to that of the pre-war period and the number of Luxembourg workers up by 125%. From 1930, the world economic crisis made itself felt: production and employment plummeted. The foreign workers were hardest hit, with two-thirds of them losing their jobs.

### A PROTECTIONIST POLICY FOR AGRICULTURE

Luxembourg agriculture, accustomed to the protected market of the Zollverein, had difficulty in coping with competition from Belgium, whose agriculture was among the most productive in Europe. A full range of protective measures were introduced in favour of Luxembourg agriculture; in 1935, it had practically withdrawn from the economic union. In 1935, about 30% of the labour force was working in agriculture, compared to 43% in 1907.

To survive, viticulture had to turn to quality wine. The area under vines was reduced drastically and cooperatives were formed.

### CONTRASTING DEVELOPMENT OF THE OTHER ECONOMIC SECTORS

Glove-making, paper-making, the textiles industry and the timber industry ended up on the verge of collapse, the leather industry declined sharply and was to disappear in 1960, the metal-processing industries experienced major adaptation difficulties. The food industries, breweries, tobacco factories and above all construction, developed favourably. Some new branches made their appearance, such as the chemicals and clothing industries. But it was above all the tertiary sector which grew in importance: from 1907 to 1935, the number of people employed in this sector rose by 87%.

**For additional analytical, business and investment opportunities information, please contact Global Investment & Business Center, USA at (202) 546-2103. Fax: (202) 546-3275. E-mail: rusric@erols.com**

## THE START OF EUROPEAN INTEGRATION (1950-1960)

The period immediately after the war, a time of reconstruction, was followed by a long period of growth, although with the risks of industrial monolithism in the background.

### THE HEIGHT OF INDUSTRIAL MONOLITHISM

From 1950 to 1960, steel production again rose appreciably, but the trend in steel production at international level showed the risks inherent in industrial monolithism. Moreover, the iron ore which had led to the creation of the Luxembourg steel industry was no longer a trump card in view of its low iron content and the gradual exhaustion of the deposits; not only did recourse to ore from the Lorraine increase, but ores richer in iron were also imported, such as those of Sweden and Brazil.

The Government started to grant capital equipment loans to promote investments in small and medium-sized industries in 1948. In 1950, the American company Goodyear, wishing to acquire a foothold in Benelux (customs union created in 1944), set up a rubber tyre factory in Luxembourg; this marked the start of industrial diversification. In 1959, the Government created the Board of Industrial Development, with the objective of attracting American investors. Even though the real industrial diversification policy would only start from 1962, the will to improve the country's infrastructure was apparent from the 1950s (extension of the airport, canalisation of the Moselle River, electrification of the railways, etc.).

### THE BUILDING OF EUROPE, A NEW ASSET

Luxembourg is a founder member of the European Coal and Steel Community (ECSC - 1951), the European Economic Community and the European Atomic Energy Community (Treaties of Rome - 1957). In 1952, the city of Luxembourg became the provisional seat of the ECSC and, through this, the first capital of Europe; other European institutions would establish themselves there subsequently.

The ECSC was responsible for a new stage in the growth of the Luxembourg steel industry. The Common Market opened up new potential markets to all economic sectors and in the immediate future it promoted immigration of EEC workers.

### A TEMPORARY EXEMPTION FOR AGRICULTURE

In the Treaty of Rome, Luxembourg was able to obtain special provisional arrangements for its agriculture, but the gradual dismantling of national agricultural protectionism was now inevitable.

The vast concentration movement recorded from the beginning of the 1950s gathered pace, as did the mechanisation of farm work. The agricultural workforce shrank by 45% between the censuses of 1947 and 1960. During the following decade, it again halved and its relative share in the total workforce fell to 7.5% in 1970 (15.0% in 1960, 26.1% in 1947).

### RENEWED RECOURSE TO FOREIGN LABOUR

The birth rate of the population had declined rapidly since the start of the 1930s. The economic recovery from the early 1950s very rapidly absorbed all the indigenous labour available and the country had to have renewed recourse to foreign labour.

**For additional analytical, business and investment opportunities information, please contact Global Investment & Business Center, USA at (202) 546-2103. Fax: (202) 546-3275. E-mail: rusric@erols.com**

# SOCIAL AND ECONOMIC DEVELOPMENT STRATEGY

## IMPORTANT INFORMATION

### DEMOGRAPHIC SITUATION

Luxembourg had 455 000 inhabitants in 2005; mean population growth in recent years has been close to 1% with a net migration rate largely exceeding the rate of natural growth[1]. Between 1970 and 2001 the population increased by over 29% and the proportion of the resident population for which foreigners accounted more than doubled. In 2003 life expectancy at birth was 81.0 for women and 75.0 for men[2]. Infant mortality is continuing to fall sharply, from 11.4 in 1980 to 7.3 in 1990 and 3.9 in 2004. The fertility rate for the population as a whole was 1.70 in 2004.

According to the projections of the Economic Policy Committee's working group on "ageing" Luxembourg will have a population of 643 000 in 2050. The fertility rate will level off at 1.8 around 2030 and life expectancy at birth will increase to 82 for men and 87 for women. The older population will increase in proportional terms between 2010 and 2030 and will level off thereafter. In 2050, the ratio of people aged 65 and over to the population aged between 14 and 64 will be around 36%. This ratio was 21% in 2005[3].

### ECONOMIC SITUATION AND PUBLIC FINANCES

After three years of relatively low growth, the pace of economic activity picked up, reaching 4.2% in 2004 and 4.0% in 2005[4]. Even though this growth is very far from the exceptional levels recorded between 1997 and 2000, it is nevertheless close to the overall rate of growth of the last twenty years.

There has been a substantial deterioration in public finances in recent years, with the budget balance falling from a surplus of 6.0% of GDP in 2000 to a deficit of 1.9% in 2005[5]. This deterioration in public finances reflects major increases in public spending not offset by concomitant increases in revenue. In recent years, however, changes in public debt have been marginal (6.5% in 2002 and 6.2% in 2005)[6]. Expenditure on social benefits amounted to

23.3% of GDP (old-age and survivors 8.7%, health care 5.8%, family benefits 4.1%, disability and long-term care 3.1%, unemployment and labour return measures 1% and social inclusion/housing 0.6%[7]).

According to the projections of the Economic Policy Committee's working group on "ageing", expenditure on social protection (pensions, health and long-term care, unemployment) and on education will increase by more than 8% of GDP up to 2050[8], pension payments accounting for most of this growth.

### EDUCATION, EMPLOYMENT AND UNEMPLOYMENT

In a context in which 37.3% of students are of foreign nationality (mostly Portuguese)[9], the system of education in Luxembourg, which is taught in French and German and not in Luxembourgish, is facing particular challenges. Gaps in school performance between natives and immigrants are pronounced and failure at school is largely connected with socioeconomic background[10]. In 2005, the average rate of early school leavers was 13.3%[11].

**For additional analytical, business and investment opportunities information, please contact Global Investment & Business Center, USA at (202) 546-2103. Fax: (202) 546-3275. E-mail: rusric@erols.com**

In 2005, 300 000 people were employed in Luxembourg, frontier workers accounting for 39% of this figure[12]. The total employment rate (63.6%) was in line with the European average (63.8%)[13]. The number of working women has increased since 1998, reaching 53.7% in 2005. This relatively low level nevertheless continues to pose a challenge from the point of view of equal opportunities[14]. The employment rate for older workers is low in comparison with the European average (31.7% in comparison with 42.5%)[15].

With a total rate of 4.5% in 2005, unemployment is among the lowest in the EU, but has doubled in six years and is higher among women (5.9%) than among men (3.5%)[16]. Between 1999 and 2005 the long-term unemployment rate increased from 0.7% to 1.2%[17] and the sharp increase in unemployment among young people (especially women) from 6.9% to 13.8%[18] is a matter for concern.

## SITUATION OF HOUSEHOLDS, RISK OF POVERTY AND INCOME INEQUALITIES

3.3% of the population live in lone-parent households (4.5% in the EU). In contrast 35.5% of the population live in households of two adults with two or more children, a percentage which is much higher than the EU average (24.5%)[19]. 13.0% of households of people aged 75 and over are living in retirement homes or assistance and care facilities[20] (EU average: 6.7%). 1% of children live in care facilities (EU average of 0.6%).

7 288 households, whose members account for 3.0% of the population, are beneficiaries of the guaranteed minimum wage scheme. In these households, 52.8% of members are female and 47.1% are male; 26.6% of the members of beneficiary households are aged under 18 and 13.8% are aged 60 and over. 60.7% of beneficiary households are made up of a single person and 17.6% of these households are lone-parent households[21].

Income inequality indicators show that Luxembourg is in a rather good situation in comparison with the European average (S80/S20 ratio of 3.7% in comparison with 4.8%[22] and Gini coefficient of 26% in comparison with 30%[23]). In a context in which the at-risk-ofpoverty threshold is the highest in the EU, the same applies to indicators of the incidence and intensity of the risk of poverty (risk level of 11% in comparison with 16%[24] and relative median gap of 17% in comparison with 23%[25]). These relatively low at-risk-of-poverty levels are largely shaped by social transfers: the pre-transfer rate is 22% (excluding old-age and survivors' pensions)[26]. The risk of exposure to poverty is particularly high for lone-parent families (21%), large families (18%), households of working age with few occupational income providers (28%), jobseekers (46%), tenants (23%)[27] and children aged 0 to 15 (18%)[28]. The poverty risk is smaller for people with jobs (8%) and people who own their homes (8%)[29]. The poverty risk of 6% among older people aged 65 and over is well below the EU average (18%)[30].

The net income from social assistance of a jobless household accounts for 74.4% of the atrisk-of-poverty threshold income for a household composed of two adults and two children[31]. The income level of people aged 65 and over is equivalent to that of people aged 15-64[32].

## STRATEGIC APPROACH

The Luxembourg population is very much in favour of its system of social protection and social inclusion. This system guarantees access to high-level health and long-term care, relatively generous unemployment benefits and old-age, disability and survivors' pensions and a minimum income providing for a decent standard of living[33].

As society is evolving, the system of social protection and social inclusion is having to take this into account and to adapt to the new circumstances and new challenges. Changes in the family

**For additional analytical, business and investment opportunities information, please contact Global Investment & Business Center, USA at (202) 546-2103. Fax: (202) 546-3275. E-mail: rusric@erols.com**

model, increasingly diverse types of family and parents' aspirations better to reconcile family and working life mean that social security in Luxembourg, in which the "male breadwinner" of the beginning of the 20th century continues to be the dominant model, needs to adapt. Luxembourg's economy is traditionally highly integrated into the European and world economy. Luxembourg's integration into the *Grande Région* continues to increase as can be seen from the growing proportion of frontier workers in domestic employment. Faced with growing labour market demand and competition with jobseekers from abroad, some groups of residents are finding it hard to find a job, with the result that unemployment is increasing. Social protection and social inclusion policies will have to be adapted in order to provide these people with more help in gaining a foothold in the labour market and to support older people so that they can continue to work in good health and with appropriate income.

The Luxembourg social protection and social inclusion system is a system which requires substantial financial resources if it is to be maintained and developed. This system has to be adjusted to the public financial resources available and steps need to be taken to improve its long-term viability.

*Guaranteeing free access to social protection services, an adequate level of benefits, a fair redistribution of income and ongoing promotion of social cohesion*

In Luxembourg, compulsory membership of the social security scheme for any paid professional occupation means that there is free access to benefits. The same applies to people in receipt of replacement income and the guaranteed minimum income who do not have any other protection. Derived rights extend scheme benefits to the spouses, lifetime partners and legitimate, legitimated, natural and adoptive children of the main insured person.

If people are unfit for work as a result of non-occupational diseases or accidents or if workers are in a situation in which they are unemployed for reasons beyond their control, social policy aims to provide replacement income in order to maintain their standard of living. All insured persons are entitled to the minimum pension after 40 years of work, irrespective of the amount of contributions paid during their working life.

As regards income assistance, Luxembourg has a universally-based safety net guaranteeing a subsistence income ensuring a decent life. Income assistance is a right and, as an expression of national solidarity, helps to maintain social cohesion.

Family policy, based on the principle of distributive justice, is a key component of social policy providing both benefits in kind and financial compensation (direct in the form of family allowances and indirect through taxation policy).

The founding principles of the health system include the free choice of a doctor and direct access to specialists and hospital clinics, and coverage of the costs of care and the need for assistance from a third person for the essential activities of daily living.

A housing plan is intended to reduce and permanently stabilise land and housing prices and thus to promote access to housing for everyone.

*Keeping high-quality social services and benefits, respecting equal opportunities for all and personal monitoring of beneficiaries*

A new action programme for the health and long-term care system has been drawn up to improve the quality of care, while respecting financial constraints.

Faced with poverty arising from an accumulation of problems, Luxembourg is implementing a strategy which includes the right to social assistance that is both preventive and curative. This assistance is intended to give the most vulnerable people access to the services and resources that they need, while developing their ability to use them to get out of difficult life circumstances.

As regards unemployment, the approach is to offer jobseekers personal job-finding plans drawn up by the relevant services and the jobseekers concerned.

In order to base its approach to the fight against exclusion connected with housing on a better knowledge of the extent of the problem, the government has asked the Centre d'Etudes de Populations, de Pauvreté et de Politiques Socio-Economiques (CEPS – Population, Poverty and Socio-Economic Policy Research Centre) to draw up a study of the number of homeless people in Luxembourg[34]

Individual social assistance is available for people who are homeless or in need of emergency assistance. Housing is set aside for the most needy.

To deal with failure at school, early and personal screening and assistance for students at risk has been introduced.

## FNANCIAL VIABILITY OF SOCIAL PROTECTION SYSTEMS

Social protection systems have to be financed so that they ensure high-quality care and an adequate level of benefits while maintaining equity between the generations. All social security schemes are financially healthy and in a condition likely to enable the adjustments needed to maintain financial viability in future decades. This favourable situation can be sustained only if the financial balance which has been achieved can be maintained, including ongoing transfers to reserves. To that end, financial resources need to be kept at their current level and, if expenditure cannot be reduced, new financial resources will have to be explicitly introduced to offset any additional financial burden on social protection schemes.

The financial situation of the Luxembourg sickness insurance scheme is evolving in a way which will make it necessary to adopt new concrete and concerted measures to maintain its future financial balance. In order to contain and curb drug prescription and health care benefits the government has asked all the partners to take an approach promoting a better match between what is useful and what is necessary. In order to ensure that the long-term care insurance budget is balanced in the future, a new law has introduced various changes to the financing of benefits. In future years, Luxembourg will have to introduce instruments able to deal with an explosion in the costs of benefits in the medium term. A think-tank will be commissioned to draw up concrete proposals to adapt pension schemes to changes in working lives, demographic ageing and its impact on the length of working life.

Despite an unemployment rate which is among the lowest in the EU, reducing and preventing unemployment are the challenges of a policy whose aim is to help significantly to limit the financial repercussions of the unemployment benefit scheme on public budgets.

The financial viability of this scheme will be underpinned by stronger incentives to work and limited-term measures with pay, which are being studied in the context of the guaranteed minimum income scheme.

In the field of family policy, the Government is drawing up a system of tax credits. An agreement on the mechanisms and method of application of this system should come into operation in the near future.

*Promoting employment and improving the labour market integration of all groups of people*

An appropriate family policy enables parents freely to choose to have a family life in parallel with a working life and to match their lifestyle to the needs of the family. By increasing the women's participation rate and enabling both parents to work while taking care of the upbringing of their children, the policies introduced are helping to strengthen employment policy and ensure the individual careers of future pensioners, which is a method par excellence of combating poverty and social exclusion.

Inclusion policy combines "income assistance" and "activation". In order to improve its efficiency, active measures acting as bridges into the employment market are being promoted.

Employment policy is both preventive and active. The aim is make the players on the employment market more responsible and return to a mentality of full employment.

Social policies in the field of welfare and old-age actively support measures to keep family members in employment in the case of childbirth (maternity leave, dispensation from work) or family problems (leave for family reasons, leave to assist a terminally ill person). Special measures have been introduced to preserve the pension entitlements of informal carers.

By helping everyone to gain the knowledge needed to participate in the knowledge society, education policy also has an impact on the fight against poverty as it helps people to find jobs. It can play a part in increasing the working population, thereby helping to ensure the viability of the social security system. Lastly, it can help to prevent poverty from being passed on from one generation to the next.

*Preserving the principle of social consultation and promoting "evidence- based" dialogue*

There has long been coordination of the stakeholders and mobilisation of the relevant parties in Luxembourg. "Tripartite" social consultation, bringing together representatives of employers, employees and the public authorities (or "quadripartite", including representatives of care providers, in the case of sickness and long-term care insurance) is a concerted approach in which consensus solutions are systematically sought for social and economic problems.

Social inclusion and social protection policies are coordinated with the Lisbon policies and with national sustainable development partly by the Joint Ministerial Committee responsible for drawing up the national plan for innovation and full employment and partly by the Joint Ministerial Committee responsible for sustainable development strategy.

When reports are drawn up, there are talks at both ministerial level and with the social partners, including non-governmental organisations.

The measures set out in this report and their impact on social inclusion and social protection policies are evaluated using comparable and reliable statistics and indicators. The list of proposed indicators (see Annex 1.4) is in line with the notion of social inclusion and social protection indicators proposed by the European Commission, while taking account of Luxembourg's specific circumstances, activities and priorities.

## KEY POLICIES

Secure living conditions are the foundation of social cohesion.

The social protection system, intended to protect the whole of the population against changes in circumstances, is an essential component of this foundation.

The priorities and initiatives set out in this report help to strengthen social cohesion and are components of the following policies:

an active employment policy, where an absolute priority is to combat unemployment,

an education and training policy in keeping with new skill needs,

a family policy enabling parents to cope with the problems of reconciling family and working life,

a policy to maintain high-performance health and long-term care systems providing the population with high-quality care,

a pensions policy intended to guarantee, under the statutory scheme, an adequate standard of living for pensioners and also to guarantee this commitment for future generations,

an active housing policy intended to step up the supply of affordable housing.

| Employment rate | 1998 | 2005 |
|---|---|---|
| Total | 60.5 | 63.6 |
| Men | 74.5 | 73.3 |
| Women | 46.2 | 53.7 |
| Employment rate of older workers | 1998 | 2005 |
| Total | 25.1 | 31.7 |
| Men | 35.2 | 38.3 |
| Women | 15.5 | 24.9 |
| Youth unemployment rate | 1998 | 2005 |
| Total | 6.9 | 13.8 |

| Early school leavers not in education or training | 2004 | 2005 |
|---|---|---|
| Total | 12.9 | 13.3 |
| Men | 12.8 | 17.0 |
| Women | 13.0 | 9.6 |

## NATIONAL ACTION PLAN FOR SOCIAL INCLUSION

2.1 Key challenges, priority objectives and targets

Following consultation with its partners[35], the Government adopted the following four overarching policy objectives for the National Action Plan for social inclusion (NAP-Inclusion) 2006-2008:

**For additional analytical, business and investment opportunities information, please contact Global Investment & Business Center, USA at (202) 546-2103. Fax: (202) 546-3275. E-mail: rusric@erols.com**

returning to full employment,

preventing failure at school and increasing skill levels,

reconciling family and working life,

access to housing.

These four overarching priorities are consistent with the strategy adopted at the time of the NAP-Inclusion 2003-2005[36] and take account of those highlighted in the Joint Report on Social Protection and Social Inclusion (JR) of 2006[37].

*2.1.1 Returning to full employment*

Social inclusion indicators show the paramount importance of labour as a factor in combating poverty[38].

Hence the need to develop a policy geared towards returning to full employment.

Employment policy, decided by the Government in consultation with the social partners in the Tripartite Coordination Committee, has two aims: to activate jobseekers as early as possible and to prevent unemployment. Particular attention will be paid to a policy of anticipation of changes in the economic and social context.

As set out in detail in 2.2 below, priority measures will be implemented in the following fields:

keeping people in jobs,

integrating all groups of people at risk of exclusion into the labour market,

improved activation of young people (aged 15-24),

integrating and keeping older workers in jobs.

Efforts to attract the largest possible number of people into the employment market will be pursued as part of a global approach bringing together the aspects of education, continuing training, reconciliation of family and working life, health and safety at work and working conditions in general.

A policy of this kind meets:

priority 1 set out in the 2006 JR and objective e) on social inclusion adopted by the European Council in March 2006 as it helps to promote participation by all in employment,

• objective d) on social inclusion as it tends to prevent the unemployment that can lead to social exclusion,

priority 3 set out in the 2006 JR as measures to eliminate disadvantages in education and training are part and parcel of the increased activation of young people towards which it is geared.

The policy envisaged will also help to meet the third challenge identified in the "country profile" of the 2006 JR, i.e.: increasing the employment rate among residents aged between 55 and 64.

*Targets*

Preliminary note:

It has been agreed at the tripartite and political level not to set numerical targets for a return to full employment. For information, reference should be made to the priorities and objectives set in the context of the Lisbon strategy, the national action plan for innovation and full employment, the opinion of the Tripartite Coordination Committee of 28 April 2006 and the Government statement of 2 May 2006.

| Indicator | Starting situation (NSR 20062008) | Target |
|---|---|---|
| Employment rate39 | Total: 63.6% Men: 73.3% Women: 53.7% | "Lisbon" target: bring the employment rate to a level as close as possible to 70% by 2010 and take steps to ensure that the proportion of working women exceeds 60% by 2010. |
| Employment rate among older workers40 | Total: 31.7% Men: 38.3% Women: 24.9% | "Lisbon" target: bring the mean employment rate in the EU for the 55-64 age group to 50% by 2010. |
| Long-term unemployment rate41 | Total: 1.2 % Men: 1.2% Women: 1.2% | Reduction of long-term unemployment. |

*Preventing failure at school and increasing skill levels*

The following factors are leading to inequalities in the education and training system[42]:

parents' socio-occupational status and family composition,

the effects of immigration,

students' gender.

As:

young people from disadvantaged families account for a substantial proportion of young people failing at school and leaving education with no qualifications,

people with no or few skills account for a substantial proportion of the long-term unemployed and beneficiaries of social assistance and welfare schemes, a policy needs to be developed to promote access to education and training, success at school and a high level of skills for all.

The priority measures discussed in detail in section 2.3 below are therefore intended to help to promote the above.

**For additional analytical, business and investment opportunities information, please contact Global Investment & Business Center, USA at (202) 546-2103. Fax: (202) 546-3275. E-mail: rusric@erols.com**

They should make it possible, in the short term, to reduce the numbers of early school leavers, reduce failure at school, increase the numbers of young people leaving school with qualifying training and thus help with social and occupational integration.

Through its goals, the policy to be implemented under this priority policy objective meets:

common objectives d) and e) on social inclusion,

priority 3 set out in the 2006 JR.

*Target*

Preliminary note:

Significant results from reforms that concern all educational streams cannot be expected over a two-year period.

| Indicator | | Starting situation (NSR 20062008) | Target |
|---|---|---|---|
| Mean rate leavers43 | of early school | EU mean: 14.9% EU men: 17.1% EU women: 12.7 % Total LU: 12.9% Men LU: 12.8% Women LU: 13% | "Lisbon" target: Reduce the rate of early school leavers in the European Union to 10% by 2010. |

*Reconciling family and working life*

The social inclusion indicators show that:

households with dependent children are more exposed to the risk of poverty than households without dependent children[44],

the at-risk-of-poverty rate for households with dependent children with a very low work intensity is four times greater than that of similar households with a very high work intensity[45],

the women's participation rate continues to be below the European average[46].

These observations justify the development of a family policy geared towards supporting families and an ongoing extension of the supply of child-minding facilities. The child-minding facilities set up should:

be flexible and financially affordable,

promote children's social integration, while supporting family and school upbringing and educational goals.

This policy is consistent with the second field of action of the NAP-Inclusion 2003-2005[47] and draws on the efforts already made on the basis of this plan[48].

Policy to reconcile family and working life meets:

**For additional analytical, business and investment opportunities information, please contact Global Investment & Business Center, USA at (202) 546-2103. Fax: (202) 546-3275. E-mail: rusric@erols.com**

common objective d) on social inclusion,

common objective e) on social inclusion and priority 1 of the 2006 JR relating to increased labour market participation.

It is also likely to play a part in meeting the challenges addressed by the following policy priorities of the 2006 JR:

priority 3 relating to the elimination of disadvantages in children's education,

priority 4 relating to the elimination of child poverty (by helping parents to find jobs).

*Targets*

| Indicator | Starting situation (NSR 2006-2008) | Intermediate targets | Target |
|---|---|---|---|
| National indicator: number of places in child-minding facilities | 8 000 places in 2006 | To 2009: 10 000 additional places | 30 000 places in 2013 |
| Employment rate of the population aged 15-24 | Total: 63.6% Women:53.7 % Men: 73.3% | Increase in the employment rate (especially women/mothers) | "Lisbon" target: Total employment rate reaching 70% in 2010 Women's employment rate exceeding 60% |

*Access to housing*

Since the housing shortage, especially as regards affordable housing for low-income households, at the end of the 1980s, the Government has implemented an active housing policy. However, despite the range of measures implemented since that time, the situation still gives cause for concern.

The aim of the "housing" plan of October 2005 is to reverse adverse trends in the housing market and to combat the housing-related exclusion of people on low incomes and/or socially disadvantaged people.

As the expression of an active and sustainable housing policy, the "housing" plan is intended not just to promote access to housing for all social groups, but also:

to improve the quality and flexibility of housing (multi-generational housing) for all types of housing (purchase/rental of a single-family home/housing in apartment blocks),

social mix (taking particular steps to ensure a balance between owners and tenants).

The plan takes a new approach towards rentals of social housing:

any new plan to build housing by a public promoter (municipalities, Housing Fund, National Company for Low-Cost Housing) must now in principle include at least 10% of dwellings for rental,

**For additional analytical, business and investment opportunities information, please contact Global Investment & Business Center, USA at (202) 546-2103. Fax: (202) 546-3275. E-mail: rusric@erols.com**

public promoters must comply with the above provision to receive substantive housing aid from the state, which may be as much as 75% of the cost of the plan to build subsidised housing for rental.

The policy envisaged is structured around the following two points, as described in detail in

2.5 below:

a housing "pact" with municipalities,

an active land control policy.

makes further progress in the housing field as stressed in the "country profile" of the 2004 JR,

meets objective d) on social inclusion and priority 5 of the 2006 JR.

By taking up the challenge posed by the current housing situation, the policy launched:

*Targets*

| Indicator | Starting situation (NSR 20062008) | Medium-/long-term target |
|---|---|---|
| National indicator of social housing and social mix: number of plans to build housing/number of social dwellings planned | 2 650 dwellings built as at 31 August 2006 under the 8th building plan | Building of 10 800 dwellings, including some 3 600 low-cost rental dwellings. |

**RETURNING TO FULL EMPLOYMENT**

*Measures implementing this priority which meets sub-objectives d) and e)*

These measures come under the following four headings.

*A. Keeping people in employment*

Policy to keep people in employment targets "employment security" rather than "job security".

Its purpose is to prevent unemployment, placing the focus on early redeployment.

For this purpose:

enterprises employing over 15 employees will have to notify the Comité de Conjoncture (Economic Committee) of redundancies for economic reasons;

the Comité de Conjoncture or the employer may launch an economic and social audit to anticipate any economic problems in an enterprise or a particular sector. This method of managing restructuring in advance will take account of repercussions on employment in other enterprises that may be involved;

**For additional analytical, business and investment opportunities information, please contact Global Investment & Business Center, USA at (202) 546-2103. Fax: (202) 546-3275. E-mail: rusric@erols.com**

a plan to keep people in employment, whose practical methods are currently being discussed by the government and the social partners, will be drawn up before collective redundancies take place. This plan should in particular enable the social partners to find alternative solutions, at all appropriate levels, to redundancies.

*B. Integrating all groups of people at risk of exclusion into the labour market*

The various "social employment initiatives" currently in operation all aim to:

provide help for a population with few links with the labour market in order to improve their employability through education and training,

manage facilities geared to the specific needs of the target population.

The purpose of Draft Law 5144 on combating social unemployment, tabled in the Chamber of Deputies in 2003 and amended by the government in 2004 and 2006, is to provide these initiatives with a legal framework in order to:

provide them with a solid foundation,

improve their effectiveness in the labour market through coordinated development,

step up their social effectiveness,

extend their scope of application to enterprises in the competitive sector,

make them more financially transparent.

The aim is to reserve the activities ultimately covered by the Draft Law for people considered by the Administration de L'Emploi (ADEM - Employment Service) to be very remote from the labour market. The underlying philosophy mirrors that of sheltered workshops for disabled workers, which are genuine economic units producing goods and services. The sole vocation of such facilities will therefore be to help jobseekers, assigned by ADEM under a common-law contract, to carry on a permanent paid occupation in conditions that are in keeping with their abilities.

*C. Better activation of young people*

On the basis of an agreement between the social partners and the government, ADEM will be under a statutory obligation to offer an active employment measure to all young people, in keeping with their education and skills, by at least the end of their sixth month of registration and preferably by the end of their third month of registration.

The spirit of enterprise will be encouraged and developed among young people.

Young people's integration into the labour market will be supported by the measures discussed under 2.3 below.

*D. Integrating older workers and keeping them in employment*

Priority will be given to the following fields of action:

**For additional analytical, business and investment opportunities information, please contact Global Investment & Business Center, USA at (202) 546-2103. Fax: (202) 546-3275. E-mail: rusric@erols.com**

continuing to promote the employability of older workers,

encouraging employers to review their age-related human resource management practices,

discouraging a culture of early retirement from work,

reforming schemes for early retirement from work,

looking for more flexible models for retirement from working life, in which components of pay can be combined with social security benefits.

*2.2.2 Responsibility for implementation and resources allocated*

Measures will be implemented by the Ministry of Labour and Employment. The government has nevertheless stressed that a return to full employment requires a responsible attitude on the part of all stakeholders in the labour market: public authorities, enterprises, unions, employees and the unemployed.

The resources needed to implement measures come from the state budget, in which € 152 130 100 has been earmarked for the "Employment Fund" in 2006, and from the European Social Fund.

*Monitoring and evaluation*

The priority objectives of a return to full employment are part and parcel of the National Reform Programme (2005) and the results obtained by the measures discussed will be monitored and evaluated by a monitoring and evaluation instrument currently being devised by the tripartite working group mentioned above[49]. As this national instrument has yet to be finalised, some common indicators that have a bearing on this issue are specified under 2.1.1 above.

*Gender mainstreaming*

The unemployment rate among women is 5.9%, while the rate among men is 3.5%[50].

The unemployment rate among young women is 16.4% while the rate among their male counterparts is 11.8%[51].

As a result of these disparities between the genders, the expected impact of measures for a return to full employment will be particularly important for women.

**PREVENTING FAILURE AT SCHOOL AND INCREASING SKILL LEVELS**

*Measures implementing this priority which meets sub-objectives d) and e)*

The measures discussed, which draw on a summary report drawn up for the European "Leonardo da Vinci" programme[52] and follow its key recommendations, are to take place at the following three levels.

*A. A preventive approach*

**For additional analytical, business and investment opportunities information, please contact Global Investment & Business Center, USA at (202) 546-2103. Fax: (202) 546-3275. E-mail: rusric@erols.com**

In order to promote success at school, the paradigm in Luxembourg is changing from education based on the reproduction of rote knowledge to education based on the acquisition of skills.

In the system preparing for technical secondary education, attended by students who do not manage to go straight from primary to secondary education, French, German and mathematics learning modules are being reformed.

As a study conducted in 2005 showed that the practice of repeated years did not improve students' chances of success, more detailed advancement criteria, follow-up and guidance measures and remedial measures have been introduced.

The "Cycle Inférieur" (Lower Cycle) pilot project is intended to reform curricula, improve student monitoring, and to provide more detailed evaluation and more effective guidance in year 9.

Under the "Neie Lycée" (New Lycée) pilot project, students from all streams of post-primary education will be able attend classes for eight hours a day, and the focus will be on interdisciplinary learning and assessment of education. The University of Luxembourg will be responsible for evaluation.

Core competences will be decided for various levels of primary and secondary education. In primary education, the notion of competences will be implemented at the same time as schools are organised by learning cycles as provided for by the reform of the schools law. The introduction of these cycles is being studied for secondary and technical secondary education.

A new "Profile for Luxembourg's language policy in education" based on the Community reference framework for languages, is being prepared. Its differentiated approach will make it possible to target the highest level of language competence for each student, although students not reaching this level will still be able to enter vocational training.

*B. Early screening and help for students at risk*

The annual survey of early school leavers that the Ministry of Education and Vocational Training (MENFP) has been running since 2005[53] is a statistical and early action instrument. The Action Locale pour Jeunes (ALJ – Local Action for Young People), a socio-educational service of the MENFP responsible for helping young people to make the transition from school to working life, has been commissioned to contact the young people surveyed as part of the study to find out why they left school and what they have been doing since then.

The following measures are intended to help young people to return to education and training:

relay classes making it possible to keep students with behavioural problems in a school environment and prepare them to return to normal classes,

more extensive supervision, more appropriate curricula and broader training prospects are to be introduced into the preparatory scheme,

teaching models aiming to develop bridging classes paving the way for qualifying training will be enhanced,

schools will inform the ALJ of students who leave school during the academic year.

*C. Helping young people at risk by implementing the voluntary guidance service (SVO) project*

The SVO project, implemented under the auspices of the Ministry of the Family and Integration, chiefly targets young people aged under 18 who have left school early, or who have completed their compulsory education without qualifications or employment and are not attending school. The aim of this project is to provide young people with stability, give them back confidence and help them to make the most of an experience which encourages them to return to education and training or to find a job. During the project, young people will be supervised by a tutor in the workplace and supported by a worker from the National Youth Service who will be responsible for monitoring them.

*D. Re-integration and remedial measures*

To prevent early school leavers from becoming excluded, and help them to gain access to a vocational qualification, the supply of qualifying and vocational integration training schemes will be increased:

vocational re-integration classes will be offered by several technical lycées and the national continuing vocational training centre,

vocational induction training, in the form of an apprenticeship contract leading to a recognised certificate (CITP), will be revised to cover more trades/families of trades.

A draft law tabled in the Chamber of Deputies on 29 June 2006[54]:

redefines the objectives and organisation of vocational guidance and induction (COIP) courses for unemployed young people aged 15-18 who have no learning opportunities,

introduces training aid for minors and a training allowance for adults aged under 25,

introduces a training bonus system rewarding young people who have successfully met the objectives set for COIP courses and who have been under apprenticeship/employment contracts for at least six months after the conclusion of the apprenticeship/employment contract.

*Responsibility for implementation and resources allocated*

The MENFP is responsible for implementing the planned measures, apart from the SVO, from both an operational and a legislative point of view. The government nevertheless stresses that schools must be developed together with the other stakeholders in the field of education, i.e. students, parents and teachers.

Ambitions in the educational field, including the competence school, have a price: while education cost € 550 000 000 in 2000, it will cost between € 1 100 000 and 1 200 000 per annum in future years

As regards the implementation of the SVO project, it should be noted that this project which is scheduled to start at the beginning of 2007, is based on concerted action by the MENFP, the ALJ network, youth centres and voluntary service facilities.

*Monitoring and evaluation*

The MENFP will follow up measures and will evaluate the impact of their implementation[56]. For this purpose, it will call on its statistical and analysis service. The service's approach, which will

**For additional analytical, business and investment opportunities information, please contact Global Investment & Business Center, USA at (202) 546-2103. Fax: (202) 546-3275. E-mail: rusric@erols.com**

take account of students' socio-economic situations, will make it possible to pinpoint the impact of educational reforms on social inclusion.

Measures connected with training and occupational integration will also be followed up within Luxembourg's tripartite structures (state, employers' and trade union organisations). School measures will be monitored by consultative structures bringing together teachers, students and parents.

*Gender mainstreaming*

Personal advancement, social integration and occupational integration require a minimum of knowledge. While the measures taken to ensure access to such knowledge are therefore important for all young people, they are of particular importance for boys. A recent study has shown that, in the Luxembourg education and training system, students' gender is a factor generating disparities and that early school leavers are predominantly male[57].

## RECONCILING FAMILY AND WORKING LIFE

*Measures implementing this policy priority which meets sub-objectives d) and e)*

The key measure here is the new concept of care for schoolchildren outside school hours in facilities known as "Maisons Relais pour enfants" (MR – Childcare Centres).

The conduct of the "Fogaflex" pilot project under the NAP-Inclusion 2003-2005, co-financed by the European Social Fund, paved the way for the development of this concept[58]. The concept was finalised in the Grand Ducal Regulation of 20 July 2005 on the approval to be given to managers of such centres.

In 2005, there were 87 MRs (with 178 local or district branches and 8000 places) under convention with the Ministry of the Family and Integration (MIFA) in 76 of Luxembourg's 166 municipalities[59]. In line with the government statement of 2 May 2006, efforts to improve the supply of MR facilities will be pursued and intensified during the reference period of the NAP-Inclusion (see 2.1.3 above).

The main distinctive features of the MR concept are as follows:

a) extended and flexible opening times (between 06:00 and 20:00 from Monday to Saturday) to take account of the various problems faced by parents,

b) participation in the life of the local communities hosting the MR, promoting the social, linguistic and cultural integration of children and families,

c) close cooperation between families and schools paving the way for synergies,

d) integration into a single facility of various mandatory and ancillary services such as:

catering at midday and refreshments at other times

supervision of recreational services and other socio-educational activities

supervision of school homework

**For additional analytical, business and investment opportunities information, please contact Global Investment & Business Center, USA at (202) 546-2103. Fax: (202) 546-3275. E-mail: rusric@erols.com**

socio-educational support

minding of children who are sick either in the MR facility or at home

social-educational, instructive or cultural activities for children and families

parental training sessions, e) slimmed-down administrative procedures for approval and the possibility of outsourcing some services to external providers, f) a twofold aim of help for families and support for employment.

The "child care in people's homes" measure, with its two strands, will also help to achieve this priority:

*"Daageselteren" (Parental assistants)*

The "Daageselteren" accommodate from four to seven children during the day and/or night and, under the Law of 8 September 1998 governing relations between the state and bodies working in the social, family and therapeutic fields, are subject to approval by the MIFA which also plays a part in their training. Conditions for obtaining such approval are set by a Grand Ducal Regulation of 29 March 2001 which supplements the above-mentioned law.

*Care in cooperation with a "Service de placement familial" (SFP – Family Placement Service)*

Four bodies managing such services are subsidised by the MIFA to organise and supervise care.

On 31 December 2005, 588 children were receiving care in people's homes in comparison with only 308 en 2000. 84% of approved parental assistants work with a family placement service[60]. In order to create a genuine network and further improve the quality of this care, the MIFA tabled a draft law in the Chamber of Deputies on 17 November 2005 regulating parental assistance work[61]. Training and social security affiliation are in particular required under this draft law.

*Responsibility for implementation and resources allocated*

In the case of the MR facilities, the main players are the MIFA and municipalities which work together closely to extend the MR network, whose concept means that municipalities can manage facilities independently. The extent to which municipal players are involved can be seen from the following details on MR managing agencies:

20.7% were non-profit associations,

4.6% were unions of municipalities,

74.7% were municipal authorities.

The state provides 50% of funding for MR infrastructure, to a maximum of € 10 000 per place. In 2006, two non-limited appropriations to a total amount of € 16 100 698 were entered in the state budget to help with the operating costs of MR facilities. The cost of extending child care facilities outside school hours is estimated at € 150 000 000 to € 180 000 000 for the period 2007-2009[63].

As regards care in people's homes, the MIFA is continuing to work with the voluntary sector which manages the SPF network: Action familiale et populaire (Family and Popular Action), the Luxembourg Red Cross, the Association of Managers of Care Centres and "Fir ons Kanner".

**For additional analytical, business and investment opportunities information, please contact Global Investment & Business Center, USA at (202) 546-2103. Fax: (202) 546-3275. E-mail: rusric@erols.com**

In 2006, the state provided funding of € 7 415 207 for the operating costs of SPF facilities under convention.

*Monitoring and evaluation*

The MIFA processes applications for approval and helps to fund MR and SPF facilities under convention. As a result, it is able closely to monitor quantitative[64] and qualitative developments in this field. This monitoring and evaluation is carried out by Division IV "Youth and Family" of the MIFA. The Centre d'Etudes de Populations, de Pauvreté et de Politiques Socio-Economiques (CEPS – Population, Poverty and Socio-Economic Research Centre) also monitors the situation as regards reconciling working and family life and its most recent study of this issue was published in February 2006[65].

*Gender mainstreaming*

Family burdens, in particular child minding, continue to be shouldered largely by women. As a result, reconciling family and working life is a particular problem for women and is a major curb on women's participation in work. With a view to equal opportunities, measures to promote reconciliation should therefore allow mothers in particular to make the most of their employment potential.

## PROMOTING ACCESS TO HOUSING

*Measures implementing this priority which meets sub-objective d)*

These measures, covering both housing for sale and for rental, including subsidised rented housing, have two main strands.

*A. A housing "pact" with municipalities*

Under this pact, the state will help all municipalities which undertake, under convention with the government, to build new housing in their area with a view to increasing their population by over 15% over a ten-year period.

The key elements of this pact are:

- the principle of a convention between municipalities and the government,
- annual capital aid of € 4 500 per new additional inhabitant in the case of a 1% population growth,
- for some municipalities, an exhaustive list of which will be drawn up by the government, a conditional increase of 50% of the amount of capital aid.

Legislation on long leases and building rights, which dates from 1824, will be revised and amended and, in order to promote use of the leasehold formula, Article 22 of the amended Law of 25 February 1979 will be amended.

*B. An active land control policy*

The state (like municipalities and public promoters) has few land reserves and its land control instruments are limited. Faced with land prices which are soaring because land is so scarce and

**For additional analytical, business and investment opportunities information, please contact Global Investment & Business Center, USA at (202) 546-2103. Fax: (202) 546-3275. E-mail: rusric@erols.com**

the demand for housing is growing, the public authorities are therefore too often unable to act. The active land management policy is intended to remedy this using the following tools:

1. Right of compulsory purchase

• Article 16 of the Constitution will be amended to make compulsory purchase possible again for reasons of public utility.

2. Right of pre-emption

• A right of pre-emption will be introduced for municipal councils for pre-emption in urban areas and for the state for the land needed to implement the regional master plans, sectoral plans and land-use plans which are mandatory.

3. Tax measures to promote the assignment of land and residential buildings

Full exemption from the capital gains to be paid by natural persons if the state or the municipality is the purchaser.

Tax exemption of 50% on the commercial profit from the sale of land to the state or to a municipality.

4. The introduction of municipal taxes to combat property retention

Special tax for non-allocation of building land for construction.

Municipalities will be able to punish a change of use of residential buildings: the draft law on the main residence lease requires prior authorisation of a change of use.

Municipalities will be able to levy a special tax to combat the non-occupation of housing: under the new law on lease contracts municipalities will be able to compel owners to declare buildings or parts of buildings which are not occupied. On the basis of the relevant file, municipalities will be able to levy the tax for prolonged non-occupation of housing set out in the above-mentioned draft law.

5. Amendment of the amended Law of 19 July 2004

This amendment is intended to reduce the retail price of serviced land.

6. Measures to develop sustainable housing

Creation of an "Urban Renovation Agency" The task of this public body will be to help, with a view to social mix, mix of urban functions and sustainable development, to draw up and implement a national programme of urban renovation in the districts set out in Chapter 4 ("Housing renovation") of the amended Law of 25 February 1979 on housing aid by offering municipalities technical, logistical and financial assistance. As a result of the criterion of social mix, less well-off households will not be excluded from these projects.

From 1 January 2009, housing aid will be awarded only if the newly built housing respects the new European standards on the energy performance of buildings.

**For additional analytical, business and investment opportunities information, please contact Global Investment & Business Center, USA at (202) 546-2103. Fax: (202) 546-3275. E-mail: rusric@erols.com**

The award of the improvement allowance will be linked to compliance with the priority recommendations issued by the expert when drawing up the buildings specification.

7. Measures to increase the number of low-cost dwellings.

The 8$^{th}$ building construction programme under which it is planned to build some 10 800 housing units, approximately 1/3 of which will be low-cost dwellings for rental, will be completed. These dwellings are intended for people whose low incomes make it impossible for them to rent housing on the private, non-subsidised, market.

In all building plots of more than one hectare, 10% of the area will be set aside for low-cost housing. For this purpose, a draft law promoting housing will be drawn up.

*Responsibility for implementation and resources allocated*

As the state and municipalities are jointly responsible for implementing the right to appropriate housing for all citizens, the housing plan is structured around a pact under which these two actors have to shoulder their responsibilities and pool their efforts.

The budget available to the housing department to achieve this objective is € 92 400 000 for the 2006 budget year alone, including € 69 300 000 for individual state aid for housing and € 23 100 000 for aid for the construction of apartment blocks. The annual cost of state aid to municipalities is estimated at € 10 000 000. In order to promote the construction of subsidised housing for rental between 2006 and 2008, the Luxembourg government intends to make € 63 500 000 available to the various public promoters in the form of aid for the construction of apartment blocks.

*Monitoring and evaluation*

The Ministerial department for housing will follow up the "Housing" plan which has just been launched and will evaluate the impact of its implementation[66]. These tasks will be carried out in particular by the Land Occupation Observatory, a service set up within the department in 2003 in order to monitor and analyse trends in the various segments of the housing and land market and to plan a housing policy in particular and a land occupation policy in general which are consistent and effective.

*Gender mainstreaming*

Housing is a major burden on the family budgets of low-income households and may become a factor in exclusion. The expected impact of the "Housing" plan measures will thus involve all members of low-income households. The focus is nevertheless on women as, in the type of household most at risk of poverty, i.e. lone-parent families, the adult is normally a woman.

## GOVERNANCE IN RELATION TO THE NAP-INCLUSION

Social inclusion policies are coordinated at both ministerial level and with the partners concerned in the following bodies[67] :

the Joint Ministerial Committee on social action,

the Higher Council for social action,

a Joint Ministerial NAP-Inclusion group,

**For additional analytical, business and investment opportunities information, please contact Global Investment & Business Center, USA at (202) 546-2103. Fax: (202) 546-3275. E-mail: rusric@erols.com**

a consultation and coordination group ("NAP-Inclusion Group") which brings together all the players and was set up by the Ministry of the Family and Integration, which coordinates social inclusion, at the time of the first NAP-Inclusion round.

Through their composition, these bodies make it possible to:

organise wide-ranging and transparent consultation with all the players involved in combating poverty and social exclusion,

propose practical measures to improve the way in which poverty and social exclusion are combated to the Government,

take an integrated approach, bringing together the multidimensional aspects of poverty and social exclusion covered by various ministries' fields of competence,

better to target measures to make them more effective,

take account of the municipal dimension of social inclusion policies.

The following meetings were held to prepare for the NAP-Inclusion 2006-2008:

6 December 2005: meeting to inform the "NAP-Inclusion Group" about the new rationalised labour framework,

6 April 2006: joint ministerial information and consultation meeting on the new labour framework, on the key elements to be considered when drawing up the NAP-Inclusion and on the timetable for preparation of the NAP,

27 April 2006: information meeting and exchange of views with the "NAP-Inclusion Group" and invitation to that Group to forward its priority policy objectives for combating poverty and social exclusion to the Joint Ministerial NAP-Inclusion group by 10 May 2006,

15 May 2006: joint ministerial consultation meeting to draw up four priority policy objectives for the NAP-Inclusion 2006-2008 from the written contributions,

12 June 2006: information meeting and exchange of views with the "NAP-Inclusion Group" to present and discuss the four priority policy objectives decided upon.

As a result of these meetings, all the players, i.e. the ministries concerned, the social partners and non-governmental organisations, took part in the process to draw up the NAP-Inclusion 2006-2008.

The views of people living in poverty were brought to the attention of the "NAP-Inclusion Group" following a round table organised on 23 March 2006 by EAPN-Lëtzebuerg, with the support of the Ministry of the Family and Integration.

Consultation of the Joint Ministerial NAP-Inclusion Group and the "NAP-Inclusion Group" will continue as the NAP-Inclusion 2006-2008 is implemented.

To help to improve information on and raise awareness of the process of social inclusion, the Ministry of the Family and Integration is a partner in the project "Local coordination of inclusion and social protection – CLIPS" launched by the Caritas Luxembourg foundation following call for

**For additional analytical, business and investment opportunities information, please contact Global Investment & Business Center, USA at (202) 546-2103. Fax: (202) 546-3275. E-mail: rusric@erols.com**

proposals VP/2006/012 financed under the Community Action Programme to combat social exclusion 2002-2006.

In order better to take up the challenges raised by the steering of inclusion strategy, identified in the “country profile” of the 2006 JR, a delegation from the Ministry of the Family and Integration took part in the peer review exercise organised under the above programme in Paris in June 2006 on the theme “Cross-cutting guidance for policies against exclusion”.

*Examples of good practice Rental of housing through NGOs*

| Name of Policy/Project | Member State |
|---|---|
| Rental of housing through NGOs | Luxembourg |
| End Purpose of the Initiative | |
| The Housing Fund (HF) is the largest public promoter in the Grand Duchy and provides social housing for rental, some of which it makes available permanently to NGOs working in the social housing field. Housing is made available under a convention signed by the parties. NGOs, in their turn, rent this housing to those persons for whom they provide social assistance under a lease contract drawn up by the HF and then carry out regular social supervision of the people in receipt of housing. The lease contract and a domiciliation order are an integral part of the convention | |
| Main Results | |
| The persons looked after by the respective NGOs benefit from rented housing which is in keeping with their particular needs and which is financially affordable. These persons are then monitored, where necessary, by the NGOs. 85 dwellings have been rented out since the beginning of the 1990s, i.e. some 6% of the Housing Fund’s total stock of rental property. | |
| Targeted Beneficiaries | Policy Focus |
| General Population Children Single-parent families UnemployedOlder people Young People People with disabilities Immigrants / Refugees Ethnic Minorities Homeless Specific Illness/disease Other Low-income households. | Social Exclusion Healthcare Long-term Care Governance |
| | Geographical Scope |
| | National Regional |
| | Implementing Body |
| | Housing Fund and NGOs |
| Context/Background to the Initiative | |
| At the beginning of the 1990s, at the request of several NGOs, the Housing Fund, which is a public body, started to rent housing from its existing stock of property to various associations willing to provide social supervision for those persons for whom they provide assistance. | |
| Details of the Initiative | |
| 1. Specific Objectives | |

**For additional analytical, business and investment opportunities information, please contact Global Investment & Business Center, USA at (202) 546-2103. Fax: (202) 546-3275. E-mail: rusric@erols.com**

| |
|---|
| - Keen to put its plans into practice in urban centres rather than in more outlying areas – with a view to promoting the social integration of these socially disadvantaged people – the Housing Fund has since the 1990s received regular requests from NGOs which share similar concerns as regards the people for whom they provide assistance, such as people with physical and mental disabilities. - In this way, socially disadvantaged people are able to find housing which is appropriate from the point of view of equipment and fittings, at an affordable rent. Social workers also provide supervision in this housing. |
| 2. How did the initiative address these objectives? |
| It should be noted that the Housing Fund makes provision, for any plan of a certain size, for a minimum number of dwellings in keeping with the needs of people with physical disabilities for instance. To carry out its construction projects, the Housing Fund receives the state aid set out in the Law of 25 February 1979 on housing aid. This law targets, among other things, promotion by the state of the construction of low-cost housing by public promoters Public promoters, including the Housing Fund, rent out these subsidised dwellings according to the criteria set by the Grand Ducal Regulation of 16 November 1998, i.e. the household's net available annual income and the weighted area of the dwelling As well as the provision of subsidised housing, some people also receive other social benefits, such as coverage of all or part of costs by long-term care insurance in the case, for instance, of a person with physical disabilities. |
| 3. What is/was the timescale for implementing the initiative? |
| As the initiative was launched some 15 years ago and the number of applications has continued to increase since then, there are no plans to wind up this initiative. |

| Monitoring and Evaluation | |
|---|---|
| | How is/was the project monitored/evaluated? |
| | Monitoring in the strict sense of the term has not taken place. However, as only a few dwellings were made available to a few associations at the beginning of the 1990s, and, 15 years later, there are 85 units for rental, i.e. some 6% of the rental property stock of the Housing Fund, this initiative seems to have been a success. |

Outcomes

| 1. | To what extent have the objectives been met? |
|---|---|
| | |

The objectives have been met as 22 associations have, over the last 15 years, benefited from one or several of these 85 rental dwellings and all 85 units continue to be managed by the same NGOs without any major problems.

2. What obstacles/risks were faced in implementing the initiative?

Nothing to report

3. How were these obstacles and risks addressed?

Nothing to report

**For additional analytical, business and investment opportunities information, please contact Global Investment & Business Center, USA at (202) 546-2103. Fax: (202) 546-3275. E-mail: rusric@erols.com**

4. Were there any unexpected benefits or weaknesses?

Nothing to report

*Monitoring of school dropouts*

| Name of Policy/Project | Member State |
|---|---|
| Monitoring of school dropouts (early school leavers) | Luxembourg |

End Purpose of the Initiative

Introduction of a method of identifying and monitoring post-primary students leaving school with no certificate (early school leavers).

Main Results

1 984 students (out of a total of 32 250) were identified as leaving post-primary education with no certificate in 2003/2004, i.e. a rate of 3.7%. The rate among men (4.3%) was higher than among women (3.1%). 27% of this overall sample continued their education in Luxembourg or abroad, 30.5% were in employment or attending a vocational integration scheme, 16.2% were unemployed and 26.3% had left the country or could not be surveyed. The majority of students leaving school early were aged 16-18 (45.5%). Students of foreign nationality are more likely to leave school early than students of Luxembourg nationality. The dropout rate was particularly high among Cape Verdean students (13.6%). The lowest rate was in secondary education, while the highest rate was in apprenticeship (CATP, CCM, CITP). The reasons most frequently given for leaving school early were learning difficulties and/or problems in adapting to the education system.

| Targeted Beneficiaries | Policy Focus |
|---|---|
| General Population Children Single-parent families UnemployedOlder people Young People People with disabilities Immigrants / Refugees Ethnic Minorities Homeless Specific Illness/disease Other  Early school leavers | Social Exclusion Healthcare Long-term Care Governance |
| | Geographical Scope |
| | National Regional |
| | Implementing Body |
| | Ministry of Education and Vocational Training |

Context/Background to the Initiative

In view of the many cases of dropping out from school reported by schools (1 984 cases according to a survey from December 2004), the Ministry of Education and Vocational Training decided to launch, in January 2005, a survey of the reasons and circumstances leading these students to leave school early

**For additional analytical, business and investment opportunities information, please contact Global Investment & Business Center, USA at (202) 546-2103. Fax: (202) 546-3275. E-mail: rusric@erols.com**

Details of the Initiative

1. Specific Objectives

To determine the extent and nature of the problem of dropping out from school. To explore the reasons why students leave school early. To provide assistance from a specialist service, the ALJ (Local Youth Action), for this target group.

2. How did the initiative address these objectives?

Students who dropped out in 2003/2004 were contacted (mostly) by telephone (or by post if they could not be contacted by telephone) by workers from the ALJ. Interviewees were questioned and their answers recorded in a questionnaire. Young unemployed people were offered an information and guidance interview with an ALJ worker.

3. What is/was the timescale for implementing the initiative?

March to May 2005: contact with the 1 984 students identified. June to September 2005: statistical analysis of replies. October 2005: Publication of results.

Monitoring and Evaluation

How is/was the project monitored/evaluated?

SCRIPT was asked to draw up the questionnaire to be used and statistically to analyse the replies. The “questionnaire” tool was evaluated by interviewing the ALJ workers with a view to repeating the operation in 2006.

Outcomes

1. To what extent have the objectives been met?

It was possible to contact 75% of the overall sample. A statistical breakdown of early school leavers by age, gender, nationality and school background was drawn up

The reasons for dropping out were recorded.

2. What obstacles/risks were faced in implementing the initiative?

It was impossible to contact over 25% of the sample (26.3%). No information was obtained on early school leavers from private schools. The use of telephone interview techniques raised a degree of mistrust.

3. How were these obstacles and risks addressed?

4. Were there any unexpected benefits or weaknesses?

A number of the young people contacted, and their parents, were pleased that a public body was taking an interest in their fate

*Governance in relation to the NAP-Inclusion*

Composition of the Joint Ministerial Committee on social action following the Law of 8 June

The Committee was set up by the amended Law of 29 April 1999, introducing the right to a guaranteed minimum income[68]. It is made up of representatives of the ministers for social security, the family, labour and employment, the interior, women's advancement, health, housing and education and vocational training.

Its role is to propose measures likely to step up the fight against poverty and social exclusion to the Government and to coordinate the work of all departments in this field.

Composition of the Higher Council on social action following the Law of 8 June 2004

The Higher Council was set up by the amended Law of 29 April 1999 and includes:

- representatives of government members whose portfolios include labour and employment, the family, social security, housing, the interior, health, education and vocational training and women's advancement;

- a representative from the national solidarity fund;

- a representative from the national social assistance agency;

- a representative from the general inspectorate for social security;

- three members appointed from among and by the directors of social assistance offices;

- four members representing the most representative trade unions;

- three members representing social work professionals;

- three members representing associations managing services in the social work field;

- three members representing employers' organisations;

- three members representing bodies active in work to combat poverty and social exclusion;

- a representative of the Economic and Social Council;

- a representative of the Population, Poverty and Socio-Economic Research Centre.

It has consultative functions for the ministers who are members of the Joint Ministerial Committee on social action. The Council reports on needs for social action and proposes methods and resources to meet them. Every three years, it sends a detailed report to the Chamber of Deputies.

Composition of the Joint Ministerial NAP/Inclusion Group:

Ministry of the Family and Integration Ministry of Labour and Employment Ministry of Social Security Ministry of Health Ministry of Education and Vocational Training Ministry of Small Business, Tourism and Housing Ministry of Justice Ministry of Equal Opportunities Ministry of

**For additional analytical, business and investment opportunities information, please contact Global Investment & Business Center, USA at (202) 546-2103. Fax: (202) 546-3275. E-mail: rusric@erols.com**

Culture, Higher Education and Research Population, Poverty and Socio-Economic Research Centre Central Statistical and Economic Research Department Composition of the "NAP-Inclusion Group":

The "NAP-Inclusion Group" includes members of the Joint Ministerial Group and the bodies, social partners and non-governmental organisations listed below.

Syvicol intermunicipal union

Social Office of the municipality of Luxembourg

Social Office of the municipality of Pétange

Social Office of the municipality of Ettelbruck

Social Office of the municipality of Esch/Alzette

Social Office of the municipality of Dudelange

Social Office of the municipality of Differdange

Social Office of the municipality of Bettembourg

OGBL (trade union)

LCGB (trade union)

Chamber of Commerce

Chamber of Labour

Chamber of Civil Servants and Public Servants

Chamber of Trades of the Grand Duchy of Luxembourg

Chamber of Private-Sector Employees

Chamber of Agriculture

Federation of Craft Trades

FEDIL - Federation of Luxembourg Industry

Union of Luxembourg Enterprises (non-profit)

General Confederation of Civil Servants

Association of care centre managers (EGCA)

National Council of Foreigners

**For additional analytical, business and investment opportunities information, please contact Global Investment & Business Center, USA at (202) 546-2103. Fax: (202) 546-3275. E-mail: rusric@erols.com**

ASTI - Immigrant Workers' Support Association

EAPN-Lëtzebuerg – Luxembourg branch of the European Anti-Poverty Network

Caritas Confederation

Luxembourg League for Prevention and Medical and Social Action

Luxembourg Red Cross

National Social Defence Committee

Maison de la Porte Ouverte Foundation

Women in Distress (non-profit)

National Council of Luxembourg Women

ATD-Quart Monde

Stëmm vun der Strooss

Wunnéngshëllef

Initiativ vu betraffenen an solidarischen Bierger géint d'Aarmut a fir Integratioun

Inter-Actions

Aarbéchtshëllef

COLABOR

Ënnerdaach Differdange

Horizon (non-profit)

## NATIONAL STRATEGY ON PENSIONS

The Member States submitted their National Strategy Reports on pensions in 2005 and a summary report was finalised by Commission departments in 2006[69]; this section therefore contains only updates on relevant changes from the 2005 National Strategy Report. At the end of 2005, the Economic Policy Committee's Working Group on "Ageing" completed its projections of expenditure connected with population ageing. The results for Luxembourg are commented upon in this section.

### ADEQUATE PENSIONS

At present the Luxembourg pension system provides adequate pensions: the at-risk-of-poverty rate is lowest for the population aged 65 and over (6% in comparison with 11% for the population as a whole)[70] and the median equivalised income of older people is the same as that of people of working age[71]. Similarly, the relative risk-of-poverty gaps are not as high for older people and the median income of all older people with income below the poverty threshold is approximately 86% of that threshold[72]. The Working Group's projections predict that the theoretical replacement rate will remain unchanged throughout the projection period (2004-2050)[73], which is the same as assuming that no change in legislation has been envisaged and that the projections keep pensions at an unchanged level throughout the projection period. In this scenario, the actual replacement rate of the general private-sector scheme, defined as the ratio between the mean amount of pensions being paid (including survivors' pensions) and the mean wage on which contributions are levied, is predicted to increase from 48% in 2005 to 63% in 2050; this increase can largely be attributed to increasingly complete working lives on the part of non-resident scheme members.

## FINANCIAL VIABILITY

As a result of population of working age which is relatively young in comparison with the European mean, the financial viability of pension schemes in Luxembourg is better than that of most Member States, although it has to be said that reforms are needed now if the scheme is to be financed in the long term. Actuarial forecasts in the Working Group's projections show that the general private-sector pension scheme will manage to retain a sufficient level of revenue to cover expenditure with an accumulation of the statutory reserve in the medium term. The system's financing problems become evident, however, from a long-term view. According to the scenario used by the Working Group, based on long-term economic growth of 3%, the contribution rate of the general private-sector scheme will have to be adjusted for the first time at latest by 2027, and if the contribution rates remain unchanged, the statutory reserve will be exhausted by 2034. The long-term deterioration of the pension system is shown by the growth of the demographic dependency rate of the system (number of pensions per 100 contributors), which is projected to increase from 42% in 2005 to 62% in 2050[74], and the growth of pensions expenditure, increasing by 7.4% of GDP by 2050[75].

## MODERNISATION, TRANSPARENCY AND COMMUNICATION

With a view to regular evaluation of the financial situation of the general private-sector pension scheme, the Inspectorate General for Social Security draws up a report at the end of each seven-year period of coverage in accordance with Article 238(6) of the Social Insurance Code which states that "For each subsequent period of coverage, the overall contribution shall be continued, or reset by special law on the basis of a technical review of the preceding period and actuarial forecasts for the new period of coverage to be drawn up by the supervisory authority". The report was presented at a press conference by the Minister for Social Security in February 2006 and in outline takes up the predictions of the Working Group on "Ageing". The report concludes that: "the financial situation of the general pension scheme is sound and in a condition likely to support the adjustments that financial viability will necessitate in future decades". Two international publications (International Monetary Fund, Organisation for Economic Cooperation and Development), presented to the public at press conferences in January and July 2006, support the report's conclusions, but stress that the general scheme will be subject to major financial pressures in future years and that reforms will have to be envisaged in the medium term to ensure the sustainability of the general scheme.

## SPECIAL CONSIDERATIONS

Following the decisions of the Tripartite Coordination Committee in April 2006, bringing together representatives of employers, employees and the public authorities, "the social partners and the Government will set up a think-tank whose task will be to draw up proposals to ensure the long-term viability of pension schemes and to study the various measures which could be envisaged to ensure such long-term viability and to adjust the pension system to developments connected with

**For additional analytical, business and investment opportunities information, please contact Global Investment & Business Center, USA at (202) 546-2103. Fax: (202) 546-3275. E-mail: rusric@erols.com**

changes in occupational careers, demographic ageing and its impact on the length of working time throughout life". This initiative, based on the conclusions of the national and international reports, is in line with the decisions of those taking part in the round table on pensions in 2001 which brought together representatives of parliamentary groups, trade unions and employers' organisations, at which agreement was reached between the social partners and the political parties to "review a number of measures, without prejudicing low-level pensions, if it transpires from the actuarial review, carried out every seven years, that the level of the reserve could fall below the statutory minimum of 1.5 times annual expenditure and that sustainable financing of pensions could not guaranteed without imposing additional charges on future generations".

Although the financial viability of social security schemes is closely linked to the level of pensions paid, steps need to be taken to ensure that the system provides income security for older people. Pension schemes are an important factor in inter- and intra-generational transfers. Pensions are a key factor in maintaining social cohesion within the population and the role of pension schemes cannot be limited solely to the payment of benefits that reflect contributions paid. Population ageing will not just create a new burden for pension schemes, but will also entail major expenditure in the fields of health care and long-term care benefits. The public authorities already provide a high level of funding for social security in Luxembourg with the result that there is little room for manoeuvre in future for additional public contributions for social security.

## NATIONAL HEALTH CARE STRATEGY

In view of the precarious financial balance of the health care system, all the players in sickness and long-term care insurance, care providers, the social partners and the state are now taking a common approach and have committed themselves to a programme of action for the health care system. This programme aims to curb additional costs and to provide better care through better spending by advocating good medical practices in the broad sense of the term.

The Scientific Council, whose task is in particular to identify, together with the main players, priority medical issues and to gather the scientific information available, has started work in this respect.

It has undertaken an initial analysis of the profiles of those prescribing certificates of incapacity for work and has in particular decided that the analysis method will be further refined so that appropriate and agreed penalties can then be introduced.

As Luxembourg occupies, as regards drug consumption, second place in Europe after France, efforts have been made to curb consumption in this field, in particular through a second campaign against the excessive use of antibiotics and a campaign to introduce generics as bioequivalent products for the conventional drugs that they replace.

With a view to improving efficiency, hospitals have started to organise a common purchasing unit. The aim is to obtain, in the relatively short term, more advantageous prices from the main suppliers not only for purchases of drugs, but also for medical devices, laboratory consumables, perfusions and the like.

In order to improve the way in which incapacity for work is handled, the legislative provisions have been improved.

In the field of sickness insurance, major changes chiefly concerning methods of payment of financial sickness benefits came into force with effect from 1 May 2005. These changes chiefly involve the methods of reporting and coverage of incapacity for work.

**For additional analytical, business and investment opportunities information, please contact Global Investment & Business Center, USA at (202) 546-2103. Fax: (202) 546-3275. E-mail: rusric@erols.com**

In order to improve the system for workers unable to work in their last job for reasons of health, infirmity or exhaustion, the Law of 25 July 2002 had introduced an internal or external redeployment procedure linked with the award of certain benefits. The new redeployment procedure was triggered when the insured person submitted a disability claim.

The Law of 1 July 2005 reorganises the occupational redeployment procedure. Workers have to submit an application to obtain the disability pension. This improves the way in which long-term incapacity for work is handled in the sense that cases are handled by sickness insurance (acute and evolving chronic diseases) or pension insurance (incapacity to work in the general labour market), or occupational redeployment measures are applied (incapacity for work in the last job).

After the Government adopted several amendments to Draft Law 5146 amending various provisions of the Social Insurance Code on long-term care insurance, the Chamber of Deputies then examined the draft law and approved it in December 2005.

While retaining the basic principles of the 1998 law, the Law of 23 December 2005 introduces a number of specific amendments in particular concerning the benefits awarded, relations with providers of assistance and care and the tasks of the Assessment and Orientation Unit.

The new text also includes the creation of a Service Quality Committee whose task is to draw up guideline proposals and reference standards, in particular as regards the quality of assistance and care, technical aids and housing adaptations.

Given that the long-term care insurance is showing a budget deficit for the first time since it was introduced in 1999, a working group and think-tank has been set up in the Ministry of Social Security in order to review the operation of the long-term care insurance. The working group will review the various aspects and fields of long-term care insurance to examine which of these fields is functioning well and also to find out where costs are likely to raise major problems in future years. In a second phase, the working group will examine remedies to the problems identified.

## HEALTH CARE

Sickness/maternity insurance provides its members and their dependants with financial protection in the event of sickness or maternity. There are two separate strands to this protection:

the system of benefits in kind, i.e. the full or partial reimbursement of expenditure on health care,

the system of benefits in cash which replaces the occupational income lost as a result of leave for sickness or maternity.

Benefits in kind are financed from contributions and by a state contribution amounting to 37% of contributions. The state is responsible for financing all maternity benefits.

From an administrative point of view, the Union des Caisses de Maladie (UCM – Union of Sickness Funds) negotiates agreements with providers, sets the rules governing the rights and duties of insured persons and plays a centralising and coordinating role in respect of payments of benefits in kind and general accounting for sickness/maternity insurance. The task of the nine other sickness funds, organised by socio-occupational criteria, is simply to ensure direct contact with insured persons, manage the membership of family members and order the reimbursement of benefits in cash and in kind not subject to the direct settlement principle which is managed directly by the UCM.

**For additional analytical, business and investment opportunities information, please contact Global Investment & Business Center, USA at (202) 546-2103. Fax: (202) 546-3275. E-mail: rusric@erols.com**

## COVERAGE OF HEALTH CARE BENEFITS

Health care in Luxembourg is covered by a compulsory insurance system modelled on the Bismarckian insurance system. It covers all persons working in a regular occupation, whether employed or self-employed, in receipt of replacement income (sickness, maternity and unemployment benefits, invalidity, old-age and survivors' pensions, guaranteed minimum wage, etc.) or having asylum-seeker status. This principle applies to everyone regardless of occupational status or income level, except for those employed by international organisations. There is no freedom of choice in the area of insurance. Derogating from the principle of individual insurance, the law grants "derived rights" to the family members of insured persons (spouses, children) or their partners in cases when they do not have their own rights. The state pays the insurance contributions of students or children not having their own or derived rights.

People not eligible for compulsory insurance may join the insurance scheme on a voluntary basis.

The single and compulsory national system has a very high level of coverage: in 2003, as an annual average, 96.3%[76] of the resident population was covered by the public scheme. Some 2.4%[77] of the population are insured with private companies. Total coverage is estimated at 99.9%.

Persons insured under sickness/maternity insurance are entitled to health-care benefits from the first day of affiliation, with the exception of insured persons who have taken out optional insurance (voluntary insurance), who are entitled to health-care benefits only after a three-month qualifying period. If affiliation lapses, entitlement to health-care benefits continues for the month in question and the following three months, provided that the person concerned has been affiliated for at least six months.

## THE SUPPLY OF CARE

Sickness/maternity insurance covers the costs of the following services: medical or other outpatient care, laboratory analyses and tests, hospital care, pharmaceutical products, rehabilitation and spa cures, curative methods and prostheses and medical transport.

Health care is readily accessible:

People are free to choose a doctor and have direct access to specialists and hospital clinics. By way of international comparison, there is a relatively high stock of equipment and acute hospital beds (644.3 per 100 000 inhabitants in 2002[78]). Hospital facilities have been designed to meet the country's demographic needs and take account of some geographical features. As a result there are no regional inequalities in health facilities.

There is an adequate number of doctors and other health professionals. In 2003, there were 1 100 doctors (general practitioners and specialists), 314 dental surgeons and 4 087 nurses and midwives[79] in Luxembourg.

The average rate of reimbursement, based on sickness/maternity insurance tariffs, was estimated at 91.8% in 2004. However, the rate of reimbursement for the various types of service may vary greatly depending on their degree of usefulness or necessity. This relatively high rate of reimbursement explains why top-up insurance schemes have not developed to any great extent in Luxembourg. The only mutual society of any size in particular covers the per diem fees paid by hospital patients and also reimburses the costs of additional services (supplements for single bedrooms, etc.) exceeding the tariffs. It also covers, to a small extent, some dental care (see Annex 4.1).

**For additional analytical, business and investment opportunities information, please contact Global Investment & Business Center, USA at (202) 546-2103. Fax: (202) 546-3275. E-mail: rusric@erols.com**

Insured persons with financial problems may be entitled to fast-track reimbursement or even the pre-financing of some expensive services.

## HEALTH INDICATORS

As a result of a supply of care that meets the population's needs in the best possible way and universal access to care, the state of health of beneficiaries continues to improve. Life expectancy was 81.0 for women and 75.0 for men in 2003[80]. According to recent surveys, 74.7% of the Luxembourg population feels very well, and only 8.6% of the population considers that it is ill or very ill[81].

Since 1970, moreover, remarkable progress has been made as regards infant and perinatal mortality. Following the introduction of a protection programme for pregnant women in 1977 infant mortality fell from 25.0 in 1970 to 4.9 in 2003[82] and the perinatal mortality rate fell from 24.7 in 1970 to 5.3 in 2003[83].

*Promoting the quality of care*

Since 2004, there has been a new action programme for the health system and sickness insurance. Its aim is to improve the quality of health care and to keep sickness insurance financially balanced.

## INVESTMENT AND PLANNING POLICY

In order to meet the real needs of a protected resident population which is growing (increase of 1.4% between 2003 and 2004), the public authorities have supported a major hospital planning and investment policy.

In order to offer patients better quality care, the state is offering financial incentives to hospitals which create synergies or merge.

*Introduction of computerised systems for medical data*

Patients' free choice and doctors' ability freely to choose treatment methods are one of the strengths of the Luxembourg health system. This freedom may nevertheless mean that medical data are not efficiently handled, with a proliferation of technical operations, redundancy and duplication which pointlessly increase expenditure and certain risks.

More effective health care and better information can be coordinated by drawing up computerised or electronic medial records so that data on a patient can be exchanged electronically (image transfers – X-rays, endoscopies, etc. – emailing of the results of biological tests, etc.).

*Establishment of a Scientific Council and recommendations for good medical practice*

The remit of the Scientific Council, made up predominantly of practitioners, is to draw up good practice recommendations in order to influence practitioners' behaviour by proposing that they base their work on guides drawn up by scientific communities. These recommendations are based on a critical analysis of a large number of scientific studies and focus on the concrete and measurable results of clinical treatments ("evidence-based medicine").

*Judicious drug use*

**For additional analytical, business and investment opportunities information, please contact Global Investment & Business Center, USA at (202) 546-2103. Fax: (202) 546-3275. E-mail: rusric@erols.com**

As regards drug consumption, it is essential to promote judicious drug use to keep beneficiaries in good health and better to control health care expenditure. Since 2004, therefore, the Ministry of Health and the AMMD[84] have launched several campaigns to promote reasonable antibiotic and psychotropic use.

*Preventive medicine*

The main preventive medicine activities covered by sickness insurance include the medical monitoring of pregnant women and infants and programmes drawn up in conjunction with the Ministry of Health.

There are currently four of these preventive medicine programmes, co-financed by social security:

The programme for early breast cancer diagnosis by mammography aimed at women aged between 50 and 69.

The hepatitis B vaccination programme for infants and adolescents.

The vaccination programme against meningococcal meningitis C targeted on older people, children and young people aged from 1 to 18.

The flu vaccination programme for the population aged 65 and over and people at particular risk (2003 vaccination rate: 49.1%).

The Ministry of Health also supports the colorectal cancer screening programme for the population aged 50 and over, as well as the fight against tuberculosis and other infectious diseases organised by the Luxembourg League for Prevention and Medical and Social Action.

Alongside these primary prevention programmes, the Ministry of Health regularly runs campaigns to raise awareness of public health issues, for instance AIDS, prevention of osteoporosis and cardiovascular diseases, and smoking.

A new tool to improve quality using the EFQM[85] method was introduced in 2006.

*Combating smoking*

On 13 July 2006 the Chamber of Deputies passed a law restricting smoking in public places.

This law bans any advertising and sponsorship, and any sale of tobacco products to adolescents aged under 16.

Smoking in public places, cinemas, theatres, sports complexes, including school recreation areas, is now banned. Smoking is allowed in restaurants provided that the restaurant has an enclosed smoking section occupying at most one quarter of the restaurant's total area. Smoking is allowed in cafes unless they offer a restaurant service. In this case, smoking is prohibited from 12:00 to 14:00 and from 19:00 to 21:00 in the evening.

*Training and continuing training*

All health care providers (especially doctors and health professionals in general: nurses, physiotherapists, etc.) must, under their codes of ethics or European directives, or under their statutes or conventions with the UCM, maintain and improve their occupational and scientific knowledge through conferences, seminars, congresses, continuing training, etc., in Luxembourg and abroad.

*Patients' rights and duties*

The Law of 28 August 1998 on hospitals enshrines the fundamental rights of patients to:

information on their state of health and appropriate treatment,

patients' informed consent for any diagnostic and treatment measure,

access to their individual medical records which they may consult in situ (in hospital) or receive in copy form,

the professional confidentiality with which health professionals must comply, and the respect of integrity and dignity,

a free choice of doctor and hospital except in emergency cases.

*The Health Portal – Informing the public*

The Health Portal, which will come into operation in 2007, is designed as a tool to serve individual and public health:

prevention and promotion of healthy living,

greater responsibility for their own health on the part of citizens,

health safety for citizens and patients,

health information accessible to all citizens,

controlled use of health resources in order better to control health expenditure.

*4.2.4 Ensuring the financial viability of accessible and high-quality care*

*Health care service provision*

In Luxembourg, most doctors work either in private practice or as approved doctors in a hospital. Most other health professionals, with the exception of physiotherapists, are employees.

It is compulsory for all providers to be approved; as a result they have to comply with the nomenclatures and tariffs set out in laws and regulations.

The professional services and treatments provided by health care providers and covered by sickness insurance are included in various nomenclatures. Insured persons pay the charges for treatments directly to providers and are then reimbursed by the sickness funds. However, laboratory tests, hospital costs excluding medical costs, and pharmaceutical costs are covered directly by the UCM (direct settlement principle).

While doctors are paid per treatment, hospitals are financed by annual budgets negotiated with the UCM. Each budget has two strands: fixed costs not linked to their work and variable costs directly proportional to their work.

In 2002, total health care expenditure amounted to 6.1% of GDP[86] and reached an amount of € 2264.9 PPP per inhabitant. As health care is covered by a compulsory social security system, public expenditure on health care accounts for the majority of total expenditure. 85.4% of financing came from public insurance (social security and Luxembourg government) and 8.9% from private insurance in 2002[88].

Trends in the financial situation of the Luxembourg sickness insurance scheme are continuing to worsen. It is estimated, for instance, that acute health care expenditure will represent 6.3% of GDP by 2050 in comparison with 5.1% in 2004, i.e. an annual variation of 1.2%[89].

In order to contain and curb health care prescription and provision, the coverage of some services is restricted under the statutes of the UCM:

In the case of pharmaceutical products, insured persons pay a variable proportion of costs depending on the indication or presumed usefulness for treatment of the prescribed drug.

There are also restrictions on the number of physiotherapy sessions covered, unless a derogation is granted by social security's medical supervisory services.

Similarly, some non-urgent care is covered only by medical prescription following authorisation from the medical supervisory services: for instance spa cures, rehabilitation and re-education treatment, physiotherapy, speech therapy and psychomotor therapy.

Dental or other prostheses are covered solely on the basis of the fund's tariffs following presentation of an estimate.

From 1 January 2005, coverage of laboratory tests conducted outside hospitals is limited to a maximum of 12 examinations per prescription in order to encourage prescribing doctors to work in a more targeted way and in waves.

*Supervisory bodies*

The Quadripartite Committee The Quadripartite Committee monitors the implementation of the measures in force and examines the efficiency of these measures with a view to improving the quality of care, ensuring that the insurance scheme remains financially balanced and maintaining the performance of the health care system.

In the light of this information, the Quadripartite Committee may propose new directions in order to ensure a high-quality health care system at a cost which can be afforded.

The Steering Committee

Under the auspices of the Ministry of Health and Social Security, a Steering Committee bringing together government experts on health and social security has been set up to monitor trends in revenue and expenditure and assist concerted action.

The remit of this Committee is to prepare for meetings of the Quadripartite Committee by supervising and coordinating the work of the various working groups examining the issues raised by the common action priorities decided.

*Introduction of a central purchasing unit*

In order to contain the increase in variable hospital costs, it is being envisaged to organise central purchasing and to introduce a single drug distribution system in each hospital.

*Incapacity for work*

A new legislative provision introduced in 2005 is intended to improve the management and coverage of long-term incapacity for work.

Financial benefits are no longer awarded after ten weeks of incapacity for work during a reference period of twenty weeks unless the insured person submits a detailed report from his or her doctor (form R4). This form enables social security's medical supervisory services to direct the insured person to the appropriate system of coverage (continued financial benefit, disability pension, occupational re-integration measure or return to work) and to disallow improper applications.

*The introduction of "generic" drugs*

In order to contain unnecessary expenditure resulting from the prescription and therefore consumption of costly branded drugs, a campaign to promote generic drugs was launched at the beginning of 2006.

A list can be consulted on the UCM website (http://www.ucm.lu/).

**LONG-TERM CARE**

The Law of 19 June 1998 introducing the long-term care insurance recognised dependence as a new social security risk alongside sickness, industrial accidents, disability and old-age.

The purpose of the long-term care insurance is to offset the costs resulting from the need for assistance from a third person for the essential acts of daily living. As part of social security, dependent persons are entitled to long-term care insurance benefits without means-testing.

This law introduces the following main provisions:

creation of a compulsory insurance whose scope of application is modelled on that of sickness/maternity insurance,

introduction for protected persons of an unconditional entitlement to benefits in kind and, as an ancillary, to cash benefits to enable them to obtain care and assistance with the essential acts of daily living from third persons,

introduction of a system of assessment, guidance and coverage for dependent persons run by the Cellule d'Evaluation et d'Orientation (Assessment and Orientation Unit) (see Annex 4.1),

• organisation of relations with providers of assistance and care in the framework of home care and residential care (see Annex 4.1),

**For additional analytical, business and investment opportunities information, please contact Global Investment & Business Center, USA at (202) 546-2103. Fax: (202) 546-3275. E-mail: rusric@erols.com**

introduction of a mixed financing system placing this new form of insurance on a sound financial basis.

The provisions of the law are based on four guiding principles, i.e.:

rehabilitation measures take priority over long-term care care,

keeping people at home takes priority over placement in residential homes,

benefits in kind take priority over cash benefits,

coverage of long-term care has to be continuous.

Long-term care insurance is administered by the UCM which makes decisions on individual cases and manages the budget.

*Ensuring access to care: universality, equity and solidarity*

Any dependent person insured under sickness/maternity insurance is eligible for benefits irrespective of their age. People insured under the compulsory scheme and people insured under a continuing insurance scheme are protected under long-term care insurance from the first day of affiliation. People who have taken out optional insurance are eligible for benefits after a qualifying period of one year.

Persons working for international organisations or receiving a pension from such organisations are not eligible for long-term care insurance benefits.

Long-term care insurance benefits are awarded if applicants have been assessed as needing assistance from a third person for the essential acts of daily living in the areas of nutrition, hygiene and mobility: the need for assistance and care has to be substantial and regular and account for at least 3.5 hours per week.

Long-term care insurance awards the following benefits in kind: benefits for the essential acts of daily living, domestic chores, support activities, products needed for assistance and care, technical aids and home adaptations.

Benefits in kind may be replaced by cash benefits, for up to a maximum of 10.5 hours per week, to ensure that highly dependent people can receive professional and high-quality care.

The insurance also provides other measures for informal carers:

coverage of care at home or respite care in a semi-permanent facility for dependent persons so that informal carers can have periods of respite,

payment of pension insurance contributions,

possibility of replacement of informal carers for three weeks to allow them to take a period of leave,

coverage of advisory services for informal carers (learning about appropriate care practices, etc.).

**For additional analytical, business and investment opportunities information, please contact Global Investment & Business Center, USA at (202) 546-2103. Fax: (202) 546-3275. E-mail: rusric@erols.com**

Persons needing assistance from a third person for some activities of daily living who are not eligible for long-term care insurance (in particular persons whose need is below the required minimum threshold) may receive the assistance which they need by paying a contribution to the cost of care services provided in a residential care context, calculated according to an income-related social tariff. The state pays the provider the difference between the beneficiary's financial contribution set according to the social tariff and the actual cost of the service.

On 23 December 2005, a new law, which retained the basic principles of the 1998 law, introduced a number of specific amendments in particular concerning the benefits awarded.

As regards access to benefits, for instance, the law provides for a derogation from the minimum threshold of 3.5 hours of care required for home adaptations, technical aids and experimental action projects.

Assessment of people's dependence by the CEO provides valuable information which can be used to improve care conditions both at home and in institutions. This information should make it possible to plan permanent and semi-permanent infrastructure in the short and medium term and to decide on services to be phased out, extended or created.

37 new construction, conversion and renovation plans for integrated centres for older people, care homes, psycho-geriatric centres and pensioners' clubs were handled by the Ministry of the Family in 2005. In addition, 15 projects for disabled people, to which the state is contributing € 88.8 million (day centres, accommodation facilities, etc.), are being drawn up.

General hospitals are at present responsible for covering and providing palliative care. They are required, especially in incurable and terminal cases, to ease the physical and mental suffering of patients, to avoid any undue prolongation of life by medical means, to maintain quality of life for as long as possible and to allow a close relative to stay permanently with the patient in circumstances that respect their dignity. Hospitals are free to organise the palliative care that they offer as they wish, either in specially adapted units or through specialist mobile teams.

The Ministry of Health and the Ministry of the Family have recently tabled a new draft law on palliative care. Through this draft law, the Luxembourg Government is intending to promote palliative care provision outside hospitals (care homes, own homes), to provide funding through social security (sickness and long-term care insurance), to prevent any criminal penalties or civil action for damages against practitioners refusing or unwilling to arrange for inappropriate examinations and treatment, to prevent any undue prolongation of life by medical means, and to offer attendance leave of up to five days to close family when people are dying. Patients may, moreover, set out their wishes in respect of the conditions, limits on and discontinuation of treatment in a document known as an "advance guideline". This document is held by the person's doctor or by another person of trust.

In order to raise awareness of palliative care, the Ministry of Health regularly organises lecture cycles aimed largely at medical practitioners and other health workers.

In parallel, the Luxembourg association for palliative care and assistance for people at the end of their lives and the bereaved offers specialist training in this field for care workers, nurses, social workers and auxiliaries working in hospitals, care and assistance networks, facilities for older people, etc.

*Promoting the quality of care*

*Standards*

Requirements to ensure the quality of long-term care are set out in two legal provisions: approval is needed to carry on an activity and an assistance and care contract has to be signed.

In practice, only assistance and care establishments and networks approved by the Ministry whose portfolio includes the family may enter into an assistance and care contract with the UCM and be entitled to remuneration from long-term care insurance in return for the services in kind that they provide for dependent persons (see Annex 4.1, Relations with providers).

The ministerial approval sets the establishment's operating conditions, in particular as regards appropriate staffing levels for the tasks that it is to perform and the infrastructure needed to ensure an appropriate quality of care and assistance. The approval covers requirements in terms of *structural* quality, however, and does not set quality standards as regards the actual care (process quality).

Assistance and care contracts set out the rights and obligations of long-term care providers within the framework of long-term care insurance. They cover both types of provider operating within long-term care insurance, i.e. assistance and care homes for persons in permanent accommodation and assistance and care networks for persons continuing to live in their own homes.

*Providing high-quality care*

Bearing in mind demographic changes among older people in Luxembourg (44 544 people aged 70 or over in 2003[90] in comparison with 45 121 people in 2004[91], i.e. an increase of 1.3%), and the creation of new facilities for old and very old people, the risk of a shortage of competent and motivated supervisory staff has become a worrying concern for the Luxembourg public authorities. Training in geriatrics and continuing training in gerontology play a key role here.

In January 2002, therefore, the Ministry of the Family, Social Solidarity and Youth, the Ministry of Culture, Higher Education and Research, Luxembourg University and the Benelux University Centre foundation signed an agreement to set up a university-level training scheme leading to a "masters in gerontology".

Training is also run jointly by the Ministry of the Family and the Ministry of Education for social/family workers. This is supplemented by lectures organised by the Ministry of the Family, in the context of "quality management", on the topic of quality in the old-age sector in Luxembourg, and courses and training days for old-age and geriatric professionals run by the RBS training institute[92].

*Improving the quality of care*

Given the current long-term care insurance deficit, a working group and think-tank has been set up at the Ministry of Social Security in order to review the operation of long-term care insurance. The working group is reviewing the various aspects and fields of long-term care insurance to examine which fields are functioning well and also to find out in which fields costs are likely to spiral out of control in future years. In a second phase, this working group will look at ways of remedying the problems identified.

In parallel with this work, the Department of Social Security is conducting a satisfaction survey among beneficiaries and their families (planned to begin in September 2006).

A Service Quality Commission has also been set up and asked to draw up proposals for guidelines and reference standards in particular for assistance and care quality, technical aids

**For additional analytical, business and investment opportunities information, please contact Global Investment & Business Center, USA at (202) 546-2103. Fax: (202) 546-3275. E-mail: rusric@erols.com**

and home adaptations. A further task of the Assessment and Orientation Unit (CEO) is to inspect the quality of the services provided for dependent persons, taking account of agreed standards.

Relations between long-term care insurance and the various type of assistance and care providers are now governed by the framework agreements negotiated with the UCM.

*Ensuring the financial viability of accessible and high-quality care*

*Financing system*

In order to cope with the burdens incumbent upon it, long-term care insurance applies a system of distribution of charges, establishing a reserve which cannot be below 10% or above 20% of the annual amount of current expenditure. This upper limit will be withdrawn when a new law on long-term care insurance comes into force in January 2007.

In terms of the resources needed to finance long-term care insurance, 45% of total expenditure comes from a state budget contribution.

In 2004, however, the state contribution was reduced to 40% of total expenditure and from 2007 the state contribution will remain fixed at the 2006 amount.

A special contribution also comes from revenue from the electricity tax.

The remainder is financed by a long-term care contribution. This contribution is levied on all persons insured under sickness/maternity insurance. It is calculated on occupational income, income from assets and replacement income. It is set at 1%, but will be raised to a rate of 1.4% from 1 January 2007.

*Supervisory bodies*

The Consultative Committee The Consultative Committee, composed of representatives of long-term care insurance beneficiaries, representatives of providers and the social partners and representatives of the managing body, is asked for its opinion on:

methods of assessing and measuring dependence, i.e. the assessment questionnaire and the assistance and care review;

experimental action projects to be run under long-term care insurance for the benefit of specific groups;

the list of appliances to be covered by long-term care insurance.

Concerted action on long-term care insurance

In order to be able improve action for dependent persons, the Minister for Social Security periodically convenes those ministers whose portfolios include the family, health and the budget, organisations working in the fields of health, the family and social action and associations representing dependent persons.

The task of this committee is to examine the operation of long-term care insurance, assistance and care networks and establishments and to issue proposals to improve the situation and the coverage of dependent persons.

**For additional analytical, business and investment opportunities information, please contact Global Investment & Business Center, USA at (202) 546-2103. Fax: (202) 546-3275. E-mail: rusric@erols.com**

## ADDITIONAL INFORMATION

*Mutual societies in Luxembourg*

Mutual societies in Luxembourg are run in accordance with the following basic principles:

solidarity: members join together with a view to mutual aid;

voluntary nature: membership of mutual societies is freely and voluntarily chosen;

lack of any profit-making motive: mutual societies are non-profit societies of people;

non-exclusion: mutual societies are open to all socio-occupational groups and no risks are excluded on grounds of age, state of health, etc.;

autonomy: members are insurers and insured persons and take part, through representatives, in the management of their society;

democracy: directors of societies are democratically elected;

social welfare: mutual societies play their part in social welfare together with the social security authorities.

The basic law (Law of 7 July 1961) on mutual societies confirms that mutual aid societies, complying with the obligations set out in the law, must be governed by mutual principles.

While the mutual societies recognised by the state are independent and autonomous, they are nevertheless subject to supervision by the Ministry of Social Security, which ensures strict compliance with the legal and regulatory provisions on both their services and financial management. The Higher Council on Mutual Societies (CSM) carries out these tasks on behalf of the Government member responsible for mutual societies, the Minister for Health and Social Security.

As a Government body, the CSM is also responsible for advising the Minister for Social Security on all matters connected with mutual societies. The relevant legislation and regulations therefore state that the Minister must ask the CSM for its opinion before approving a mutual aid society, or approving its statutes or subsequent amendments of statutes. If societies are merged or dissolved, the CSM also carries out liquidation operations prior to ministerial approval.

There are no mandatory rules on the services provided by mutual societies. They are set by the statutes of each society and must be approved, before they come into force, by the Minister for Social Security.

Mutual societies offer the following services:

full or partial coverage of ineligible health care costs (services not covered by the sickness funds of the compulsory scheme);

funeral costs, allowances in the event of accidents or disability;

family allowances (birth grants, grants at the time of other family events such as marriages).

**For additional analytical, business and investment opportunities information, please contact Global Investment & Business Center, USA at (202) 546-2103. Fax: (202) 546-3275. E-mail: rusric@erols.com**

Some of the services listed above are offered by services or societies set up by mutual aid societies as a whole, predominantly the Caisse médico-chirurgicale mutualiste (CMCM – Mutual Medical and Surgical Fund).

*The Cellule d'évaluation et d'orientation (CEO – Assessment and Orientation Unit)*

The CEO is a public service answerable to the Minister for Social Security and attached for administrative purposes to the Inspectorate General for Social Security.

In addition to its tasks of assessing and deciding on the benefits to which dependent people are entitled, the CEO is also required to:

give opinions on the award of benefits in kind and in cash, the products needed for assistance and care, appliances and home adaptations, and opinions in cases of withdrawal, reduction or cancellation of benefits;

propose, where appropriate, what re-education and rehabilitation measures are needed;

propose whether to keep people in their own homes or admit them to assistance and care institutions;

centralise data on supply and demand as regards assistance and care institutions and specialist day centres, a task which has up to now not been carried out;

assess the urgency of applications to enter care institutions.

A further task of the CEO is to provide information and advice on long-term care for all the bodies working in the field.

The CEO is organised on an interdisciplinary basis. It includes health professionals, doctors, nurses, psychologists, occupational therapists, physiotherapists, social workers and administrative staff. To carry out its tasks, it may, where appropriate, call on outside experts.

*Relations with providers*

The two main types of provider in long-term care insurance are assistance and care institutions and assistance and care networks.

**ASSISTANCE AND CARE INSTITUTIONS**

Assistance and care institutions are institutions accommodating dependent people day and night and providing them with the care required by their state of dependence.

Assistance and care networks

The network is an organised unit of one or more natural or legal persons, operating throughout a geographical area, with different and complementary competences in order to provide and coordinate all the care needed by dependent people.

The network structure means that dependent people can deal with a single person. It also makes it possible to ensure the continuity of assistance and care when people are living at home.

**For additional analytical, business and investment opportunities information, please contact Global Investment & Business Center, USA at (202) 546-2103. Fax: (202) 546-3275. E-mail: rusric@erols.com**

Approval

Since 1999, any natural or legal person has required ministerial approval to work in the social, socio-educational, medical and social and treatment fields. The work subject to such approval in particular includes:

day or night care and accommodation for more than three people at once;

provision of consultation and aid, and care, assistance, guidance, social training and vocational aid and guidance services.

The approval sets out all the conditions under which the work for which it is issued can be performed. In particular, it sets out:

the type of population for which the work in question is intended;

standards as regards the number and qualifications of staff required to perform the work;

standards as regards staff supervision;

requirements as regards the infrastructure in which the work is performed: safety, hygiene, cleanliness, specific adaptations needed for the population for which the work is intended;

requirements as regards the timetable for the performance of the work;

methods of supervising compliance with these requirements and penalties.

The assistance and care contract

Long-term care insurance providers undertake to provide and coordinate all the assistance and care that dependent people need, not just assistance and care under long-term care insurance but all health care under sickness/maternity insurance and all services and persons involved with the dependent person. This enables a global and multidisciplinary approach to the person requiring care. It also means that dependent people are in contact with only one service for all of their care.

Providers undertake to ensure that care is continuous, both during the day and at night, every day of the year. This provision also applies when people are living at home.

Providers undertake to document the assistance and care provided according to particular methods. There are two strands to the documentation of assistance and care: external documentation in which the provider provides proof that the assistance and care has been provided, and internal documentation. The internal documentation is in practice the dependent person's care log in which the provider enters all the relevant information on the dependent person being cared for. This documentation is drawn up according to standard rules. The internal documentation in particular includes all personal identification details, prior information, medical data, a full care history, care methods, treatments, clinical supervision and data on action by other providers.

Providers undertake to conclude a care contract with each person cared for which sets out the rights and obligations of both.

**For additional analytical, business and investment opportunities information, please contact Global Investment & Business Center, USA at (202) 546-2103. Fax: (202) 546-3275. E-mail: rusric@erols.com**

An assistance and care contract cannot be concluded with an institution which has not been approved to carry on the activities that it offers.

Key to the standard assistance and care review

Place: environment in which the assistance and care may be provided, H = home, I = assistance and care institution.

TRW: Time required per week; TRWS1: TRW weighted by the intensity coefficient; TRWS2: TRWS1 weighted by the qualification coefficient.

Child intensity coefficient (ci): For children, the additional need for assistance from a third person in comparison with an able-bodied and mentally unimpaired child of the same age is calculated from a development scale. The mean of the scores obtained for the child on this scale for each activity of daily of living makes it possible to calculate an individual intensity coefficient which is applied to the standard times for adults in order to calculate the additional time needed for the assistance and care required by the child.

MRQ: Minimum qualification required for assistance and care: 1 (none – 0.7); 2 (socialfamily worker – 1); 3 (carer – 1); 4 (nurse – 1.3); 5 (psychiatric nurse – 1.3); 6 (occupational therapist – 1.5); 7 (physiotherapist – 1.5); 8 (psychologist – 1.9); 9 (educator – 1.1); 10 (social worker – 1.5).

The following qualifications are still accepted, without any change to the MRQ for assistance and care: graduate hospital nurse, anaesthetic nurse, graduate educator, psychomotor specialist, curative pedagogue, speech therapist.

In comparison with its neighbours, Luxembourg is an exception as the proportion of total expenditure on drugs for which generics account is practically zero. While, in terms of turnover, the prescription of generics averages above 12% in Europe, the figure for the Grand Duchy is below 2%[93]. In terms of prescription volume, the figure for Luxembourg is probably below 5%, while Belgium is announcing around 10% for 2005. In neighbouring countries (Netherlands, Germany, United Kingdom), over 50% of all prescriptions are for generics.

The proportion of generics could easily be increased, especially as a result of the arrival of new generics containing compounds which are prescribed in large volumes (the anti-ulcer drug omeprazol and the cholesterol-reducing agent simvastatin), without the quality of patent care being reduced in any way.

New compounds which are still protected by patent (and for which there is as yet no competition on price) account for a very substantial proportion of reimbursements for drugs. A number of these compounds treat new diseases or are clearly more effective than preceding treatments. In many cases, however, the new compound represents only a very limited medical advance[94].

In the case of a fairly substantial proportion of prescribed drugs, there is now an equivalent treatment alternative which is less expensive (generic drug or original drug at a lower price). While drugs are therefore a very important factor in the sickness insurance budget, substantial savings could nevertheless be made with no adverse effects on quality.

1. Why prescribe generics?

Generics are copies which are essentially the same as the original drug. After the exclusive right to the original has lapsed, any laboratory may produce a generic drug,

**For additional analytical, business and investment opportunities information, please contact Global Investment & Business Center, USA at (202) 546-2103. Fax: (202) 546-3275. E-mail: rusric@erols.com**

i.e. a drug containing the same active principle which has been shown to be bioequivalent to the original branded drug. Before it is marketed, a marketing authorisation has to be obtained for the drug. During this procedure, the generic drug has to satisfy the same criteria of safety, effectiveness and quality as the original drug.

While generics are therefore equivalent from this point of view, they also make it possible to curb increases in health expenditure.

Generics cost patients less. The first generic that arrives on the market is generally much less expensive than the original (20 to 40%). Through competition, generics help to reduce the price of original drugs once the research costs for those drugs have been offset (i.e. when the patent lapses).

Generic drugs may therefore help to contain increases in the sickness insurance budget, releasing funds for new drugs to treat new needs which offer a significant medical contribution. There are no adverse effects on research, therefore, as the pharmaceutical industry is in contrast encouraged to develop new drugs when the profit margin on drugs whose patents have lapsed decreases.

The campaign to prescribe generics aims to promote the use of generics when they offer an alternative but equivalent form of treatment, but are much less expensive. The doctor's concern must nevertheless be to limit any prescription to what is useful and necessary in view of the patient's state of health.

2. Generic or original whose patent has lapsed?

The arrival of a generic is often needed to trigger a reduction of the price of the original whose patent has lapsed. Whether doctors then prescribe generics or originals if their price has fallen to the same level as the generic, the advantages for the patient and for sickness insurance are the same.

Alignments of the prices of originals to generics therefore need to be taken into account in the penetration level of generics. However, in Luxembourg, generic use is the lowest in Europe and the margin for reduction is substantial.

3. The campaign aims to make the public and doctors more aware of generics

The campaign targets the systematic prescription of the least expensive drug when this drug represents an alternative treatment of equivalent quality.

The campaign is being launched for the first time in 2006 and aims to make patients much more aware with a view to changing attitudes towards drug prescription which are still too conservative.

Taking a pragmatic approach, the campaign is initially limited to seven active principles selected because it is felt that all the preliminary procedures as regards marketing and the Luxembourg medical environment have been completed. This initiative will nevertheless be extended to other products. It is hoped that the approach now being taken will become a permanent way of curbing sickness insurance expenditure by encouraging a responsible attitude to drug prescription and consumption.

a) Informing providers and making them more aware:

**For additional analytical, business and investment opportunities information, please contact Global Investment & Business Center, USA at (202) 546-2103. Fax: (202) 546-3275. E-mail: rusric@erols.com**

A lack of information and awareness on the part of doctors is one of the main reasons for the failure to use less expensive products.

It is often difficult for doctors to find their way in a market in which the products on offer and the prices charged change rapidly. To remedy this, a comparative list showing key comparative information on the active principles selected will be made available to prescribing doctors on the Internet[95] and attached to the round robin sent to all doctors. The comparative list published on the Internet will be updated every month.

The Minister for Health and Social Security particularly welcomes the support of the AMMD (Association of Physicians and Dental Surgeons) and the Union of Pharmacists for the campaign launched today. The success of the campaign depends largely on the support of the professionals who advise patients when issuing and making up prescriptions.

While the poster and leaflet awareness campaign primarily targets patients, professionals will also be informed and made aware through a collective letter signed by the Minister, the AMMD, the Union of Sickness Funds (UMC) and the Union of Pharmacists. A second letter will enclose a poster focusing on the campaign themes for prescribing doctors and pharmacists, who will be invited to display it in their waiting or consulting rooms or in their pharmacies, together with leaflets for patients. These may be ordered free of charge from the UCM.

b) Informing patients and making them more aware:

One of the factors in the low level of use of generic drugs is that patients know too little about them and are therefore wary of taking them.

So that prescribing doctors can continue to play their advisory role in a dispassionate way, a public information campaign will start in mid-February 2006.

This campaign targets generic drugs, as any information campaign which is to be effective has to give a simple message. It has therefore been decided to focus on a simple message about the existence, quality and lower cost of generic drugs, as too little is often known about these drugs with the result that people are wary of them. The aim of the campaign is therefore to allay public mistrust. The use of original drugs whose price has dropped may nevertheless provide the same financial savings.

c) Prescription by DCI:

When they write out prescriptions, doctors are not always aware of all the brands available on the market or those available from the pharmacist to whom the patient goes to have the prescription made up.

While it has been possible for some years to prescribe using the International Common Denomination (DCI)[96], i.e. using the name of the compound, doctors have not been very aware of this option.

When writing out prescriptions, doctors may opt for a brand name (original or generic) or the DCI. They are still free, therefore, to offer the treatment they think fit.

If the doctor chooses the DCI, the pharmacist provides the patient either with a generic or with a branded drug whose price has fallen to the same level. If the doctor prescribes using the DCI and there is no generic or cheaper alternative, the pharmacist provides the original compound.

**For additional analytical, business and investment opportunities information, please contact Global Investment & Business Center, USA at (202) 546-2103. Fax: (202) 546-3275. E-mail: rusric@erols.com**

# IMPORTANT GOVERNMENT AND BUSINESS CONTACTS

## CHAMBRE DE COMMERCE DU GRAND-DUCHÉ DE LUXEMBOURG

Bureaux : 7, rue Alcide de Gasperi
Adresse postale : L-2981 Luxembourg
Tél. : (+352) 42 39 39 - 1 (Standard)
Fax : (+352) 43 83 26
E-mail : chamcom@cc.lu

| **Services** | **Téléphone** | **E-mail** |
|---|---|---|
| Affiliation, cotisations | 42 39 39 - 250 | affiliation@cc.lu |
| Bourse d'entreprises | 42 39 39 - 354<br>42 39 39 - 332 | sarah.tamai@cc.lu<br>paola.pierotti@cc.lu |
| Commerce extérieur | 42 39 39 - 310 | comex@cc.lu |
| Certificats numériques | 42 39 39 - 310 | globalsign-lux@cc.lu |
| Conseil et assistance aux PME | 42 39 39 - 330 | pme@cc.lu |
| Centre de formalités | 42 39 39 - 330 | centre.de.formalites@cc.lu |
| Centre d'arbitrage de la Chambre de Commerce | 42 39 39 - 300 | iccl@cc.lu |
| Etudes économiques | 42 39 39 - 350 | carlo.thelen@cc.lu |
| Euro Info Centre PME/PMI | 42 39 39 - 333 | eic@cc.lu |
| Formation professionnelle initiale | 42 39 39 - 210 | formprof@cc.lu |
| Formation professionnelle continue | 42 39 39 - 220 | formcont@cc.lu |
| Formation professionnelle accélérée | 42 39 39 - 220 | formcont@cc.lu |
| Mutualité d'assistance aux commerçants | 26 47 42 42 | |
| Mutualité de cautionnement et d'aide aux commerçants | 42 39 39 - 339 | mcac@cc.lu |
| Office du Ducroire | 42 39 39 - 320 | odl@cc.lu |
| Publications | 42 39 39 - 380 | merkur@cc.lu |
| Service juridique | 42 39 39 - 360 | pme@cc.lu |

## Accountancy and Banking Supervision Committee

LESSEL Carlo, Président (Banque Générale du Luxembourg S.A.)
Suppléant: SCHROEDER Daniel (Banque Générale du Luxembourg S.A.)

CRELOT André-Marie, Vice-Président (Kredietbank S.A. Luxembourgeoise)
Suppléant: DE LIEVRE Marc (Kredietbank S.A. Luxembourgeoise)

DEBRY Jean-Luc (Svenska Handelsbanken S.A.)
Suppléant: FIORDALSIO Marie-France (Nordea Bank S.A.)

DONNEAUX Eric (Nomura Bank (Luxembourg) S.A.)
Suppléant: PALLUCCA Agueda (Bank of Tokyo-Mitsubishi (Luxembourg) S.A.)

DOS SANTOS Emmanuel (J.P. Morgan Bank Luxembourg S.A.)
Suppléant: OLIVIER Jérôme (Brown Brothers Harriman (Luxembourg) S.C.A.)

DURAND Philippe (Crédit Agricole Indosuez Luxembourg)
Suppléant: ELSEN Guy (Banque de Luxembourg)

ENGEL Doris (Banque et Caisse d'Epargne de l'Etat, Luxembourg)
Suppléant: BELLI Rodolphe (Banque et Caisse d'Epargne de l'Etat, Luxembourg)

GERAETS Jo (ABN AMRO Bank (Luxembourg) S.A.)

HAMEN Frank (Banque LBLux S.A.)
Suppléant: ZISSELSBERGER Manfred (Deutsche Bank Luxembourg S.A.)

HOSTE Marc (Banque BCP S.A.)
Suppléant: HAYES Robin (Banco Bradesco Luxembourg S.A.)

KAINZ Gerhard (Pfandbrief Bank International S.A.)
Suppléant: SIEMANN Walter (EUROHYPO Europäische Hypothekenbank S.A.)

PAULY Paul (UBS (Luxembourg) S.A.)
Suppléant: SPRUNCK Daniel (VP Bank (Luxembourg) S.A.)

SCHUMACKER Jean-Pol (Fideuram Bank (Luxembourg) S.A.)
Suppléant: UNSEN Christian (Société Européenne de Banque S.A.)

SERGIEL Philippe (PricewaterhouseCoopers sàrl)
Suppléant: WEYDERT Marianne (PricewaterhouseCoopers sàrl)

SOLBREUX Sylviane (Dexia Banque Internationale à Luxembourg)
Suppléant: GOFFLOT Jean-Louis (Dexia Banque Internationale à Luxembourg)

Assistent:

LINSTER Marc (Banque Centrale du Luxembourg)
Suppléant: DAWANCE Bruno (Banque Centrale du Luxembourg)

MOAYED SANANDAJI Vafa (Deloitte & Touche S.A.)

**Audit Committee**

HAAS Pia, Président (Dexia Banque Internationale à Luxembourg)
Suppléant: PLAKIDES Ariane (Dexia Banque Internationale à Luxembourg)

BLAISE Adelin (Kredietbank S.A. Luxembourgeoise)
Suppléant: HANSEN Daniel (Kredietbank S.A. Luxembourgeoise)

BOUREAU Guy (BNP Paribas Luxembourg)
Suppléant: CHRISTOPHE Frédéric (Banque de Luxembourg)

BURR Graham (ABN AMRO Bank (Luxembourg) S.A.)
Suppléant: CHILLET Patrick (ING Luxembourg S.A.)

GASPAR Paul (Banque et Caisse d'Epargne de l'Etat, Luxembourg)
Suppléant: SCHAMBOURG Jean-Nicolas (Banque et Caisse d'Epargne de l'Etat, Luxembourg)

HAGEMEIER Gerd (Erste Europäische Pfandbrief- und Kommunalkreditbank A.G.)

HAUBERT Cécile (State Street Bank Luxembourg S.A.)
Suppléant: MONDONI Jacqueline (Brown Brothers Harriman (Luxembourg) S.C.A.)

MAJEWSKI Jean-René (Credem International (Lux) S.A.)
Suppléant: MERTENS Hugo (Banca Lombarda International S.A.)

OLINGER Marc (Banque Générale du Luxembourg S.A.)
Suppléant: PETRY Roger (Banque Générale du Luxembourg S.A.)

PERVEZ Ajmal A. (Nomura Bank (Luxembourg) S.A.)
Suppléant: DREES Laurent (Bank of Tokyo-Mitsubishi (Luxembourg) S.A.)

RAU Axel (DZ BANK International S.A.)
Suppléant: HOFFMANN Nico (Dresdner Bank Luxembourg S.A.)

SCHMITZ Alex (Banque Safra-Luxembourg S.A.)

WEISSENBACHER Catherine (Credit Suisse (Luxembourg) S.A.)
Suppléant: ESPEN Huguette (United European Bank (Luxembourg) S.A.)

**Markets Committee**

DIBUS Reinolf, Président (EUROHYPO Europäische Hypothekenbank S.A.)
Suppléant: KELLOW Clive (Erste Europäische Pfandbrief- und Kommunalkreditbank A.G.)

TRUYENS Denis, Vice-Président (ING Luxembourg S.A.)
Suppléant: VAN DEN AMEELE Chris (ABN AMRO Bank (Luxembourg) S.A.)

CAYTAN Luc (Kredietbank S.A. Luxembourgeoise)
Suppléant: FISCHER Rafik (Kredietbank S.A. Luxembourgeoise)

**For additional analytical, business and investment opportunities information, please contact Global Investment & Business Center, USA at (202) 546-2103. Fax: (202) 546-3275. E-mail: rusric@erols.com**

GIALLOMBARDO Giovanni (UniCredito Italiano SpA, Luxembourg Branch)

KOHLL Aly (Banque et Caisse d'Epargne de l'Etat, Luxembourg)
Suppléant: CROCHET Alain (Banque et Caisse d'Epargne de l'Etat, Luxembourg)

LICOPPE François (Crédit Lyonnais Luxembourg S.A.)
Suppléant: KAUFFMANN Bertrand (Société Générale Bank & Trust)

PARDANAUD Gérard (Danske Bank International S.A.)

PEFFER Claude (ING BHF-BANK International S.A.)
Suppléant: FRIEDRICH Norbert (DZ BANK International S.A.)

SCHON Claude (Dexia Banque Internationale à Luxembourg)
Suppléant: MUNSTER Henry (Dexia Banque Internationale à Luxembourg)

SCHULTE Martin (Pfandbrief Bank International S.A.)

THESING Walter (UBS (Luxembourg) S.A.)
Suppléant: TÜFFERS Frank (VP Bank (Luxembourg) S.A.)

THILL Jean (Banque Générale du Luxembourg S.A.)
Suppléant: RIES Alain (Banque Générale du Luxembourg S.A.)

VIGNOLLE Giorgio (Banca Popolare Commercio e Industria International S.A.)
Suppléant: Di STEFANO Marco (Banca Popolare dell' Emilia Romagna Intl S.A.)

Assistent:

ZENNER François (Banque Centrale du Luxembourg)
Suppléant: WELSCHER Patrick (Banque Centrale du Luxembourg)

**Fiscal Committee**

NEU Francis, Président (Banque Générale du Luxembourg S.A.)
Suppléant: HOFFMANN André (Banque Générale du Luxembourg S.A.)

LOESCH-SCHROEDER Annette, Vice-Président (Banque de Luxembourg)
Suppléant: MOINIL Dominique (Crédit Lyonnais Luxembourg S.A.)

BARP Gianfranco (Banco Popolare di Verona e Novara S.c.r.l., Luxembourg Branch)
Suppléant: BROCCA Massimo (Fideuram Bank (Luxembourg) S.A.)

BASTENDORFF Gilles (Bank of Tokyo-Mitsubishi (Luxembourg) S.A.)

CABAY Béatrice (Banque Degroof Luxembourg S.A.)
Suppléant: DELHERS Isabelle (ING Luxembourg S.A.)

DE VULPIAN Olivier (Erste Europäische Pfandbrief- und Kommunalkreditbank A.G.)

HOCHWEILER André (Dexia Banque Internationale à Luxembourg)
Suppléant: DELFORGE Laurence (Dexia Banque Internationale à Luxembourg)

HUBERT Olivier (Kredietbank S.A. Luxembourgeoise)
Suppléant: BATARDY Frederic (Kredietbank S.A. Luxembourgeoise)

KLAR Christian (WestLB International S.A.)
Suppléant: MERTENS Peter (HVB Banque Luxembourg)

LÖYTYNOJA Hanna (Clearstream Banking)

MAHAUX Jacques (Crédit Agricole Indosuez Luxembourg)
Suppléant: AUGIER Marc (Société Générale Bank & Trust)

PAULY Paul (UBS (Luxembourg) S.A.)
Suppléant: KRAEMER Markus (Credit Suisse (Luxembourg) S.A.)

PUTZEIS Caroline (J.P. Morgan Bank Luxembourg S.A.)
Suppléant: DENOTTE Charles (Citibank International plc, Luxembourg Branch)

WARINGO Paul (Banque et Caisse d'Epargne de l'Etat, Luxembourg)
Suppléant: WILMES Jean-Claude (Banque et Caisse d'Epargne de l'Etat, Luxembourg)

**Pension funds Committee**

MAHAUX Jacques, Président (Crédit Agricole Indosuez Luxembourg)
Suppléant: KELLER Mario (Banque de Luxembourg)

BOFFERDING Jacques (Banque Générale du Luxembourg S.A.)
Suppléant: FEIERSTEIN Mario (Banque Générale du Luxembourg S.A.)

FISCHER Rafik (Kredietbank S.A. Luxembourgeoise)
Suppléant: CAEYMAEX Jean-François (Kredietbank S.A. Luxembourgeoise)

HELFFERICH Thomas (UBS (Luxembourg) S.A.)

HUET Catherine (Société Européenne de Banque S.A.)
Suppléant: HEYNDERICKX Eddy (Banca Lombarda International S.A.)

LEONARD Alain (Banque Degroof Luxembourg S.A.)
Suppléant: LEONARD Philippe (ABN AMRO Bank (Luxembourg) S.A.)

PRESBER Julian J.H. (State Street Bank Luxembourg S.A.)
Suppléant: LALOYAUX Pierre (Citibank International plc, Luxembourg Branch)

SCHULTE Gesa (Dresdner Bank Luxembourg S.A.)
Suppléant: SANTNER Markus (Deutsche Bank Luxembourg S.A.)

Suppléant: CELLIER André (Dexia Banque Internationale à Luxembourg)

Assistent:

**For additional analytical, business and investment opportunities information, please contact Global Investment & Business Center, USA at (202) 546-2103. Fax: (202) 546-3275. E-mail: rusric@erols.com**

BERG Luc (Dexia Life & Pensions)
BRAUSCH Freddy (Linklaters Loesch)
ELVINGER Jacques (Etude Elvinger, Hoss & Prussen)
GRULMS Fernand (PECOMA International S.A.)
HOFFMANN Robert (ALFI - Association Luxembourgeoise des Fonds d'Investissement)
KIEFFER Michel (Banque et Caisse d'Epargne de l'Etat, Luxembourg)
KREMER Claude (Etude Arendt & Medernach)
SCHOLS Patrick (Swiss Life (Luxembourg) S.A.)

**Legal Committee**

HOFFMANN André, Président (Banque Générale du Luxembourg S.A.)
Suppléant: WIANS Gaby (Banque Générale du Luxembourg S.A.)

BOURIN Philippe (Kredietbank S.A. Luxembourgeoise)
Suppléant: GOUDEN Patrick (Kredietbank S.A. Luxembourgeoise)

BÜTZOW Bernd-Dieter (Banque LBLux S.A.)
Suppléant: VANDENBULCKE Christophe (Deutsche Bank Luxembourg S.A.)

DELHAYE Joseph (Banque et Caisse d'Epargne de l'Etat, Luxembourg)
Suppléant: THOMA Françoise (Banque et Caisse d'Epargne de l'Etat, Luxembourg)

FALTZ Christiane (ABN AMRO Bank (Luxembourg) S.A.)
Suppléant: CAMMAERT Serge (Banque Delen Luxembourg)

JØRGENSEN Lise (Danske Bank International S.A.)
Suppléant: VAN DER MOLEN Jeroen (Nordea Bank S.A.)

KRAEMER Markus (Credit Suisse (Luxembourg) S.A.)
Suppléant: DE VOS Yves (VP Bank (Luxembourg) S.A.)

LALOYAUX Pierre (Citibank International plc, Luxembourg Branch)

LIES Charlotte (Dexia Banque Internationale à Luxembourg)
Suppléant: HOCHWEILER André (Dexia Banque Internationale à Luxembourg)

LINON Jacques (Société Européenne de Banque S.A.)
Suppléant: GRANGE Guillaume (Sanpaolo Bank S.A.)

LÖSCHNER Jost (HVB Banque Luxembourg)
Suppléant: KLAR Christian (WestLB International S.A.)

LÜHRING Anette (Erste Europäische Pfandbrief- und Kommunalkreditbank A.G.)

PARIZE Harold (Bank of Bermuda (Luxembourg) S.A.)

PLAT Stéphane (Société Générale Bank & Trust)
Suppléant: DUMONT Christel (Crédit Lyonnais Luxembourg S.A.)

POSTAL Daniel (BNP Paribas Luxembourg)
Suppléant: DELVAUX Cosita (Banque de Luxembourg)

**For additional analytical, business and investment opportunities information, please contact Global Investment & Business Center, USA at (202) 546-2103. Fax: (202) 546-3275. E-mail: rusric@erols.com**

SCHEIDECKER Katia (Cabinet d'avocats Aloyse May)
Suppléant: JACOBY Steve (Kremer Associés & Clifford Chance)

**Committee on Means of Payment, Computer Systems and Organization**

BARTOLINI Gian Marco, Vice-Président (Banque de Luxembourg)
Suppléant: MALLICK Thierry (BNP Paribas Luxembourg)

LATRAN Guy, Vice-Président (Dexia Banque Internationale à Luxembourg)
Suppléant: KLAUNER Théo (Dexia Banque Internationale à Luxembourg)

COULONVAL Hervé (State Street Bank Luxembourg S.A.)
Suppléant: BIDAINE Yves (Citibank International plc, Luxembourg Branch)

DANHYER Joël (ABN AMRO Bank (Luxembourg) S.A.)
Suppléant: THENY Pascal (ING Luxembourg S.A.)

KOCKELMANN Jürgen (Norddeutsche Landesbank Luxembourg S.A.)
Suppléant: HAAG Helmut (DekaBank Deutsche Girozentrale Luxembourg S.A.)

LAMHENE Patrick (Banque Générale du Luxembourg S.A.)
Suppléant: CAROFF Patrice (Banque Générale du Luxembourg S.A.)

LEQUEUX Joël (Nordea Bank S.A.)

MARTINO Jean-Luc (Kredietbank S.A. Luxembourgeoise)
Suppléant: MEUX Philippe (Kredietbank S.A. Luxembourgeoise)

PLEBANI Giancarlo (Banca Lombarda International S.A.)
Suppléant: KASHANI RAD Lorenzo (IMI Bank (Lux) S.A.)

PROMMENSCHENKEL Richard (Banco Bradesco Luxembourg S.A.)

RICARD Jean-Philippe (PricewaterhouseCoopers sàrl)
Suppléant: SCHMITZ Stephan (PricewaterhouseCoopers sàrl)

SIMON Bernard (Société de la Bourse de Luxembourg S.A.)
Suppléant: HOFFMANN Marcel (Société de la Bourse de Luxembourg S.A.)

WAGENER Serge (Banque et Caisse d'Epargne de l'Etat, Luxembourg)
Suppléant: MELCHIOR Jacques (Banque et Caisse d'Epargne de l'Etat, Luxembourg)

WILMES Serge (UBS (Luxembourg) S.A.)
Suppléant: DIDERRICH Rolf (VP Bank (Luxembourg) S.A.)

Assistent:

BECK Pierre (Banque Centrale du Luxembourg)
Suppléant: GERMEAUX Guy (Banque Centrale du Luxembourg)

BORSA Jean-Pierre (CETREL S.C.)

**For additional analytical, business and investment opportunities information, please contact Global Investment & Business Center, USA at (202) 546-2103. Fax: (202) 546-3275. E-mail: rusric@erols.com**

DAMSCHEN Pascale (Commission de Surveillance du Secteur Financier)
Suppléant: FRANCK Jean-Luc (Commission de Surveillance du Secteur Financier)

MOLLING Marc (Entreprise des Postes et Télécommunications)
Suppléant: SAUBER François (Entreprise des Postes et Télécommunications)

**Committee Professional Obligations**

HONDEQUIN Alain, Président (UBS (Luxembourg) S.A.)
Suppléant: DE VOS Yves (VP Bank (Luxembourg) S.A.)

BÜTZOW Bernd-Dieter (Banque LBLux S.A.)
Suppléant: KEIPES Renée (HVB Banque Luxembourg)

CROCHET Patrice (BNP Paribas Luxembourg)
Suppléant: BERSCHEID Roland (Société Générale Bank & Trust)

DE POVER Marie-France (Kredietbank S.A. Luxembourgeoise)
Suppléant: GOUDEN Patrick (Kredietbank S.A. Luxembourgeoise)

DELHAYE Joseph (Banque et Caisse d'Epargne de l'Etat, Luxembourg)
Suppléant: SCHAAL Claude (Banque et Caisse d'Epargne de l'Etat, Luxembourg)

DIESCHBURG Romain (ING Luxembourg S.A.)
Suppléant: BERTON Christine (Bank Sarasin Benelux S.A.)

DUPONT Gérard (Banque Générale du Luxembourg S.A.)
Suppléant: OLINGER Marc (Banque Générale du Luxembourg S.A.)

FREY Jean-Louis (Sanpaolo Bank S.A.)
Suppléant: ZACCHINO Francesco (Banca Nazionale del Lavoro International S.A.)

PARIZE Harold (Bank of Bermuda (Luxembourg) S.A.)

VEYDER Frank (Dexia Banque Internationale à Luxembourg)
Suppléant: d'ANSEMBOURG Charles-Antoine (Dexia Banque Internationale à Luxembourg)

WAGNER Evelyne (American Express Bank (Luxembourg) S.A.)
Suppléant: PÉREZ José Luis (The Bank of New York (Luxembourg) S.A.)

Assistent:

MEYERS Véronique (Institut de Formation Bancaire, Luxembourg)

**Investment funds Committee**

BOFFERDING Jacques (Banque Générale du Luxembourg S.A.)
Suppléant: HEGER Jean-Paul (Banque Générale du Luxembourg S.A.)

D'ORAZIO Serge (Kredietbank S.A. Luxembourgeoise)
Suppléant: RIES Stéphane (Kredietbank S.A. Luxembourgeoise)

**For additional analytical, business and investment opportunities information, please contact Global Investment & Business Center, USA at (202) 546-2103. Fax: (202) 546-3275. E-mail: rusric@erols.com**

GELHAY Jean-Michel (Banque Degroof Luxembourg S.A.)
Suppléant: SUTTOR Paul (ING Luxembourg S.A.)

HILDEBRANDT Holger (DekaBank Deutsche Girozentrale Luxembourg S.A.)
Suppléant: KAUFFMANN Pascale (HVB Banque Luxembourg)

PARIZE Harold (Bank of Bermuda (Luxembourg) S.A.)

PAULY John (Dexia Banque Internationale à Luxembourg)
Suppléant: BECHET Marc-André (Dexia Banque Internationale à Luxembourg)

RIDOLE Christian (J.P. Morgan Bank Luxembourg S.A.)
Suppléant: ALLDIS John (Citibank International plc, Luxembourg Branch)

STILMANT Eric (Union Bancaire Privée (Luxembourg) S.A.)
Suppléant: GELLERSTAD Christian (Pictet & Cie (Europe) S.A.)

THILL Nico (Banque de Luxembourg)
Suppléant: LASCH Georg (BNP Paribas Luxembourg)

THOMMES Camille (Banque et Caisse d'Epargne de l'Etat, Luxembourg)
Suppléant: NICKELS Norbert (Banque et Caisse d'Epargne de l'Etat, Luxembourg)

Suppléant: BOUCHOMS Pierre (Sanpaolo Bank S.A.)
Suppléant: VAN HUMBEECK Yvan (Bank of Tokyo-Mitsubishi (Luxembourg) S.A.)

Assistent:

LENTZ Jean-Robert (PricewaterhouseCoopers sàrl)

**Committee of the Promotion of the Financial Centre**

HAMER Charles, Président (Crédit Agricole Indosuez Luxembourg)
Suppléant: AHLBORN Pierre (Banque de Luxembourg)

MESTAT Alain, Vice-Président (Banque Privée Edmond de Rothschild Europe)
Suppléant: GONNE Philippe (United European Bank (Luxembourg) S.A.)

BOSI Stéphane (Sanpaolo Bank S.A.)
Suppléant: DI VINCENZO Fabio (Banca Nazionale del Lavoro International S.A.)

CATRY Philippe (ING Luxembourg S.A.)
Suppléant: DEN HOEDT Victor (Bank Sarasin Benelux S.A.)

D'HONDT Christian (Kredietbank S.A. Luxembourgeoise)
Suppléant: JANSEN Xavier (Kredietbank S.A. Luxembourgeoise)

FINCK Jean-Claude (Banque et Caisse d'Epargne de l'Etat, Luxembourg)
Suppléant: QUEUDEVILLE Guy (Banque et Caisse d'Epargne de l'Etat, Luxembourg)

**For additional analytical, business and investment opportunities information, please contact Global Investment & Business Center, USA at (202) 546-2103. Fax: (202) 546-3275. E-mail: rusric@erols.com**

GUILLAUME Paul (State Street Bank Luxembourg S.A.)
Suppléant: HACKENBERG Henri (Brown Brothers Harriman (Luxembourg) S.C.A.)

RATHLE Fouad E. (Garanti Bank Luxembourg Branch)

SCHNEIDER Kik (Banque Générale du Luxembourg S.A.)
Suppléant: MARGUE Jean-Louis (Banque Générale du Luxembourg S.A.)

SPETZ Jean-Luc (EUROHYPO Europäische Hypothekenbank S.A.)
Suppléant: SCHULTE Martin (Pfandbrief Bank International S.A.)

WARLAND Valérie (Dexia Banque Internationale à Luxembourg)
Suppléant: GILLIERON Eric (Dexia Banque Internationale à Luxembourg)

WEBER Alain (Banque LBLux S.A.)
Suppléant: KOPPERS Josef (DZ BANK International S.A.)

**Security Committee**

BORSCHETTE Patrick, Président (Banque Générale du Luxembourg S.A.)
Suppléant: HENTGEN Marc (Banque Générale du Luxembourg S.A.)

THEIS François, Vice-Président (Banque de Luxembourg)
Suppléant: TURCI Marco (Crédit Lyonnais Luxembourg S.A.)

CAPELLE Jean (ING Luxembourg S.A.)
Suppléant: LAMOCK Fabrice (Bank Sarasin Benelux S.A.)

CECCACCI Anna-Vera (Société Européenne de Banque S.A.)
Suppléant: MURGIA Jean-Pierre (Sanpaolo Bank S.A.)

FELTEN Carlo (Kredietbank S.A. Luxembourgeoise)
Suppléant: JACOB Benoît (Kredietbank S.A. Luxembourgeoise)

GIERES Gaston (Banque et Caisse d'Epargne de l'Etat, Luxembourg)
Suppléant: POLATI Maurice (Banque et Caisse d'Epargne de l'Etat, Luxembourg)

KRANK Martin (Nordea Bank S.A.)

SCHEUREN Romain (Dexia Banque Internationale à Luxembourg)
Suppléant: WALTZING Olivier (Dexia Banque Internationale à Luxembourg)

SCHMIT Marc (UBS (Luxembourg) S.A.)
Suppléant: PETER Philippe (VP Bank (Luxembourg) S.A.)

WIETHOFF Klaus (Dresdner Bank Luxembourg S.A.)
Suppléant: SCHULZE Uwe (Norddeutsche Landesbank Luxembourg S.A.)

Assistent:

BOLLENDORFF Claude (Association pour la Santé au Travail du Secteur Financier)

**For additional analytical, business and investment opportunities information, please contact Global Investment & Business Center, USA at (202) 546-2103. Fax: (202) 546-3275. E-mail: rusric@erols.com**

MARCHIONI Alain (Banque Raiffeisen)
Suppléant: ATTEN Bob (Banque Raiffeisen)

MULLER Jeannot (Entreprise des Postes et Télécommunications)

ZEIMES Marc (Banque Centrale du Luxembourg)
Suppléant: GESCHWINDT Christian (Banque Centrale du Luxembourg)

## Social Committee

PLANCHARD Etienne, Président (Banque de Luxembourg)
Suppléant: DALVIT René (Société Générale Bank & Trust)

SAUSSEZ Dominique, Vice-Président (Dexia Banque Internationale à Luxembourg)
Suppléant: DHONT Alain (Dexia Banque Internationale à Luxembourg)

ANDRÉ Jean-Pierre (Bank of Tokyo-Mitsubishi (Luxembourg) S.A.)

DOMKEN Lilette (ING Luxembourg S.A.)
Suppléant: HARNOIS Viviane (ABN AMRO Bank (Luxembourg) S.A.)

IVANOVA Vio (J.P. Morgan Bank Luxembourg S.A.)
Suppléant: PRIEUR Catherine (Citibank International plc, Luxembourg Branch)

MIGNANI Paolo (Dresdner Bank Luxembourg S.A.)
Suppléant: FEY Christian (DekaBank Deutsche Girozentrale Luxembourg S.A.)

MULLER Annie (Kredietbank S.A. Luxembourgeoise)
Suppléant: HEMMER Dominique (Kredietbank S.A. Luxembourgeoise)

NICOLA Danielle (Credit Suisse (Luxembourg) S.A.)
Suppléant: KOENIG Stephanie (UBS (Luxembourg) S.A.)

RIBONNET Sandrine (Sanpaolo Bank S.A.)
Suppléant: JONCQUEL Rosanna (Société Européenne de Banque S.A.)

ROLLINGER Edmond (Banque et Caisse d'Epargne de l'Etat, Luxembourg)
Suppléant: BALTES Myriam (Banque et Caisse d'Epargne de l'Etat, Luxembourg)

SCHUMAN Thierry (Banque Générale du Luxembourg S.A.)
Suppléant: GREGORIUS Patrick (Banque Générale du Luxembourg S.A.)

SIEMANN Walter (EUROHYPO Europäische Hypothekenbank S.A.)
Suppléant: LÜHRING Anette (Erste Europäische Pfandbrief- und Kommunalkreditbank A.G.)

## SELECTED CHAMBERS AND ASSOCIATIONS

Chambre des Métiers du Grand-Duché du Luxembourg

2, Circuit de la Foire Internationale

L-1016 Luxembourg

Tel.: 00352 / 42 67 67-1

Fax: 00352 /42 67 87

Email: promotion@chambre-des-metiers.lu

URL: www.chambre-des-metiers.lu

Chambre de Commerce du Grand-Duché du Luxembourg

7, rue Alcide de Gasperi

L-2981Luxembourg

Tel: 00352 / 42 39 39-1

Fax: 00352 /43 83 26

Email: chamcom@cc.lu

URL: http://www.cc.lu

CEPS

Instead

Rue Emile Mark

L-4501 Differdange

Tel.: 00352 / 58 58 55-526/527

Fax: 00352 / 58 55 53

Email: monique.borsenberger@ci.rech.lu

URL:www.ceps.lu

Comité international de l'environnement

des 5 régions (CIE5) asbl

1, av. de la gare

L-1611 Luxembourg

Tel: 00352 / 48 70 31

Fax: 00352 / 40 41 61

EURES Pôle européen de développement ( PED)

Fédértion des industriels luxembourgeois (FEDIL)

7, rue Alcide de Gasperi

L-2981Luxembourg

Tel.: 00352 / 43 53 66-1

Fax.: 00352 / 43 23 28

Email: fedil@fedil.lu

URL: www.fedil.lu

Forum entreprise, le magazine transfrontalier du Dirigeant

300c, route de Thionville

L-5801 Hesperange

Tel.: 00352 / 40 84 69

Fax: 00352 / 48 20 78

Email: icouset@yahoo.com

URL: ---

IRI asbl

Institut Régional Intracommunautaire

1, av. de la gare

L-1017 Luxembourg

Tel: 00352 / 48 70 31

Fax: 00352 / 40 41 61

Email: iri@pt.lu

URL:www.iri.lu

Maison de la Grande Région

14, rue Ste Zithe

L-2763 Luxembourg

Tel.: 00352 / 478-69 90

Les offices statistiques de la Grande Région Saar-Lor-Lux- Rhénanie-Palatinat-Wallonie

B.P. 48
L-4501 Differdange
Tel.: 00352 / 58 58 55-549
URL:www.ped.org

URL:www.grande-region.lu

EuroRégio
SAARLORLUX RHIN ASB
1, av. de la gare
L-1611 Luxembourg
Tél.: 00352 / 29.71.46
Fax.: 00352 / 40.41.61

Statec -
et des études économiques
6, bd Royal
L-2013 Luxembourg
Tél.: 00352 478-42 19 / 42 68
Fax: 00352 / 46 42 89
Email: statec.post@statec.etat.lu
URL: www.statec.lu

| | |
|---|---|
| Chambre de Commerce du Grand-Duché de Luxembourg | http://www.cc.lu/ |
| Chambre des Métiers du Grand-Duché de Luxembourg | http://www.cdm.lu/ |
| F E D I L | http://www.fedil.lu/ |
| Ministère de l'Economie | http://www.etat.lu/ECO/ |
| Ministère de la Culture, de l'Enseignement Supérieur et de la Recherche | http://www.gouvernement.lu/gouv/fr/doss/mcesr/index.html |
| SNCI | http://www.snci.lu |
| CRP Gabriel Lippmann | http://www.crpgl.lu/ |
| CRP Henri Tudor | http://www.crpht.lu/ |
| CRP - Santé | http://www.crp-sante.lu/ |
| Technoport Schlassgoart | http://www.technoport.lu/ |
| Centre de veille technologique | http://www.cvt.lu/ |
| Centre des resources de l'environnement | http://www.crte.lu/ |
| Business Initiative | http://www.123go-creation.org/ |
| Innovation Relay Centre Network | http://www.cordis.lu/irc/ |
| CORDIS | http://www.cordis.lu/ |
| EUREKA | http://www3.eureka.be/ |
| Welcome to Europa | http://europa.eu.int/ |
| Ideal-IST | http://www.dlr.de/ideal-ist |
| IPR-Helpdesk | http://www.ipr-helpdesk.org/ |
| IRC-Deutschland | http://www.irc-deutschland.de/ |
| Leonardo da Vinci | http://europa.eu.int/comm/education/leonardo/leonardo2_en.html |

**For additional analytical, business and investment opportunities information, please contact Global Investment & Business Center, USA at (202) 546-2103. Fax: (202) 546-3275. E-mail: rusric@erols.com**

# LUXEMBOURG EMBASSIES ABROAD

| | |
|---|---|
| **Austria** | 81 Sternwartestrasse<br>A-1180 Vienna<br>Tel. 478 2142/43 / Fax. 478 2144 |
| **Belgium** | 75 avenue de Cortenbergh<br>B-1000 Brussels<br>Tel. 737 5700/06 / Fax. 737 5710 (Embassy)<br>Fax. 737 5709 (Consulate General) |
| **China** | 21 Nei Wu Bu Jie<br>100600 Beijing<br>Tel. 6513 59 37 / Fax. 6513 72 68 |
| **Denmark** | 5 Fridtjof Nansens Plads<br>DK-2100 Copenhagen<br>Tel. 35 26 82 00 / Fax. 35 26 82 08 |
| **France** | 33 avenue Rapp<br>75007 Paris<br>Tel. 1 45 55 13 37 / Fax. 1 45 51 72 29 |
| **Greece** | Skoufa 11-13<br>Kolonaki<br>10673 Athens<br>Tel. 364 39 58 / Fax. 363 87 61 |
| **Germany** | Adenauerallee 108<br>D-53113 Bonn<br>Tel. 21 40 08/09/00 / Fax. 22 29 20 |
| **Italy** | 90 Via di Sante Croce in Gerusalemme<br>I-00185 Rome<br>Tel. 772 01 177 / Fax. 772 01 055 |
| **Japan** | Nibancho TS Building 4F<br>2-1 Nibancho<br>Chiyoda-Ku<br>102-0084 Tokyo<br>Tel. 81-3-3265-9621 / Fax. 81-3-3265-9624 |
| **Netherlands** | Nassaulaan 8<br>2514 JS The Hague<br>Tel. 703 60 75 16 / Fax. 703 56 33 03 |
| **Malaysia** | Menara Keck Seng Building (16th Floor)<br>203 Jalan Bukit Bin Tang<br>55100 Kuala Lumpur<br>Tel. 24 33 134 / Fax. 24 33 157 |
| **Portugal** | Rua das Janelas Verdes 43<br>P-1200 Lisbon<br>Tel. 396 27 81 / Fax. 601 410 |
| **Russian Federation** | Khrouchtchevsky Pereoulok 3 |

| | |
|---|---|
| | Moscow<br>Tel. 220 21 11 / Fax. 220 21 10 |
| **Spain** | Calle Claudio Coello 78<br>E-28001 Madrid<br>Tel. 435 91 64 / Fax. 577 48 26 |
| **Switzerland** | 45 Kramgasse B.P. 619<br>CH-3000 Berne 8<br>Tel. 311 47 32 / Fax. 311 00 19 |
| **United Kingdom** | 27 Wilton Crescent<br>London SW1X 8SD<br>Tel. 0207-235 6961 / Fax. 0207-235 9734 |
| **U.S.A.** | 2200 Massachusetts Avenue N.W.<br>Washington D.C. 20008<br>Tel. 265 41 71/72 / Fax. 328 82 70 |
| **Vatican** | 20 via Casale S. Pio V<br>I-00165 Rome<br>Tel. 660 4901 / 660 00 915 |
| **Andorra** | Luxembourg Embassy, Madrid |
| **Belorus** | Luxembourg Embassy, Moscow |
| **Canada** | Luxembourg Embassy, Washington |
| **Cyprus** | Luxembourg Embassy, Athens |
| **Czech Republic** | Luxembourg Embassy, 5 rue Notre Dame, L-2240 Luxembourg |
| **Finland** | Luxembourg Embassy, Copenhagen |
| **Georgia** | Luxembourg Embassy, Moscow |
| **Hungary** | Luxembourg Embassy, Vienna |
| **Ireland** | Luxembourg Embassy, London |
| **Iceland** | Luxembourg Embassy, London |
| **Kazakhstan** | Luxembourg Embassy, Moscow |
| **Korea** | Luxembourg Embassy, Tokyo |
| **Liechtenstein** | Luxembourg Embassy, Berne |
| **Malta** | Luxembourg Embassy, Rome |
| **Mexico** | Luxembourg Embassy, Washington |
| **Mongolia** | Luxembourg Embassy, Beijing |

| | |
|---|---|
| **Norway** | Luxembourg Embassy, Copenhagen |
| **Poland** | Luxembourg Embassy, 5 rue Notre Dame, L-2240 Luxembourg |
| **Romania** | Luxembourg Embassy, Athens |
| **Slovenia** | Luxembourg Embassy, Vienna |
| **Slovak Republic** | Luxembourg Embassy, 5 rue Notre Dame, L-2240 Luxembourg |
| **Sweden** | Luxembourg Embassy, Copenhagen |
| **Ukraine** | Luxembourg Embassy, Moscow |
| **Vietnam** | Luxembourg Embassy, Beijing |

**Please note:**
**In countries where there is no Luxembourg Embassy, please address yourselves to the Belgian and/or Netherlands Embassy.**

## US AND COUNTRY CONTACTS

Embassies
American Embassy
22 Boulevard Emmanuel-Servais
L-2535 Luxembourg
Tel: +352/ 46-01-23
Fax: +352/ 46-14-01

U.S. Mail Address
U.S. Embassy
Unit 1410
APO AE 09126-1410

Ambassador: James Hormel
Contact: Monica Kwiecinski, Political
and Economic Specialist

The Commercial Service in Brussels is responsible for business conducted in Luxembourg.

American Embassy
27 Boulevard du Regent
B-1000 Brussels, Belgium
Tel: +32/2 508-2425
Fax: +32/2 512-6653
http://www.us-embassy.be

Contact: George Knowles, Commercial Counselor, Angela Dawkins, Commercial Attaché

U.S. Mail Address:
U.S. Embassy
FCS/EMB
PSC 82, Box 002
APO AE 09710

Embassy of the Grand Duchy of Luxembourg
2200 Massachusetts Ave. NW
Washington, DC 20008
Tel: (202) 265-4171
Fax: (202) 328-8270

Ambassador: Arlette Conzemius

Luxembourg Consulates
17 Beekman Place
New York, NY 10022
Tel: (212) 888-6664
Fax: (212) 888-6116

Contact: Mr. Jean Graff, Consul General

One Sansome Street Suite 830
San Francisco, CA 94104
Tel: (415) 788-0816
Fax: (415) 788-0985

Contact: Mr. Patrick Nickels, Consul General

Chambers of Commerce
AmCham-Luxembourg
31, Blvd Konrad Adenauer
L-1124-Luxembourg - Kirchbourg
Tel: +352/ 42-39-39-390
Fax: +352/ 43-17-56
http://www.amcham.lu

Contact:
Dr. Gilbert E. McNeill, Executive Director
Email: gilbert.mc-neill@amcham.lu

Chambre de Commerce du Luxembourg
31, Blvd. Konrad Adenauer
L-2981 Luxembourg - Kirchbourg
Tel: +352/ 42-39-39-311
Fax: +352/ 43-83-26
http://www.cc.lu

Contact: Mr. Jean-Claude Vesque
Manager, Department of Foreign Trade

Luxembourg trade and industry associations
Fédération des Industriels Luxembourgeois
(Federation of Luxembourg Enterprises)
31, Blvd Konrad Adenauer L-1124-Luxembourg - Kirchbourg
Tel: +352/ 43-53-66-1 Fax: +352/ 43-23-28
http://www.fedil.lu

# SELECTED BUSINESS CONTACTS

## RISK MANAGEMENTS

**ALAIN BASTIN** - President

Dexia-BIL
Risk Management: Directeur Adjoint
69, Rte d'Esch
L-2953 Luxembourg
Tel: +/352/45.90-44.06
Fax: +/352/45.90-32.38
@: alain.bastin@dexia-bil.com

**THIERRY LOPEZ** - Vice President

KBL Group
Head of Group Risk Management
43, Bd Royal
L-2955 Luxembourg
Tel: +/352/47.97-30.90
Fax: +/352/47.97-73.675
@: thierry.lopez@kbl-bank.com

**VAFA MOAYED** - Secretary

Deloitte & Touche
Partner
3, route d'Arlon
L-8009 Strassen
Tel: +/352/451.452-424
Fax: +/352/451.452.24.04
@: vmoayed@deloitte.lu

**MARC DEMEY** - Treasurer

DEXIA Group
ALM & Market Risk Management
7-11, Quai André Citroën
F-75015 Paris
Tél: ( + 33 ) 1 43 92 79 50
Fax: ( + 33 ) 1 43 92 80 73
@: marc.demey@dexia.com

## ACCOUNTING AND AUDITING

| | Telephone | Fax |
|---|---|---|
| Audit Royal SA<br>B P 878 L-2018 Luxembourg | +352 227381 | +352 227071 |
| CITCO (Luxembourg) SA<br>25A Boulevard Royal, 9th Floor L-2449 Luxembourg | +352 472323 | +352 472473 |
| Delma & Cie Sarl<br>59 rue GD Charlotte 9515 Wiltz, Luxembourg | +352 950574 | +352 959111 |
| Fiduciaire Rutledge & Associés SA<br>7 Rue Pierre D'Aspelt L-1142 Luxembourg | + 352 450450 | +352 452531 |
| Fiduciaire Générale de Luxembourg<br>(Member of Deloitte Touche Tohmatsu International) 3 Route D'Arlon, Strassen L-8009 Luxembourg | +352 451451 | +352 45145404 |
| Fiduciaire Nationale SARL<br>"Lys Royal 1", 2 Rue Tony Neuman L-2241 Luxembourg | + 352 461910 | +352 461914 |

| | | |
|---|---|---|
| FISOGEST S.A. | | |
| 16, Rue de Nassau, L-2213 Luxembourg | Telephone<br>+352 26441866 | Fax<br>+352 26441864 |

## BANKING SERVICES AND ASSET MANAGEMENT

| | | |
|---|---|---|
| Aurea Finance Company | | |
| 50 rue Basse, 7307 Steinsel L-7307 Luxembourg | Telephone<br>+352 3333011 | Fax<br>+352 33330130 |
| Bank Leumi (Luxembourg) SA | | |
| 6D Route de Treves, Senningerberg L-2633 Luxembourg | Telephone<br>+352 346390 | Fax<br>+352 346396 |
| CITCO (Luxembourg) SA | | |
| 25A Boulevard Royal, 9th Floor L-2449 Luxembourg | Telephone<br>+352 472323 | Fax<br>+352 472473 |
| Citibank (Luxembourg) SA | | |
| 58 Boulevard Grand Duchesse Charlotte L-1330 Luxembourg | Telephone<br>+352 4514141 | Fax<br>+352 451414253 |
| Corporate Funds Management Services SA | | |
| Galerie Kons, 4th Floor, 26 Place de la Gare P O Box 1375, L-1013 Luxembourg | Telephone<br>+ 352 489061 | Fax<br>+352 492369 |
| EFG Private Bank (Luxembourg) SA | | |
| 5 rue Jean Monnet, P O Box 897 L-2018 Luxembourg | Telephone<br>+352 4207241 | Fax<br>+352 420724650 |
| Rabobank Luxembourg SA | | |
| 287-289 Route d'Arlon L-1150 Luxembourg | Telephone<br>+ 352 457 8801 | Fax<br>+352 452396 |

## OFFSHORE COMPANY REGISTRATION

| | | |
|---|---|---|
| ABN AMRO Trust Company (Luxembourg) SA | | |
| 4 rue Jean Monnet, P O Box 415 L-2180 Luxembourg | Telephone<br>+352 4271711 | Fax<br>+352 421961 |
| CITCO (Luxembourg) SA | | |
| 25A Boulevard Royal, 9th Floor L-2449 Luxembourg | Telephone<br>+352 472323 | Fax<br>+352 472473 |

**For additional analytical, business and investment opportunities information, please contact Global Investment & Business Center, USA at (202) 546-2103. Fax: (202) 546-3275. E-mail: rusric@erols.com**

| | | |
|---|---|---|
| Corporate Services International SA<br>2b Boulevard Joseph II L-1840 Luxembourg | Telephone<br>+352 440931 | Fax<br>+352 440973 |
| Ermitage Luxembourg SA<br>Forum Bourse, 3rd Floor, 17 rue des Bains BP44, L-2010 Luxembourg | Telephone<br>+ 352 4604041 | Fax<br>+352 460405 |
| Fiduciaire Nationale SARL<br>"Lys Royal 1", 2 Rue Tony Neuman L-2241 Luxembourg | Telephone<br>+352 461910 | Fax<br>+352 461914 |
| Fiduciaire Royal SA<br>BP 878 L-2018 Luxembourg | Telephone<br>+352 227381 | Fax<br>+352 227071 |
| Hoogewerf & Cie<br>19 rue Aldringen L-1118 Luxembourg | Telephone<br>+352 460025 | Fax<br>+352 460027 |
| Paddock SA<br>3a Rue Kroll L-1882 Luxembourg | Telephone<br>+352 495924 | Fax<br>+352 402525 |
| Trust International Luxembourg SA<br>3 rue des Bains L-1212 Luxembourg | Telephone<br>+352 224051 | Fax<br>+352 224055 |

## TRUST MANAGEMENT

| | | |
|---|---|---|
| ABN AMRO Trust Company (Luxembourg) SA<br>4 rue Jean Monnet, P O Box 415 L-2180 Luxembourg | Telephone<br>+352 4271711 | Fax<br>+352 421961 |
| AMS Trust (Luxembourg) S A<br>595 rue de Neudorf L-2220 Luxembourg | Telephone<br>+352 3488911 | Fax<br>+352 438890 |
| CITCO (Luxembourg) SA<br>25A Boulevard Royal, 9th Floor L-2449 Luxembourg | Telephone<br>+352 472323 | Fax<br>+352 472473 |
| Ermitage Luxembourg SA<br>Forum Bourse. 3rd Floor. 17 rue des Bains | Telephone | Fax |

| | | |
|---|---|---|
| BP44, L-2010 Luxembourg | +352 4604041 | +352 460405 |
| FISOGEST S.A. | | |
| 16, Rue de Nassau, L-2213 Luxembourg | Telephone<br>+352 26441866 | Fax<br>+352 26441864 |
| Insinger Fund Administration (Luxembourg) SA/ Insinger Trust (Luxembourg) SA | | |
| 66 avenue Victor Hugo L-1750 Luxembourg | Telephone<br>+ 352 229444 | Fax<br>+352 229466 |
| Intertrust (Luxembourg) SA | | |
| 3 Boulevard Prince Henri L-1724 Luxembourg | Telephone<br>+352 221888 | Fax<br>+352 221899 |
| MeesPierson Trust (Luxembourg) S A | | |
| 10 rue Antoine Jans, P O Box 239 L-2012 Luxembourg | Telephone<br>+ 352 4768671 | Fax<br>+352 476867229 |
| Trust International Luxembourg SA | | |
| 3 rue des Bains L-1212 Luxembourg | Telephone<br>+352 224051 | Fax<br>+352 224055 |

## LUXEMBOURG TOURIST OFFICES WORLDWIDE

**Luxembourg**
Ministère du Tourisme (Administrative Head Office)
6 Avenue E. Reuter
PO Box 86
L-2937 Luxembourg
Tel: +352 478-1
Fax: +352 47 40 11
email: ministere.tourism@cmt.etat.lu

Office National du Tourisme (ONT)
1 Rue du Fort Thüngen
PO Box 1001
L-1010 Luxembourg
Tel: +352 42 82 82-1
Fax: +352 42 82 82-38
email: info@ont.lu
Web: http://www.ont.lu

***Belgium:***
c/o Luxembourg Embassy
75 Avenue de Cortenbergh
B-1000 Brussels
Tel: + 32 (0)2 646 0370
Fax: + 32 (0)2 648 6100

***Denmark:***
Vester Farimagsgade 1
DK-1606 Copenhagen V
Tel: +45 (0)33 91 61 91
Fax: +45 (0)33 91 63 91

***England:***
122 Regent Street
London W1B 5SA
Tel: +44 (0)20 7434 2800
Fax: +44 (0)20 7734 1205
email: tourism@luxembourg.co.uk
web: http://www.luxembourg.co.uk/

***France:***
21 Boulevard des Capucines
75002 Paris
Tel: +33 (0)1 47 42 9056
Fax: +33 (0)1 40 07 0043
email: luxfr@club-internet.fr

***Germany:***
Bismarck Strasse 23/27

D-41061 Mönchengladbach
Tel: +49 (0)2161 20 88 88
Fax: +49 (0)2161 274 220

Luxemburgische Botschaft
Abteilung Tourismus
Klingelhöferstrasse 7
D-10785 Berlin
Tel. +49 (0)30 25 75 77-3
Fax. +49 (0)30 25 75 77-55
email: Luxemburg_Kontakt@t-online.de

***Netherlands:***
8 Nassau Laan
NL-2514 JS Den Haag
Tel: +31 (0)70 364 9041
Fax: +31 (0)70 356 3303

***U.S.A.:***
17 Beekman Place
New York 10022
Tel: (212) 935 8888
Fax: (212) 935 5896
email: luxnto@aol.com
web: http://www.visitluxembourg.com/

# ART GALLERIES IN LUXEMBOURG

Further information about Luxembourg's Art Galleries

**Am Tunnel**

16 Rue Zithe
L-2954 Luxembourg
Tel: (+352) 40155901
Fax: (+352) 40155904
Mon-Fri 11-17h30, guided visits at 14h15

**Art du Verre**

4 Avenue de la Liberté
L-1930 Luxembourg
Tel: (+352) 47 18 18
50 works in Glass are permanently on display.

**Beaumont**

39 Avenue Monterey
L-2163 Luxembourg
Tel: (+352) 46 23 43

Casino Luxembourg - Forum d'Art Contemporain

PO Box 345
41 Rue Notre-Dame
L-2013 Luxembourg
Tel: (+352) 22 50 45
Fax: (+352) 22 95 95
email: casino-luxembourg@ci.culture.lu
Open: Mon, Wed, Fri, Sat, Sun: 11 a.m. to 6 p.m.
Thurs late opening: 11 a.m. to 8 p.m.
Closed Tuesdays.

La Cité

1 rue Louvigny
L-1946 Luxembourg
Tel:(+352) 22 36 89

**Edition 88**

4 Rue Louvigny
L-1946 Luxembourg
Tel: (+352) 47 45 99

**Erna Hécey**

25 Boulevard Prince Henri Ier
1724 Luxembourg
Tel: (+352) 24 11 74
Fax: (+352) 24 15 89

**Léa Gredt**

1B Rue Beaumont
L-1219 Luxembourg
Tel: (+352) 4 11 48

**de Luxembourg**

39 Avenue Monterey
L-2163 Luxembourg
Tel: (+352) 46 68 36

**Orfèo**

28 Rue des Capucins
L-1313 Luxembourg
Tel: (+352) 22 23 25
Fax: (+352) 22 23 25
Open: Tue-Sat 10-12 and 14-17h
Jewelry, Ceramics, Painting and Sculpture

**Schweitzer**

24 Avenue Monterey
L-2163 Luxembourg
Tel: (+352) 46 90 56

photogalerie rol schleich

1 rue Auguste Charles
L-1326 Luxembourg - Bonnevoie
Tel: (+352) 48 41 41
Fax: 48 41 50
email schleich@pt.lu

**Simoncini**

20bis Rue Louvigny
L-1946 Luxembourg
Tel: (+352) 47 55 15

**Toxic New Art**

34 Avenue de la Gare
L-1610 Luxembourg
Tel: (+352) 48 42 24

## BUS & COACH OPERATORS IN LUXEMBOURG

| COMPANY | PHONE/ FAX: (+352) | CONTACT | ADDRESS | BUSSES/ COACHES | MINIBUSSES |
|---|---|---|---|---|---|
| **Altmann** | 66 87 37<br>67 64 17 | Mr Victor Altmann | 12 Rue des Forges<br>L-5770 Weiler-la-Tour | 4 | n.a. |
| **Bartholme** | 92 05 08<br>92 10 64 | Mr Guy Bartholme | 5 Grand'Rue<br>L-9710 Clervaux | 6 | 1 |
| **Bollig** | 72 86 32<br>72 93 92 | Mr Edmond Michels | Rue Alferweiher<br>L-6412 Echternach<br>email: bollig@ping.lu | 6 | n.a. |
| **Clement** | 78 04 54 1<br>78 95 88 | Mr Clement | Rue d'Altlinster<br>L-6163 Bourglinster<br>email: clement@cmdnet.lu | 15 | n.a. |
| **Demy Cars** | 39 60 31<br>39 60 31 | Mr Jos Schandeler | 44 Rue de Clairefontaine<br>L-8460 Eischen | 54 | n.a. |
| **Demy Cars** | 30 01 46<br>30 89 96 | Mr Nanquette | 22 Rue de Kehlen<br>L-8295 Keispelt | 54 | n.a. |
| **Engelberty** | 51 95 03<br>51 00 72 | Note: Deals exclusively with school children transport | 1A Rue de la Chapelle<br>L-3378 Livange | n.a. | n.a. |
| **Frisch E.** | 49 61 51<br>40 28 74 | Mr Emile Frisch / Miss Katie Lommer | 5 Rue Jules Fischer<br>L-1522 Luxembourg | 20 | n.a. |
| **Frisch F.** | 64 95 95<br>64 08 79 | Mrs Marie-Dominique Lagodny / Mr Emile Frisch | 7 Rue Principale<br>L-8805 Rambrouch<br>email: contact@frisch.lu | 35 | n.a. |
| **Huberty** | 50 74 21<br>50 07 35 | Mr Lucien Huberty | 325 Route de Longwy<br>L-4831 Rodange | 3 | n.a. |
| **Koob** | 80 85 75<br>80 33 68 | Mr Constant Simon | 22 Rue Principale<br>L-8606 Bettborn | 14 | n.a. |
| **La Fraise** | 33 94 94<br>33 94 95 | Mr Marc Jacobs | 1 Rue Paul Eyschen<br>L-7317 Steinsel | 23 | n.a. |
| **Meyers** | 99 06 03<br>90 90 31 | Mrs Alixe Meyers | 30 Rue Principale<br>L-9183 Schlindermanderscheid<br>email: meycars@pt.lu | 5 | n.a. |
| **Musel Express** | 58 21 40<br>58 46 67 | Mr Pierre Cloos | 20 Route du Vin<br>L-5445 Schengen | 3 | n.a. |

| | | | | | |
|---|---|---|---|---|---|
| **Pletschette** | 35 00 85<br>35 79 07 | Mr Joseph Pletschette<br>Mr Gilbert Remy | 10 Unterstmühle<br>L-5414 Canach<br>email: info@autocars-pletschette.lu | 13 | n.a. |
| **Rapide des Ardennes** | 64 00 11<br>64 90 27 | Mrs Nelly Schammo | 43 Rue de la Poste<br>L-8824 Perlé | 4 | n.a. |
| **Ross** | 99 42 57<br>99 48 76 | Mr Raymond Ross | 58 Rue de Hoffelt<br>L-9773 Troine<br>email: ross@pt.lu | 5 | n.a. |
| **Sales-Lentz** | 65 11 65 651<br>65 11 65 444 | Service location bus | Z.I. Bommelscheuer B.P. 39<br>L-4901 Bascharage<br>email: info@sales-lentz.com | Yes (largest Bus/Coach tour-operator in Luxembourg) | Yes |
| **Siedler** | 56 50 99<br>56 32 33 | Mr Edmond Siedler | 28 R. des Légionnaires<br>L-3780 Tetange | 4 | 9 equipped for disabled transport |
| **Simon** | 80 85 75<br>80 33 68 | Mrs Constant Simon | 39 Esplanade<br>L-9227 Diekirch | 45 | n.a. |
| **Simon-Tours** | 50 77 69<br>50 28 10 | Mr Roger Simon-Gindt | 92 Porte de Lamadeleine<br>L-4744 Pétange | 4 | n.a. |
| **Autobus Stephany** | 99 81 32<br>99 88 12 | Mrs Denise Stephany | 27 Rue de Wilwerdange<br>L-9911 Troisvierges<br>email: stephany@pt.lu | 15 | 2 |
| **Unsen Freres** | 62 14 61<br>62 00 55 | Mr Ferdinand Unsen | 4 Rue Principale<br>L-8817 Eschette | 18 | n.a. |
| **Vandivinit** | 66 83 41<br>66 15 79 | Mr Alfred Vandivinit / Mr Romain Vandivinit | 13 Kiischtestrooss<br>L-5683 Dalheim<br>email: vandivinit@dialup.nacamar.lu | 12 | n.a. |
| **Wagener** | 88 82 17<br>81 77 98 | Mr Norbert Frising | 12 Rue de Michelbouch<br>L-9170 Merzig | 6 | n.a. |
| **Voyages Emile Weber** | 35 95 75<br>35 97 99 | Mr Fernand Heinisch / Mr Jos Müller | 15 Rue d'Oetrange<br>L-5411 Canach<br>email: webmaster@vew.lu | 65 | n.a. |
| **Zenners René** | 66 40 96<br>66 40 96 25 | Mr René Zenners | 32 Route du Vin<br>L-5495 Wintrange | 3 | 2 |

Note also, the Association of Bus and Coach Operators: "Fédération luxembourgeoise des exploitants d'autobus et d'autocars": email: info@ccl.dot.lu Tel: 43 94 44

Please note that whilst this list was compiled with all due care, the Luxembourg Tourist Office cannot be held responsible for any inaccuracies.

# CONTACTS IN LUXEMBOURG

Luxembourg Embassy
27 Wilton Crescent

London
SW1X 8SD

Tel: 020 7235 6961
Fax: 020 7235 9734

### BELGIUM/LUXEMBOURG CHAMBER OF COMMERCE

Berkeley House
73 Upper Richmond Road
London
SW15 2SZ

Tel: 020 8877 3025
Fax: 020 8877 3961
email: info@blcc.co.uk

### DEPARTMENT OF TRADE & INDUSTRY (DTI) EUROPE DESK

Room 950
Kingsgate House
66/74 Victoria Street
London
SW1E 6SW

Tel: 020 7215 8885
Fax: 020 7215 8884

### KREDIETBANK (S.A.) LUXEMBOURGEOISE

Founders Court
Lothbury
London
EC2R 7HE
Tel: 020 7282 3304
Fax: 020 7282 3306
email: maria.horbaczewska@kblux.co.uk

### BANQUE INTERNATIONALE À LUXEMBOURG

Shackleton House
Hay's Galleria
4 Battle Bridge Lane
London
SE1 2GZ

Tel: 020 7556 3000
Fax: 020 7556 3055

**UK LUXEMBOURG SOCIETY**

George Kieffer, Honorary Secretary

email: georgekieffer@msn.com

**UNIVERSITY OF SHEFFIELD**

Dr. G Newton - Director

Centre for Luxembourg Studies
Arts Tower
Sheffield
S10 2UJ
Tel: (0114) 282 4396
email: g.newton@sheffield.ac.uk

## INCOMING, INCENTIVE & CONFERENCE ORGANISERS IN LUXEMBOURG

| Company | Telephone Fax (+352) | Incoming | Incentive | Conference Congress | Themed Programmes |
|---|---|---|---|---|---|
| Destination Europe<br>15, rue d'Oetrange<br>L-5411 Canach<br>email:travel@destination-europe.com | T: 35 65 75 226 F: 35 00 64 | Yes | Yes | - | Yes |
| Eurolux Tours<br>2 Rue Bellevue<br>L-5412 Canach<br>email: eurolux2@pt.lu | T: 35 75 65<br>F: 36 75 66 | Yes | - | - | Yes |
| European Express<br>22 Blvd de la Foire<br>L-1528 Luxembourg<br>email: tours@european-express.com | T: 45 41 41<br>F: 45 57 30 | Yes | Yes | - | Yes |
| I.T.O.C. SA<br>7, rue Kalchesbruck<br>L-1852 Luxembourg<br>email: itoc@hermesnet.com | T: 42 22 88-1 F: 42 22 88-250 | - | - | Yes | - |
| Luxembourg City Convention Bureau<br>P.O. Box 181<br>L-2011 Luxembourg<br>email: convention.bureau@luxembourg-city.lu | T: 22 75 65<br>F: 46 70 73 | Yes | Yes | Yes | Yes |
| Luxembourg Congrès<br>"Hémicycle" - 1 Rue du Fort Thüngen | T: 4302-577751 F: 4302- | - | Yes | Yes | - |

**For additional analytical, business and investment opportunities information, please contact Global Investment & Business Center, USA at (202) 546-2103. Fax: (202) 546-3275. E-mail: rusric@erols.com**

| | | | | | |
|---|---|---|---|---|---|
| Plateau de Kirchberg<br>L-1499 Luxembourg<br>email: info@luxcongress.lu | 57575 | | | | |
| Mediation<br>137 Val St Croix<br>L-1371 Luxembourg<br>email: mediation@mediation-sa.lu | T: 45 67 45<br>F: 45 67 47 | - | Yes | Yes | Yes |
| Meetincs S.A.<br>11 Rue Beatrix de Bourbon<br>L-1225 Luxembourg<br>email:meetincs@compuserve.com | T: 45 99 45 - 1<br>F: 45 99 45 - 210 | Yes | Yes | Yes | Yes |
| New Spirit SARL<br>38, rue Pierre Krier<br>L-1880 Luxembourg<br>email:webmaster@newspirit.lu | T: 40 62 71<br>F: 48 07 76 | - | Yes | Yes | Yes |
| Voyages Emile Weber<br>15 Rue d'Oetrange<br>L-5411 Canach<br>email:<br>destination.luxembourg@vew.lu | T: 35 65 75-1<br>F: 35 97 99 | Yes | - | - | - |
| Wezenberg Incentive Travel Service<br>PO Box 2479<br>75 Rue M Gehrend<br>L-1024 Luxembourg<br>email: wits@pt.lu | T: 40 23 32<br>F: 48 18 01 | Yes | Yes | Yes | Yes |

# MAJOR BANKS OPERATION IN LUXEMBOURG

### CENTRAL BANK

**Address** Banque centrale du Luxembourg
2, boulevard Royal
L-2983 LUXEMBOURG **Central Telephone** (+352) 4774-1 **Central Fax** (+352) 4774-4901
**General Secretariat** Communication, Press and Publications
Fax: (+352) 4774-4910

E-mail: sg@bcl.lu **Cash Department** Fax: (+352) 4774-4960
E-mail: cashdep@bcl.lu **IT Department** Fax: (+352) 4774-4975
E-mail: it@bcl.lu **Monetary Affairs, Economics Analyses and Statistics Department** Fax: (+352) 4774-4920
E-mail: mes@bcl.lu **Banking Operations Department** Fax: (+352) 4774-4950 ou -4951(Middle-Office)
E-mail: fo@bcl.lu (Front-Office)
E-mail: bo@bcl.lu (Back-Office) **Payment Systems Department** Fax: (+352) 4774-4952
E-mail: paysys@bcl.lu **Internal Administration Department** Fax: (+352) 4774-4930
E-mail: admint_bcl@bcl.lu
Human Resources Section
E-mail: reshum@bcl.lu
Accounting and Budget control Section

E-mail: combud@bcl.lu **Organisation and Risk Management** Fax: (+352) 4774-4910
E-mail: or@bcl.lu **Internal Audit** Fax: (+352) 4774-4970
E-mail: audit@bcl.lu

**A**
ABN AMRO Bank (Luxembourg) S.A.
Agence de Transfert de Technologie Financière, Luxembourg
Allgemeine Deutsche Direktbank International S.A.
American Express Bank (Luxembourg) S.A.
Argentabank Luxembourg S.A.
Artesia Bank Luxembourg
Association des Banques et Banquiers, Luxembourg
Association pour la Santé au Travail du Secteur Financier
**B**
Banca Antoniana Popolare Veneta, Luxembourg Branch
Banca di Roma International
Banca Lombarda International S.A.
Banca Nazionale del Lavoro International S.A.
Banca Popolare Commercio e Industria International S.A.
Banca popolare dell'Emilia Romagna (Europe) International S.A.
Banca Popolare di Novara, Succursale de Luxembourg
Banca Popolare di Verona - Banco S.Geminiano e S.Prospero s.c.a.r.l.
Banco di Sicilia International S.A.
Banco Itaú Europa Luxembourg S.A.
Banco Mercantil de São Paulo International S.A.
Banco Totta & Açores, Succursale de Luxembourg
Bank Leumi (Luxembourg) S.A.
Bank of Bermuda (Luxembourg) S.A.
Bank of China Luxembourg Branch
Bank of Tokyo-Mitsubishi (Luxembourg) S.A.
Bankgesellschaft Berlin International S.A.
Banque Audi (Luxembourg) S.A.
Banque Banespa International S.A.
Banque BCP S.A.
Banque Carnegie Luxembourg S.A.
Banque Colbert (Luxembourg) S.A.
Banque Continentale du Luxembourg S.A.
Banque de Commerce et de Placements S.A., Luxembourg Branch
Banque de l'Europe Méridionale - BEMO, Succursale de Luxembourg
Banque de Luxembourg
Banque Degroof Luxembourg S.A.
Banque Delen Luxembourg
Banque Dewaay S.A., Succursale de Luxembourg
Banque du Gothard (Luxembourg) S.A.
Banque du Gothard, Succursale de Luxembourg
Banque et Caisse d'Epargne de l'Etat, Luxembourg
Banque Fédérative du Crédit Mutuel, Succursale de Luxembourg
Banque Ferrier Lullin (Luxembourg) S.A.
Banque Générale du Luxembourg S.A.
Banque Hapoalim (Luxembourg) S.A.
Banque Invik S.A.
Banque IPPA & Associés S.A.
Banque Leu (Luxembourg) S.A.
Banque Nagelmackers 1747 (Luxembourg) S.A.
Banque Pictet (Luxembourg) S.A.

Banque Populaire du Luxembourg S.A.
Banque Privée Edmond de Rothschild Luxembourg
Banque Raiffeisen
Banque Safra-Luxembourg S.A.
Bausparkasse Schwäbisch Hall AG, Niederlassung Luxemburg
BFI Bank Luxembourg, Niederlassung der BFI Bank AG Dresden
BHF-BANK International S.A.
BHW Bausparkasse AG, Niederlassung Luxemburg
BNP Paribas Luxembourg
Brown Brothers Harriman (Luxembourg) S.C.A.
Bunadarbanki International S.A. (Luxembourg) «B.I. Bank»

**C**

Caixa Geral de Depósitos, Succursale de Luxembourg
Cardine Banca S.p.A., Succursale de Luxembourg
CCLux, Centrale de Communications Luxembourg S.A.
CETREL S.C.
Citibank International plc, Luxembourg Branch
Clearstream Banking
Commerzbank International S.A.
Cornèr Banque (Luxembourg) S.A.
Cortal Bank
Credem International (Lux) S.A.
Crédit Agricole Indosuez Luxembourg
Crédit Européen S.A.
Crédit Industriel d'Alsace et de Lorraine, Succursale de Luxembourg
Crédit Lyonnais Luxembourg S.A.
Credit Suisse (Luxembourg) S.A.

**D**

Danske Bank International S.A.
DekaBank Deutsche Girozentrale Luxembourg S.A.
Deutsche Bank Luxembourg S.A.
Deutsche Postbank International S.A.
Dexia Banque Internationale à Luxembourg
Dexia Nordic Private Bank Luxembourg S.A.
Discount Bank S.A.
Dresdner Bank Luxembourg S.A.
DZ BANK International S.A.

**E**

East-West United Bank S.A.
EFG Private Bank (Luxembourg) S.A.
Erste Europäische Pfandbrief- und Kommunalkreditbank A.G.
EUROPA BANK AG
Europäische Hypothekenbank S.A.

**F**

F. van Lanschot Bankiers (Luxembourg) S.A.
Fairbank S.A.
Fideuram Bank (Luxembourg) S.A.
Frankfurter Sparkasse, Niederlassung Luxemburg
Frankfurter Volksbank eG, Niederlassung Luxemburg
Freie Internationale Sparkasse S.A.

**G**

Garanti Bank Luxembourg Branch

**H**

Hauck & Aufhäuser Banquiers Luxembourg S.A.
HSBC Republic Bank (Luxembourg) S.A.

HSBC Trinkaus & Burkhardt (International) SA
HVB Banque Luxembourg
**I**
IBL Investment Bank Luxembourg S.A.
IKB International
IMI Bank (Lux) S.A.
ING Bank (Luxembourg) S.A.
Institut de Formation Bancaire, Luxembourg
**J**
J.P.Morgan Bank Luxembourg S.A.
John Deere Bank S.A.
**K**
Kaupthing Bank Luxembourg S.A.
Kölner Bank eG, Niederlassung Luxemburg
Kookmin Bank Luxembourg S.A.
Kredietbank S.A. Luxembourgeoise
**L**
Lampebank International S.A.
Landesbank Rheinland-Pfalz International S.A.
Landesbank Schleswig-Holstein International S.A.
LBLux S.A.
Lloyds TSB Bank plc, Luxembourg Branch
**M**
M.M.Warburg & CO Luxembourg S.A.
Mizuho Trust & Banking (Luxembourg) S.A.
Mutuel Bank Luxembourg
**N**
Natexis Banques Populaires (Luxembourg) S.A.
Nikko Bank (Luxembourg) S.A.
Nomura Bank (Luxembourg) S.A.
Norddeutsche Landesbank Luxembourg S.A.
Nordea Bank S.A.
**P**
Pfandbrief Bank International S.A.
PROFIL (Fédération des professionnels du secteur financier, Luxembourg)
Prudential-Bache International Bank Limited, Luxembourg Branch
**R**
Rabo Robeco Bank (Luxembourg) S.A.
Rolo Banca 1473 S.p.A., Succursale de Luxembourg
**S**
Sal. Oppenheim jr. & Cie. Luxemburg S.A.
Sanpaolo Bank S.A.
SEB Private Bank S.A.
Société de la Bourse de Luxembourg S.A.
Société Européenne de Banque S.A.
Société Générale Bank & Trust
State Street Bank Luxembourg S.A.
Sumitomo Trust and Banking (Luxembourg) S.A.
Svenska Handelsbanken S.A.
Swedbank (Luxembourg) S.A.
**T**
The Bank of New York (Luxembourg) S.A.
The Bank of New York Europe Limited, Luxembourg Branch
**U**
UBS (Luxembourg) S.A.

**For additional analytical, business and investment opportunities information, please contact Global Investment & Business Center, USA at (202) 546-2103. Fax: (202) 546-3275. E-mail: rusric@erols.com**

Unibanco - União de Bancos Brasileiros (Luxembourg) S.A.
Union Bank of Norway International S.A.
United European Bank (Luxembourg) S.A.
**V**
Volksbank Hannover eG, Niederlassung Luxemburg
VP Bank (Luxembourg) S.A.
**W**
WestLB International S.A.
WGZ-Bank Luxembourg S.A.
Wüstenrot Bausparkasse AG, Niederlassung Luxemburg

## *THE* FEDERATION OF LUXEMBOURG INDUSTRIALISTS *(FEDIL)*

**The *Federation of Luxembourg Industrialists* (FEDIL)** was founded in 1918 as the representative professional association of Luxembourg's industry. **FEDIL** unites nearly all the small, medium and large sized industries of the Grand-Duchy, as well as a growing number of companies in the industrial services sector.

**FIGURES**

**420** companies
**60.000** wage-earners
**55** mia LUF/year of wage mass
**250** mia LUF/year of exports
**120** mia LUF/year of added value

**SECTORS**

Steel Industry
Metal Transformation Industry
Chemical and Para-chemical Industry
Non-Metallic Mineral Products Industry
Construction and Finishing
Quarries
Agriculture and Food Industry
Beverages and Tobacco Industry
Printing and Paper Converting
Textile Industry
Wood Industry
Electric and Electronic Industry
Energy
Communication
Data Processing
Transport and Handling
Waste Management and Transport
International Trade
Building Maintenance and Cleaning
Security and Surveillance Services
Management Consulting Firms
Patent Agents
Pharmaceutical Products

Temporary Work
Various Industrial Services

**MEMBERS**

The Federation of Luxembourg Industrialists' members are all based in Luxembourg and can be divided into 3 different categories:

1. Industrial companies
2. Industrial services companies
3. Service companies closely linked to the industrial sector

Within FEDIL, companies belonging to the same sector may form a professional section. More or less 420 companies as well as 13 professional associations are members of FEDIL today:

Luxembourg Brewers Federation
Federation of the Luxembourg Food-Processing Industry
Luxembourg Lift Federations
Association of Luxembourg Manufacturers and Founders
Association of Luxembourg Building and Public Works Contractors
Association of Fancy Paste Producers
Association of Luxembourg Rubber Industries
Association of Luxembourg Steel Industries
Association of Luxembourg Sparkling Wine Producers
Association of Luxembourg Building Material Producers
Luxembourg Saw-Mills Association
International Trade Association
Association of the Luxembourg Petrol Industry
Union of the Luxembourg Temporary employment Agencies

National institutions in which FEDIL represents its members:

*Economic affairs*

Comité de Conjoncture
Commission consultative du Commerce extérieur
Commission des Prix
Commission des Prix de la Construction
Commission du Bâtiment
Conseil supérieur de la Statistique
Groupe Luxembourgeois de l'Association internationale pour la Protection de la Propriété industrielle
Luxdevelopment
Luxinnovation
Office du Ducroire
Office luxembourgeois pour l'Accroissement de la Productivité
Société Nationale de Crédit et d'Investissement

*Social affairs*

Comité du Travail féminin

Commission consultative auprès de l'Inspection du Travail et des Mines (I.T.M.)
Commission nationale de l'Emploi
Conseil national de l'Immigration
Ecole Supérieure du Travail (E.S.T.)
Office national de Conciliation
Organes de la Sécurité sociale
Service de Santé au Travail de l'Industrie (STI)

*Others*

The Luxembourg Chamber of Commerce
National Tripartite Committee on Employment Questions
The Economic and Social Council

*Participations*

FEDIL participates in the following organisations:

| | |
|---|---|
| Handling and management off industrial waste | GEDELUX S.A. |
| Research and development | LUXINNOVATION |
| Economic Cooperation | LUXDEVELOPMENT |
| Health and Safety at work | S.T.I. Asbl |

## ORGANIZATION

For the achievement of its objectives, FEDIL functions throughout the following bodies:

The General Assembly of the members
The Board, which groups managers from each sector
Three Committees of Experts: Economic and Fiscal Affairs, Social Affairs and Industrial Affairs
Ad-hoc working groups which examine present-day questions and punctual problems

## ACTIVITIES

FEDIL assists and advises its members. These tasks cover each sector of social and economic life such as the right of establishment, investment aid, foreign trade, community legislation, innovation aid, labour legislation, collective agreements, social security, work and training, etc....

FEDIL is constantly in touch with the authorities, economic circles, politicians and trade unions. Thus, the association is directly involved in the preparation of economic and social decisions, as it is represented in numerous deliberative bodies.

The Industry departement of the Euro Info Center (E.I.C.) and the environmental counseling office are also organised within the FEDIL secretariat. The E.I.C. deals with european questions in relation to whereas the latter studies companies' problems with regard to environment protection.

**For additional analytical, business and investment opportunities information, please contact Global Investment & Business Center, USA at (202) 546-2103. Fax: (202) 546-3275. E-mail: rusric@erols.com**

LUXINNOVATION GIE, a service for promoting and assisting Innovation has been created by a joint convention between FEDIL, the Ministry of the Economy and the Luxembourg Chamber of Commerce.

On the European level, FEDIL is a member of the Union of Industrial and Employers' Confederations of Europe (UNICE). As a representative organisation of Luxembourg's employers, FEDIL contributes to the activities of the International Labour Conference in Geneva. The organisation is also a member of the International Organisation of Employers (OIE) and of the Business and Industry Advisory Committee (BIAC) of the OECD.

**For additional analytical, business and investment opportunities information, please contact Global Investment & Business Center, USA at (202) 546-2103. Fax: (202) 546-3275. E-mail: rusric@erols.com**

# TRAVEL TO LUXEMBOURG

## US STATE DEPARTMENT SUGGESTIONS

**COUNTRY DESCRIPTION**: Luxembourg is a highly developed stable constitutional monarchy. Tourist facilities are widely available.

**ENTRY REQUIREMENTS**: A passport is required. A visa is not required for American citizens for business or tourist stays of up to 90 days. For further information concerning entry requirements for Luxembourg, travelers can contact the Embassy of Luxembourg at 2200 Massachusetts Avenue, N.W., Washington, D.C. 20008, Tel. (202) 265-4171/72, or the Luxembourg consulates general in New York or San Francisco.

**CRIME INFORMATION**: Luxembourg has a low crime rate. However, during the tourist season, pickpocketing, theft from vehicles, and theft of unattended baggage can occur. The loss or theft abroad of an U.S. passport should be reported immediately to the local police and the nearest embassy or consulate. U.S. citizens can refer to the Department of State's pamphlet *A Safe Trip Abroad* for ways to enjoy a more trouble-free voyage. The pamphlet is available from the Superintendent of Documents, U.S. Government Printing Office, Washington, D.C. 20402, via the Internet at http://www.access.gpo.gov/su docs, or via the Bureau of Consular Affairs home page at http://travel.state.gov.

**MEDICAL FACILITIES**: Medical facilities are available, but may be limited outside urban areas. Serious medical problems requiring hospitalization and/or medical evacuation to the United States can cost thousands of dollars or more. Doctors and hospitals often expect immediate cash payment for health services.

**MEDICAL INSURANCE**: U.S. medical insurance is not always valid outside the United States. U.S. Medicare and Medicaid programs do not provide payment for medical services outside the United States. Uninsured travelers who require medical care overseas may face extreme difficulties. Check with your own insurance company to confirm whether your policy applies overseas, including provision for medical evacuation. Ascertain whether payment will be made to the overseas hospital or doctor or whether you will be reimbursed later for expenses you incur. Some insurance policies also include coverage for psychiatric treatment and for disposition of remains in the event of death. Useful information on medical emergencies abroad, including overseas insurance programs, is provided in the Department of State, Bureau of Consular Affairs brochure *Medical Information for Americans Traveling Abroad*, available via the Bureau of Consular Affairs home page or autofax: (202) 647-3000.

**OTHER HEALTH INFORMATION**: Information on vaccinations and other health precautions may be obtained from the Centers for Disease Control and Prevention's hotline for international traveler's at 1-877-FYI-TRIP (1-877-394-8747); fax 1-888-CDC-FAXX (1-888-232-3299), or via their Internet site at http://www.cdc.gov.

TRAFFIC SAFETY AND ROAD CONDITIONS: While in a foreign country, U.S. citizens may encounter road conditions that differ significantly from those in the United States. The information below concerning Luxembourg is provided for general reference only, and may not be totally accurate in a particular location or circumstance.

Safety of Public Transportation: Good
Urban Road Conditions/Maintenance: Good

**For additional analytical, business and investment opportunities information, please contact Global Investment & Business Center, USA at (202) 546-2103. Fax: (202) 546-3275. E-mail: rusric@erols.com**

Rural Road Conditions/Maintenance: Good
Availability of Roadside Assistance: Good

Luxembourg has a modern, well-maintained system of highways and secondary roads. In mountainous areas, winding roads and cyclists sometimes slow traffic, and roads can be congested during rush hour in the Luxembourg City environs. Visitors should drive defensively in high volume commuter and tourist traffic, or during winter fog and ice.

For specific information concerning Luxembourg driver's permits, vehicle inspection, road tax and mandatory insurance, contact the Luxembourg National Tourist Office in New York at 212-935-8888, or via the Internet at http://www.visitluxembourg.com. For international driving permits contact AAA or the American Automobile Touring Alliance.

**AVIATION SAFETY OVERSIGHT**: The U.S. Federal Aviation Administration (FAA) has assessed Luxembourg Civil Aviation Authority as category 1- in compliance with international aviation safety standards for oversight of Luxembourg air carrier operations.

For further information, travelers may contact the Department of Transportation within the U.S. at 1-800-322-7873, or visit the FAA Internet home page at http://www.faa.gov/avr/iasa.htm. The U.S. Department of Defense (DOD) separately assesses some foreign air carriers for suitability as official providers of air services. For information regarding the DOD policy on specific carriers, travelers may contact DOD at (618) 229-4801.

**CUSTOMS REGULATIONS**: Luxembourg customs authorities encourage the use of an ATA (Admission Temporaire/Temporary Admission) Carnet for the temporary admission of professional equipment, commercial samples, and/or goods for exhibitions and fair purposes. ATA Carnet Headquarters, located at the U.S. Council for International Business, 1212 Avenue of the Americas, New York, NY 10036, issues and guarantees the ATA Carnet in the United States. For additional information call (212) 354-4480, send an e-mail to atacarnet@uscib.org, or visit http://www.uscib.org for details.

**CRIMINAL PENALTIES**: While in a foreign country, a U.S. citizen is subject to that country's laws and regulations, which sometimes differ significantly from those in the United States and may not afford the protections available to the individual under U.S. law. Penalties for breaking the law can be more severe than in the United States for similar offenses. Persons violating Luxembourg law, even unknowingly, may be expelled, arrested or imprisoned. Penalties for possession, use, or trafficking in illegal drugs in Luxembourg are strict and convicted offenders can expect jail sentences and heavy fines.

**CHILDREN'S ISSUES**: For information on international adoption of children, international parental child abduction, and international child support enforcement issues, please refer to our Internet site at http://travel.state.gov/children's_issues.html or telephone (202) 736-7000.

**REGISTRATION AND EMBASSY LOCATION**: Americans living in or visiting Luxembourg are encouraged to register with the Consular Section of the U.S. Embassy in Luxembourg and obtain updated information on travel and security within Luxembourg. The Embassy is located at 22 Boulevard Emmanuel Servais in Luxembourg City, Telephone (352) 46-01-23.

## LIVING IN LUXEMBOURG

**We must make it quite clear that we are only a Tourist Office, and that it is not in our remit to help you move to Luxembourg, or relocate there, or find work, or get set up in Luxembourg, or ...**

We are however so often faced with such questions, that we have decided to put together this page which purports to help those of you who are looking for further information on the general subject of "living in Luxembourg" and/or "moving to Luxembourg", and to give you whatever help we can in this area. Our general disclaimer applies.

Relocation companies, please note that we do *not* give you permission to print out this page, and to sell the information to your customers.
Please instead direct customers to this page: http://www.luxembourg.co.uk/living.html. Thank you.

Please note that this page is very much in its infancy, and we would love to hear from you with any further suggestions as to what to include here. Please contact us by email to: living@luxembourg.co.uk.

If you've not already done so, please read our page on Luxembourg, a linguistic puzzle, which will brief you on Languages in our country, and gives contact points for language courses.
Our introduction to the country as a whole Luxembourg in a Nutshell could be of much use to you, as indeed could be many of the pages we list on our index page.

The Book "Living in Luxembourg", produced by the American Women's Club of Luxembourg (AWCL) is another most useful resource on our country. Especially for Americans moving to Luxembourg, this book has a tremendous wealth of information to make the transition easier.

Contact the AWCL (American Women's Club of Luxembourg) 52 rue Marie-Adelaide, L-2128, Luxembourg-Belair, weekdays from 10 a.m. to 5 p.m.

**ACCOMMODATION**

If you are looking for longer term accommodation other than Hotels & Guesthouses, eg Flats / houses / apartments, or perhaps even office space, may we direct you to contact one of the many estate agents in Luxembourg. At the time of writing, we know only of two such organisations which also have a full web presence:

www.lth-lux-immo.lu
www.dataimmo.lu

You would also be well-advised to consult the local papers, most of which are written in French and German. Two broadsheet papers have a particularly noteworthy web presence, and list their Small Ads sections [which include accommodation (check sub "Immobilier")] at:

Luxemburger Wort
tageblatt

There is only one (weekly) english-language newspaper, the Luxembourg News, which sometimes lists accommodation to let. For further info:

Luxembourg News
25 rue Philippe II
L-2340 Luxembourg
Tel: 46 11 22 1
Fax: 47 00 56
email: email@news.lu

**For additional analytical, business and investment opportunities information, please contact Global Investment & Business Center, USA at (202) 546-2103. Fax: (202) 546-3275. E-mail: rusric@erols.com**

## SOCIAL

Of much relevance to the subject of "living" in Luxembourg is the twice-yearly listing of Luxembourg Clubs and Associations published by the "Luxembourg News" (cf above) "**Luxembourg Accueil**" has nearly 1000 members representing 35 different nationalities and was established in 1977 to provide information about living in Luxembourg and to help people become integrated. The association holds a variety of activities ranging from language, cooking & art classes to visits of sites of interest and newcomers' coffee mornings.
Contact:

Luxembourg Accueil
10, Bisserwee
L-1238 Luxembourg
Tel: 4 17 17
open Mon-Fri: 9-12

Our page of Events in Luxembourg lists useful pointers for other social entertainment

## SCHOOLS

You might have children who need schooling while you're working in Luxembourg. In our above-mentioned Luxembourg, a linguistic puzzle, we also briefly describe the use of languages in Luxembourg schools. Check the Ministry of Education's website for a schematic overview of the Luxembourg School System (pages in French). In our London office, we are only aware of 3 schools that offer schooling in English:

**St George's International School Luxembourg**

Rue des Marguerites
L-2127 Weimershof
Tel: 42 32 24
Fax: 42 32 34
email: st.georges@online.lu

St George's welcomes puplis of all nationalities and offers a British style education for children aged two and a half to eleven. Small classes with beneficial teacher-pupil ratios make for a friendly and caring environment.

**École Européenne**

23 Boulevard Konrad Adenauer
Tel: 43 20 82-1
Fax 43 67 38

Please note that the original purpose of the "European School" was to provide schooling for the kids of people employed by the European Community. Therefore, they will only accept students *if* they have room after they have allocated the children of European Community employees.

**The American International School of Luxembourg**

188, Avenue de la Faïencerie
Limpertsberg
L-1511 Luxembourg
Tel: 47 00 20

While Luxembourg does not have a university per se, there are nevertheless three institutions that offer Higher Education:

The "Sacred Heart University at Luxembourg" is the only American accredited MBA programme in the Grand Duchy, and as such, it is a very popular choice with those seeking to maintain or introduce an American connection into their studies. The degree is also recognised by the Luxembourg government, and registration with the Ministry of National Education and Professional training bestows EU-wide recognition.

As well as offering the full MBA course, which takes between one and a half and three years to complete -depending on the canidate's other commitments- the University has recently introduced four Graduate Professional Certificate Programmes. These are designed for those people who do not want to pursue the full MBA but are keen to study a certain field. Thus the certificates are in Fundamentals of Management, Finance, and Team Leadership as well as an advanced course of Team Leadership. These courses can be taken individually, or the credits can count towards an MBA.
For more details about the "Sacred Heart University", contact the Luxembourg Campus on Tel: (+352) 22 76 13 or fax: (+352) 22 76 23, or write to: 25b, Boulevard Royal, 7th floor, L-2449 Luxembourg.

The Miami University Dolibois European Center, Luxembourg offers study abroad in Luxembourg for a semester or a year.
The Open University currently has about 200 students in Luxembourg. The University was established in 1963 and is Britain's largest and most innovative university with a world-wide reputation for the quality of its teaching. Students study part-time "at home", using multimedia supports (videos, cassettes) alongside the more traditional methods such as texts and books. For more details on the widde range of courses offered, please contact Liv-Ellen Kennedy on Tel: (+352) 32 91 14, or fax: (+352) 32 56 50, or email l.e.kennedy@open.ac.uk

Looking through the Luxembourg Telephone directory sub "école" might give you further details. Also of note is the fact that the Luxembourg Telephone Directory is on the web. Parents might also like to contact the Luxembourg Youth Club at:
**Centre Information Jeunes**

76 Boulevard de la Petrusse
L-2320 Luxembourg
Tel: 40 55 50 Further relevant places for getting more information on the subject of Schooling are:
**Ministère de l'Education Nationale**
29 Rue Aldringen
L-2926 Luxembourg
Tel: 4798-1
**Service d'Orientation Scolaire**
280 Route de Longwy
L-1940 Luxembourg
And on the web, you'll find a much useful listing of Luxembourg Schools on the web

## BRINGING PETS INTO LUXEMBOURG

Importing pets to Luxembourg from the UK: An October '94 regulation requires an "Export Health Certificate" for the pets. For Birds, this is available from the "Ministry of Agriculture, Food & Fisheries" (Import/Export of Birds section; Tel: 020 7904 6373)

Note that there are different regulations for Cats & Dogs: They must be vaccinated against Rabies and have a relevant certificate. Note also that there is currently a 6 months quarantaine on re-entry into the UK! (Jan '99)

Please also note that some airlines may require you to have a "Pet Health Certificate" for the flight.

### FURTHER INFORMATION

Of course, this brief page can only but give you some pointers as to where to enquire further.
Our list of Luxembourg Embassies Worldwide might be of use to you
You might like to look through our list of selected WWWeb Links to Luxembourg, or search this site.

The "*Salary Calculator*" at www.homefair.com includes Luxembourg, and gives comparative salaries for many places.

The "American Women's Club of Luxembourg" has published an excellent 300-page book guide (A5 format) to "Living in Luxembourg", which takes a lot of the pain out of the research work. This guide is available from:

American Women's Club of Luxembourg

7 Rue de Luxembourg
L-8184 Kopstal
Grand Duchy of Luxembourg
Tel: (+352) 30 74 34 LuxNYT addresses itself to Luxembourgers and Danes who want to move / live in Luxembourg (much of this site is in the Danish and Lëtzebuergesch language

## BUSINESS TRAVEL

### BUSINESS CUSTOMS

**Business Hours**
Government offices are open Monday through Friday from 8:00 a.m.-12:30 p.m. and from 1:30 p.m.-5:00 p.m. Banks are open Monday through Friday from 9:00 a.m.-4:30 p.m. Private companies are generally open from 8:00 a.m.-5:00 p.m. while shops and stores open at 9a.m. and close at 6:00 p.m.

**Languages**
Luxembourgish, also spelled lëtzebuergesch, is the native language spoken in the majority of homes. It has been recognized as the national language since 1984; while both French and German remain official languages. German is the language of instruction beginning in first grade; French begins shortly thereafter. French is the official language of the administration, jurisdiction, parliament, education, and some literary circles. Daily newspapers are written mainly in German with some articles written in French. Many Luxembourgers are also able to speak English, especially in the business and government sectors.

**Time**
GMT +1 (same as Berlin, Rome, Brussels, Amsterdam, Vienna, Paris, Madrid, etc.)

**Travel Advisory and Visas**
Visas are not required for U.S. citizens traveling in Luxembourg for less than 90 days. Resident visas are difficult to obtain for non-EU citizens. To obtain a residence visa, it is necessary to have a working permit, which are limited to managerial positions in foreign-owned companies and people with special skills that are unavailable in Luxembourg. It usually takes eight to twelve months to obtain a working permit and 18 months to obtain a professional card. Specialized lawyers established in Luxembourg can assist in the process.

**Currency and Credit Cards**
The Luxembourg Franc is the local currency, which is inter-exchangeable with the Belgian Franc. Most hotels and restaurants take credit and charge cards (Visa, MasterCard (Eurocard), American Express, or Diners Club).

**Voltage**
220/380 volts AC 50 three-phase current.

Work Week

Monday through Friday, 40 hours/week.

### BUSINESS INFRASTRUCTURE

Public transportation is readily available, and Luxembourg has excellent communication links with the rest of the world. Luxembourg is also home to extraordinarily rich media coverage, which offers the broadest selection of television channels in Europe. TV viewers currently have access to a broad range of programs from around the world via satellite. The country is blessed with an intense and varied cultural life, and is highly regarded for its acceptance of foreign goods and persons and its overall lifestyle and family oriented values system.

U.S. business travelers are encouraged to obtain a copy of the Key Officers of Foreign Service Posts: Guide for Business Representatives available for sale by the superintendent of documents, U.S. Government Printing Office, Washington, D.C. 20402; Tel. (202) 512-1800; Fax (202) 512-2250. Business travelers to Luxembourg seeking appointments with U.S. Embassy Luxembourg officials should contact the Commercial Section in advance. The Commercial Section in Brussels can be reached by telephone at +32/2 508-2425, by fax at +32/2 512-6653, or by email at brussels.office.box@mail.doc.gov.

Please contact:
ESIMSO
37 Rue de la Gare
L-9420 Vianden
Tel: (+352) 83 42 57
Fax: (+352) 84 90 81
You might also like to contact the City Tourist Office for guided tours. Their offers are on the web at: http://www.luxembourg-city.lu/touristinfo/html/luxembourg_city/discover/offer_for_tour.html

## RAILWAY FARES FROM LUXEMBOURG

As an indication, we list here some railway fares (in Belgian=Luxembourg Francs) for railway journeys from Luxembourg, valid at the time of input, March 2000. We aim to update these fares as and when necessary, but please note that no guarantees are given as to the exactitude of these fares.
For the most uptodate exchange rates, check out Olsen and Associates' excellent Currency converter

For further information, seat reservation, and confirmation of fares, travellers are advised to contact the Luxembourg Railways (CFL) on tel: (+352) 4990-4990, or on fax: (+352) 49 35 32

Railway Travellers might be interested to note that a porter service is available at Luxembourg Railway station from 6 a.m. to 8 p.m. at a cost of 50 Flux per item of luggage (max 150 Flux). This porter service may be ordered in advance on tel: (+352) 4990 4475

If you require timetable information, please note that the Railserver of the German Railways at: http://www.bahn.de offers a most useful email service with timetables from all German stations (and many a Belgian and French station too), to Luxembourg.

If you need any further help with regards to Luxembourg Railways, please either
telephone: +44 (0)20 7434 2800
or fax: +44 (0)20 7734 1205

# PUBLIC TRANSPORT IN LUXEMBOURG

## LUXEMBOURG CITY

The City of Luxembourg is served by an efficient network of buses run by the *"Autobus municipaux de la Ville de Luxembourg"*. The main centre of the capital city is very compact and eminently walkable, in spite of the cliffs and ramparts which so characterise the old fortress city. (cf City map). There is no underground or tramway service, but there are very interesting plans to improve on the existing link from the airport to the railway station via a direct connection, and to build a new Railway-Tram that will travel on the national Railway lines, and function as a tram once within the confines of Luxembourg City. Alas, the latter will not be ready until the next millenium...

The recent introduction of Night Buses has seen a remarkable decrease in the amount of late-night traffic and noise. For further details on these and other City Bus services, see www.autobus.lu or telephone: (+352) 4796 2975.

Unless you can show a pass, a ride on a City bus will set you back a flat fare of 40 Luxembourg Francs (some 90 UK pence). This "short distance" ticket is valid for one hour (or ±10 km) from purchase on the whole of Luxembourg's public transport network, and also allows transits between city and country buses and trains.

The Luxembourger is justly proud of the geographical variety of his small country. Especially if you're only on a short visit to the country, you should not miss out on visiting the Ardennes hills and forests, the wine-making valley of the Moselle, or the lovely "Little Switzerland" - also known as *Müllerthal* - and the "Minette", the *Land of the Red Earth*. From the capital, you are no more than 1 hour away from anywhere within Luxembourg. Browse our Country Picture Gallery if you feel you need convincing that a trip to Luxembourg's countryside (some ten minutes from the City Centre) is worth the effort ;-)

## NATIONAL TICKETS

A so-called **"Oeko-Pass"** (as in economical or even ecological network ticket) is available at railway stations throughout the country, and at the airport. It covers unlimited travel on all forms of public transport (city buses, trains and country coaches) for one day (which is considered to last until 8 am the next morning) throughout the country. It is not valid on sightseeing buses.

You can purchase a single ticket for 160 Francs (Luxembourg = Belgian Franc) [roughly £2.50], or a block of 5 such tickets for 540 Francs [± £9]. For other currencies, check out Olsen & Associates' excellent Currency converter

Other forms of such network tickets include monthly tickets (1300 Fr roughly 26 ukp). People over 65 years of age, and mini-groups (eg large families) can benefit from a reduction of 50% (but you'll need certain cards for this, available from the Luxembourg Railways).

It is also well worth investigating the LuxembourgCard which also includes free transport, and in addition gives you free entry to 34 attractions thoughout the country for about five pounds a day for a single user, or ten pounds a day for a family of five.

## RAILWAY TIMETABLES

From May 30, 1999, the Luxembourg Railways run to the new "Horaire Cadencé" schedule (which builds on last year's "Takt 98"), meaning that there is at least 1 train every hour to every station at the same time of every hour between 8 a.m. and 8 p.m. This represents a great improvement on the previous system, and deserves a full round of applause for CFL, the Luxembourg Railways!

Details of the new timetable can be found at: http://www.cfl.lu/f/horcad99/horcad99.htm, where a clickable map gives you timings for all trains to all stations on the Luxembourg Railway Network.

The Information service of CFL, the Luxembourg National Railways (also giving Country Bus information), can be contacted direct by Tel: (+ 352) 4990-4990 or (+ 352) 4990-5572 [every day GMT: 5 a.m. to 19 p.m.] and by Fax: (+ 352) 49 35 32.

Talking about **Railways**, it is perhaps well worth duplicating here some of the links presented elsewhere on this site:
The Railserver of the Deutsche Bahn (German Railways) at: http://www.bahn.de offers a most useful email service with timetables from all German stations (and many a Belgian and French station too), to Luxembourg.

The english enquiries page for HaCon, now owned by "Deutsche Bahn" offers a pan-european railway timetable. While this server is perhaps not always the quickest (seen the amount of requests), it does though cover the entire country admirably well, including the bus routes run by CFL, the Luxembourg railways. Of course, it also gives connections to Luxembourg from abroad. A CD-ROM version of this timetable is available from HaCon. Incidentally, our office uses the same timetable.

In this context, the Belgian Railways website is also worthy of note, as is the French equivalent service offered at www.sncf.fr.

## PUBLIC TRANSPORT MAPS

Just for completeness sake, we have placed here a Railway Network Map, albeit that this is now somewhat superseded by the above Takt'98, but the old version may be easier to get to grips with, if you are not entirely familiar with the geographical layout of Luxembourg's Railway Network. We also have added a schematic plan of public transport in Luxembourg, which includes both trains and national coaches

Further information on Europe's railways is available at the excellent European RailServer.

For those who have a keen interest in Luxembourg's railways, you really ought to visit: http://dbertens.www.cistron.nl/rail/runner.htm and/or www.surf.to/trains

# PACKAGES TO LUXEMBOURG

Here's a list of the main UK based Tour Operators offering packages to Luxembourg

## SHORT BREAKS / CITY BREAKS

| Name / Address | Tel / Fax | Accommodation featured |
|---|---|---|
| Aeroscope<br>Scope House<br>Hospital Road<br>Moreton-in-Marsh<br>Glos GL56 0BQ | Tel: 01608 650103<br>Fax: 01608 651295<br>aerscope@aol.com | Best Western: Hotel International **** - Luxembourg City |
| Cresta<br>Tabley Court<br>Victoria Street<br>Altrincham<br>Cheshire WA14 1EZ | Tel: 0870 161 0900<br>Fax: 0870 169 0797<br>cresta@crestaholidays.co.uk | Hôtel Christophe Colomb *** - Luxembourg City<br>Hôtel Parc Belair **** - Luxembourg City |
| Crystal Holidays<br>Crystal House<br>The Courtyard<br>Arlington Road<br>Surbiton<br>Surrey KT6 6BW | Tel: 020 8241 5040<br>Fax: 020 8390 6378<br>travel@crystalholidays.co.uk | |
| Moswin Tours<br>Moswin House<br>21 Church Street<br>Oadby<br>Leicester LE2 5DB | Tel: 01162 719922<br>Fax: 01162 716016<br>sales@moswin.freeserve.co.uk | Best Western Hôtel International **** - Luxembourg City<br>Hotel Inn-Side Residence **** |
| Motours<br>Buckingham House<br>Longfield Road<br>Tunbridge Wells<br>Kent TN2 3DQ | Tel: 01892 686666<br>Fax: 01892 686677<br>sales@motours.co.uk | Parc Belle-Vue *** - Luxembourg City<br>Hôtel-Restaurant International **** - Clervaux<br>Hôtel-Restaurant La bonne Auberge *** - Gaichel |
| Travelscene<br>Travelscene House<br>11-15 St. Ann's Road<br>Harrow<br>Middx HA1 1AS | Tel: 020 8427 4445<br>Fax: 020 8861 4154<br>reservations@travelscene.co.uk | Hotel Italia - Luxembourg City<br>Hôtel Intercontinental ***** - Luxembourg City |

## COACH HOLIDAYS

| Name / Address | Tel / Fax | Tour details |
|---|---|---|
| Crusader Holidays<br>Crusader Business Park<br>Stephenson Road West<br>Clacton-on-Sea | Tel: 01255 425 453<br>Fax: 01255 222 683 | 4/5 day breaks staying in Novotel **** - Luxembourg City, with optional excursions<br>Various departures for 2001 (Feb 9/23; |

For additional analytical, business and investment opportunities information, please contact Global Investment & Business Center, USA at (202) 546-2103. Fax: (202) 546-3275. E-mail: rusric@erols.com

| | | |
|---|---|---|
| Essex CO15 4HP | | Mar 9/23; Apr 13/20; Jul 9/23; Aug 6/20; Sep 3; Oct 5/12/26; Nov 9/23). 4 days from £139 / 5 days from £199 |
| Harry Shaw City Cruiser<br>Mill House, Mill Lane,<br>Binley<br>Coventry<br>CV3 2DU | Tel: (024) 764 555 44<br>Fax: (024) 766 35 684 | 5 days/ 4 nights Breaks from £169.95 per person.<br>Optional excursions to: The Ardennes & Clervaux; Luxembourg City Tour; The Moselle Valley; Little Switzerland & Echternach.<br>Various departures for 2001 (April 6; May 18, June 22, October 12, 19, 26) |
| Leger Travel<br>Sunway House<br>Canklow Meadows<br>West Hawtry Road<br>Rotherham S60 2XR | Tel: 01709 833 812<br>Fax: 01709 820 114<br>reservations@leger.co.uk | Hôtel Mercure *** - Luxembourg City |
| Skills Coach Holidays<br>1, St Peters Street<br>Radford<br>Nottingham NG7 3EL | Tel: 0115 978 4645<br>Fax: 0115 942 0788<br>enquiry@skills.co.uk | Luxembourg, Ardennes & Moselle Valley<br>Hôtel-Restaurant Bel-Air ****<br>Echternach |
| Travelsphere<br>Compass House<br>Rockingham Road<br>Market Harborough<br>Leicestershire LE16 7QD | Tel: 01858 410 818<br>Fax: 01858 434 323<br>telesales@travelsphere.co.uk | Grand Hotel - Vianden<br>5 days / 4 nights, with optional excursions, various departures throughout the year, from £ 149 |

## CAMPING HOLIDAYS

| Name / Address | Tel / Fax | Accommodation featured |
|---|---|---|
| Canvas Holidays Ltd<br>12 Abbey Park Place<br>Dunfermline<br>Fife KY12 7PD | Tel: (01383) 644000<br>Fax: (01383) 620075 | Camping "Nommerlayen" (Nommern) |
| Caravan Club<br>East Grinstead House<br>East Grinstead<br>West Sussex RH19 1UA | Tel: 01342 316101<br>Fax: 01342 410258 | Camping "Um Gritt" (Bourscheid)<br>Camping "Romantique" (Walsdorf)<br>Camping "Birkelt" (Larochette) |
| Carefree<br>The Camping & Caravanning Club<br>Greenfields House<br>Westwood Way<br>Coventry CV4 8JH | Tel: 01203 422024<br>Fax: 01203 422010 | Camping "Auf Kengert" (Medernach) |
| Eurocamp Travel Ltd<br>Hartford Manor<br>Greenbank | Tel: 01606 78 78 70<br>Fax: 01606 78 70 36 | Camping "Birkelt" (Larochette) |

**For additional analytical, business and investment opportunities information, please contact Global Investment & Business Center, USA at (202) 546-2103. Fax: (202) 546-3275. E-mail: rusric@erols.com**

| | | |
|---|---|---|
| Northwich<br>Cheshire CW8 1HW | | |
| Eurosites<br>Wavell House<br>Holcombe Road<br>Helmshore<br>Rossendale<br>Lancs BB4 4NB | Tel: 0870 751 0000<br>Fax: 0870 751 0011<br>eurosites@airtours.com | Camping "Birkelt" (Larochette) |
| Keycamp Holidays<br>92-96 Lind Road<br>Sutton<br>Surrey SM1 4PL | Tel: 0870 7000 123<br>Fax: 0870 7000 711<br>info@keycamp.co.uk | Camping "Birkelt" (Larochette) |
| Select Site Reservations<br>Travel House<br>34 Brecon Road<br>Abergavenny<br>Gwent NP7 5UG | Tel: 01873 859876<br>Fax: 01873 859544<br>general@select-site.com | Camping "Auf Kengert" (Medernach) |

## TOUR ORGANISERS

| Address | Details |
|---|---|
| Peltours<br>attn: Mr Saul<br>Sovereign House<br>11/19 Ballards Lane<br>London N3 1UX<br>Tel: 020 8346 9144<br>Fax: 020 8343 0579<br>sales@peltours.com | Specialised in Tailor-made Tours to European Destinations |
| Trans Europe Tours<br>(formerly Heart of Europe Tours)<br>attn:Alan Burton<br>3 Orwell View Road<br>Shotley<br>IPSWICH IP9 1NW<br>Tel & Fax: 01473 787160<br>alan@heartofeurope.com | Specialises in Tailor-made Tours to European Destinations |

## GROUP TOUR ORGANISERS

| Address | Details |
|---|---|
| Groupways Leisure Ltd<br>Overseas House | Specialised in Tailor-made packages for groups<br>worldwide. 3/4 days packages to Luxembourg in all |

**For additional analytical, business and investment opportunities information,**
**please contact Global Investment & Business Center, USA**
**at (202) 546-2103. Fax: (202) 546-3275. E-mail: rusric@erols.com**

| | |
|---|---|
| Broadway Court<br>The Broadway<br>Chesham<br>Bucks HP5 1EG<br>Tel: 01494 792722<br>Fax: 01494 792723<br>sales@groupways.co.uk | types of hotels, including deluxe. |
| JAC Education Services<br>62 - 64 Chancellors Road<br>London W6 9RS<br>Tel: 020 8741 8894<br>Fax: 020 8748 8846 | 3 day tours programme to Luxembourg based on the Luxembourg City Youth Hostel and the Hôtel Mercure ***. From £ 54 per person |
| Sibbald Travel<br>10 Queensferry Street<br>Edinburgh EH2 4QX<br>Tel: 0131 225 3334<br>Fax: 0131 225 5544 | Tours of the European Institutions for groups |
| Top Class Travel<br>Jardine House<br>6 Laird Street<br>Coatbridge ML5 3LJ<br>Tel: 01236 433433<br>Fax: 01236 426442 | Tailor-made packages for groups<br>Sells directly to the public only |
| Young Travellers Ltd<br>Travel House 34 Station Road<br>London SE20 7BQ<br>Tel: 020 8778 6850 Fax: 020 8778 9754<br>schooltravel@young-travellers.co.uk | Specialised in School Groups |

## TRAVEL AGENCIES IN LUXEMBOURG

| Agency Name/ Contact | Address | Telephone (+352) | Fax (+352) |
|---|---|---|---|
| American Express International Inc. | 34 Avenue de la Porte-Neuve<br>L-2227 Luxembourg | 22 85 55 | 22 85 50 |
| BBL Travel | Bâtiment Jean Monnet<br>L-1615 Luxembourg | 43 74 12/13 | 42 21 69 |
| BBL Travel | 25 Rue des Bains<br>L-2015 Luxembourg | 47 02 81 | 47 17 21 |
| BBL Travel | 3 Rue J Pierret<br>L-2350 Luxembourg | 29 60 49 | 29 60 51 |
| Carlson Wagonlit Travel | 105 Grand-Rue<br>L-1661 Luxembourg | 46 03 15-1 | 46 24 32 |
| Généraltour | 134A Avenue du X Septembre<br>L-2550 Luxembourg | 44 06 86 | 44 02 01 |

| | | | |
|---|---|---|---|
| Magic Tours | 54 Avenue de la Faïencerie<br>L-1510 Luxembourg | 46 90 30 | 46 90 34 |
| Nittler All-Tours<br>Margot Busco-Nittler | 22 Boulevard de la Foire<br>L-1528 Luxembourg | 45 34 39 | 45 33 14 |
| Nouvelles Frontières | 16 Rue des Bains<br>L-2449 Luxembourg | 46 41 40 | 46 41 42 |
| Ocean-Tours | 13 Rue Pierre Hentges<br>L-1726 Luxembourg | 49 26 53 | 49 36 39 |
| Panorama<br>Gaby Maul | 14a Rue des Bains<br>L-1212 Luxembourg | 22 58 01 | 47 56 63 |
| Royal Tours | 142-144 Boulevard de la Pétrusse<br>L-2330 Luxembourg | 40 62 63 | 40 62 53 |
| Voyages Sales-Lentz<br>Mr Sales | 5 Rue de la Résistance<br>L-4942 Bascharage | 46 18 18-1 | 47 22 41 |
| Select Travel | 8 Rue Notre-Dame<br>L-2440 Luxembourg | 46 40 40 | 46 42 42 |
| Sotour - La Bourse aux Voyages<br>Bob Goerens<br>email:air@sotour.com | 15, Place du Théâtre<br>L-2010 Luxembourg | 46 15 14 1 | 47 26 50 |
| Sun Days | 17 Avenue Emile Reuter<br>L-2420 Luxembourg | 46 06 05/02 | 48 23 19 |
| Táki-Tálá (Voyages) | 11 Rue Zithe<br>L-2763 Luxembourg | 40 09 25 | 40 08 69 |
| Travel Pro<br>Mr Benoit Lejeune | 22-24 Boulevard Royal<br>L-2449 Luxembourg | 46 95 45 | 46 95 22 |
| Travel Ring International | 4 Boulevard Royal<br>L-2449 Luxembourg | 22 99 85 | 22 99 84 |
| Viva Vacances | 35 Rue Glesener<br>L-1631 Luxembourg | 29 13 13 | 29 13 10 |
| Voyages 4 Saisons | 11 Avenue de la Liberté<br>L-1931 Luxembourg | 22 11 88 | 2 25 72 |
| Voyages Flammang | 3 Place de la Gare<br>L-1616 Luxembourg | 48 51 02 | 29 24 71 |
| Voyages Flammang CIT | 38 Rue Phillippe II<br>L-2340 Luxembourg | 22 51 50 | 22 03 34 |
| Voyages Wasteels | Place de la Gare<br>L-1616 Luxembourg | 48 63 63 | 48 26 51 |
| Voyages Emile Weber | 138 Boulevard de la Pétrusse<br>L-2330 Luxembourg | 40 28 28-1 | 48 44 20 |

**For additional analytical, business and investment opportunities information, please contact Global Investment & Business Center, USA at (202) 546-2103. Fax: (202) 546-3275. E-mail: rusric@erols.com**

# SUPPLEMENTS

## CONTACT INFORMATION

**Chamber of Commerce**

Mail address: L-2981 Luxembourg Offices: 7, rue Alcide de Gasperi · Luxembourg (Kirchberg)

**International Department**

Phone: (+352) 42 39 39-315/360 · Fax: (+352) 43 83 26 E-mail: international@cc.lu · Homepage: www.cc.lu

**Office du Ducroire**

Phone: (+352) 42 39 39-320 · Fax: (+352) 42 39 39-821 E-mail: odl@cc.lu Homepage: www.ducroire.lu

**Enterprise Europe Network**

Phone: (+352) 42 39 39-333 · Fax: (+352) 43 83 26 E-mail: een@cc.lu Homepage: www.cc-een.lu/www.een.lu

**Ministry of the Economy and Foreign Trade**

Phone: (+352) 24 78 41 61 · Fax: (+352) 22 34 85 E-mail: info@eco.public.lu · Homepage: www.eco.public.lu Offices: 19-21, boulevard Royal · L-2449 Luxembourg

**Ministry of Finance**

Phone: (+352) 24 78 26 19 · Fax: (+352) 47 52 41 E-mail: ministere-finances@fi.etat.lu · Homepage: www.fi.etat.lu Offices: 3, rue de la Congrégation · L-1352 Luxembourg

**Ministry of Foreign Affairs**

Phone: (+352) 24 78 24 78 · Fax: (+352) 22 31 44 E-mail: boite.officielle@mae.etat.lu · Homepage: www.mae.lu Offices: 5, rue Notre-Dame · L-2240 Luxembourg

**Ministry of Small and Medium-Sized Businesses and Tourism**

Phone: (+352) 24 78 47 15 · Fax: (+352) 24 78 47 40 E-mail: info@mcm.public.lu · Homepage: www.mcm.public.lu Offices: 6, boulevard Royal · L-2449 Luxembourg

**Luxembourg for Finance**

Phone: (+352) 27 20 21-1 E-mail: info@lff.lu · Homepage: www.lff.lu Mail address: P.O. Box 904 · L-2019 Luxembourg Offices: 59, boulevard Royal · L-2449 Luxembourg

**For additional analytical, business and investment opportunities information, please contact Global Investment & Business Center, USA at (202) 546-2103. Fax: (202) 546-3275. E-mail: rusric@erols.com**

**Luxembourg for Business**

Phone: (+352) 24 78 41 16 · E-mail: info@luxembourgforbusiness.lu Homepage: www.luxembourgforbusiness.lu Offices: 19-21, boulevard Royal · L-2449 Luxembourg The

# IMPORTANT WEBSITES

## ORGANISATIONS PROFESSIONNELLES

ABBL : www.abbl.lu
L'Association des banques et banquiers Luxembourg est une organisation professionnelle regroupant la quasi-totalité des banques établies à Luxembourg.
Confédération Luxembourgeoise du Commerce : www.clc.lu
La Confédération Luxembougeoise du Commerce regroupe des professionnels du commerce, du transport et des services. Les Fédérations qui constituent la Confédération Luxembourgeoise du Commerce (clc) représentent 20% du produit intérieur brut, 10.000 entreprises et 50.000 emplois.
Fédération des Industriels : www.fedil.lu
La Fédération des Industriels Luxembourgeois (FEDIL) est l'association professionnelle représentative des grandes, moyennes et petites industries du Grand-Duché ainsi que d'un nombre croissant d'entreprises de services industriels.
HORESCA : www.horesca.lu
La Fédération Nationale des Hôteliers, Restaurateurs et Cafetiers du Grand-Duché de Luxembourg, représente quelque 2.500 entreprises et quelque 10.000 salariés.

## CHAMBRES DE COMMERCE

### LUXEMBOURG

AMCHAM : www.amcham.lu
The American Chamber of Commerce Luxembourg ASBL (AMCHAM) is an international voluntary organization of business persons committed to fostering bilateral trade and investment between the United States and Luxembourg.
British Chamber of Commerce for Luxembourg : www.bcc.lu
The overall objectives of the independent BCC include promoting the interests of its members and, besides the development of relations between Luxembourg and the United Kingdom, encompass the need to maintain and develop links with the many countries with which the Grand Duchy has commercial ties.

### GRANDE REGION SAAR-LOR-LUX

La Chambre de Commerce du Grand-Duché de Luxembourg entretient des relations privilégiées avec les CCI de la Grande Région Saar-Lor-Lux : la CCI de la Moselle, la CCI de Meurthe-et-Moselle, la CCI Libramont, la IHK Trier, la IHK Pfalz et la IHK Saarland. Ces Chambres défendent ensemble les intérêts de 125.000 membres ressortissants de l'industrie, du commerce et du secteur des services par une large gamme de services spécialisés. Avec le Centre d'information Vector les CCI de la Grande-Région proposent un répertoire détaillé des entreprises installées dans cette région économique.

Centre d'information Vector : www.saarlorlux.org
Le Centre d'information Vector réunit des informations sur la Grande-Région Saar-Lor-Lux et propose un répertoire détaillé des entreprises installées dans cette région économique.

IHK Saarland : www.saarland.ihk.de/
Die Industrie- und Handelskammer des Saarlandes (IHK Saarland) vertritt die Interessen der 38.500 Unternehmen der gewerblichen Wirtschaft im Saarland.
IHK Trier :www.ihk-trier.de/index_d.htm
Die Industrie- und Handelskammer Trier ist die Selbstverwaltungsorganisation der Unternehmen aus Industrie, Handel und Dienstleistungen im Regierungsbezirk Trier. Die IHK ist als Körperschaft des öffentlichen Rechts organisiert. Dies bedeutet, daß sie neben ihren Dienstleistungen für die Wirtschaft auch hoheitliche Aufgaben erfüllt. Rund 20.000 Unternehmen gehören zur Zeit der IHK Trier an, davon sind 5.600 im Handelsregister eingetragen.
IHK Pfalz : www.ihk.de/ludwigshafen
Seit mehr als 150 Jahren betreut die Industrie- und Handelskammer für die Pfalz die Region, die heute der südlichste Teil und wirtschaftliche Schwerpunkt des Landes Rheinland-Pfalz ist. Die IHK für die Pfalz ist das Selbstverwaltungsorgan von rund 57.000 regionalen Betrieben aus Industrie, Handel und Dienstleistungen.
CCI Libramont : www.ccilb.be/
Emanation directe des entreprises du Luxembourg belge et de leur adhésion, la Chambre de commerce et d'industrie de Libramont est l'organisme dont elles se sont dotées comme point de ralliement, toutes catégories d'activités et de tailles confondues.
CCI Meurthe-et-Moselle: www.nancy.cci.fr/index4.shtml
Etablissement public géré par des chefs d'entreprise élus, la Chambre de Commerce et d'Industrie de Meurthe-et-Moselle contribue au développement économique et favorise l'activité commerciale, industrielle ou de services.
CCI Moselle : www.moselle.cci.fr/
La C.C.I.M. est un "parlement économique" dont la mission est de contribuer au développement du département de la Moselle.
Digital Chamber Network (Belgique) : www.cci.be/
Le Digital Chamber Network regroupe les différentes Chambres de Commerce et d'Industrie belges.

**INTERNATIONAL**

Eurochambres : www.eurochambres.be
L'association des Chambres de Commerce et d'industrie européennes représente 33 associations nationales de Chambre de Commerce et d'Industrie, un réseau européen de 1.300 Chambres locales comptant plus de 14 millions d'entreprises membres en Europe.
International Chamber of Commerce : www.iccwbo.org
ICC is the world business organization, the only representative body that speaks with authority on behalf of enterprises from all sectors in every part of the world.
World Chambers Network : www.worldchambers.com/
WCN's mission is to open up the global market and increase sales and trade opportunities for dynamic, entrepreneurial, growing businesses. WCN fosters open and comprehensive exchange of business information on products, services, markets and resources ; establishes an electronic commerce network that links companies and their customers around the world and allows each participating Chamber to serve as a unique content provider and become an electronic commerce facilitator.

**GOUVERNEMENT ET INSTITUTIONS PUBLIQUES**

Gouvernement : www.gouvernement.lu
Le site officiel du Gouvernement luxembourgeois.
Ministères et Administrations du Grand-Duché de Luxembourg : www.etat.lu
Chambre des députés : www.chd.lu
Les 60 membres de la Chambre des Députés sont élus sur la base du suffrage universel et représentent la volonté du peuple luxembourgeois.

Legilux : www.legilux.lu
Legilux.lu est le portail juridique du Gouvernement du Grand-Duché de Luxembourg.
Conseil d'Etat : www.etat.lu/CE/
Le Conseil d'Etat donne son avis sur tous les projets et propositions de loi ainsi que sur toutes autres questions qui lui auraient été déférées par le Grand-Duc ou le Gouvernement. Le Conseil d'Etat est souvent considéré comme le "gardien de la Constitution".
Conseil économique et social : www.etat.lu/CES/
Le Conseil Economique et Social fut institué par la loi du 21 mars 1966 dans le but de doter les pouvoirs publics d'un organe consultatif des forces vives de la Nation pour l'examen systématique des problèmes concernant la vie économique et sociale du pays.
Banque centrale du Luxembourg : www.bcl.lu
Depuis le 1er janvier 1999, la BCL conduit les opérations de l'Eurosystème à Luxembourg (l'Eurosystème comprend la BCE et les onze banques centrales nationales des pays participant à la zone euro).
Mémorial : www.etat.lu/memorial/
Le journal officiel du Grand-Duché de Luxembourg comprend le Recueil de Législation (Mémorial A), le recueil Administratif et Economique (Mémorial B) et le Recueil des Sociétés et Associations (Mémorial C).

**EUROPE**

**UNION EUROPÉENNE**

Dialogue with Business : http://europa.eu.int/business/
«Dialogue with Business» provides European companies with on-line access to information and advice on EU matters. The site is a One Stop Internet Shop from which enterprises can gain access to all information and advice they need to do business in the Single Market.
EUROPA : http://europa.eu.int/index-fr.htm
EUROPA est le serveur officiel de toutes les institutions de l'Union Européenne.
Parlement Européen : www.europarl.eu.int/sg/tree/fr/default.htm
A l'heure actuelle 375 millions d'Européens de 15 pays participent, à travers leurs 626 députés au Parlement européen, à la construction de l'Europe.
EUR-OP : http://eur-op.eu.int/general/fr/index.htm
Le serveur de l'Office des Publications de l'Union Européenne.
SCADPLUS : http://europa.eu.int/scadplus/
Le Service central automatisé de documentation propose des informations générales sur les politiques de l'Union européenne

**GOUVERNEMENTS DE l'UE**

Allemagne : www.bundesregierung.de
Autriche : www.austria.gv.at/
Belgique : http://belgium.fgov.be/
Danemark : www.danmark.dk
Finlande : http://virtual.finland.fi

France : www.premier-ministre.gouv.fr
Espagne : www.la-moncloa.es/
Grande-Bretagne : www.number-10.gov.uk/
Grèce : www.primeminister.gr
Irlande : www.irlgov.ie/
Italie : www.palazzochigi.it
Luxembourg : www.gouvernement.lu
Pays-Bas : www.minbuza.nl
Portugal : www.primeiro-ministro.gov.pt
Suède : www.regeringen.se

**EURO**

EURO : http://europa.eu.int/euro/
Le serveur EURO rassemble toutes les informations utiles et actuelles sur la monnaie unique.

**CREATION D'ENTREPRISES**

Portail Luxembourgeois de l'Innovation et de la Recherche : www.innovation.public.lu
Outil bilingue français/anglais entièrement gratuit, destiné aux porteurs de projets innovants, aux personnes actives dans la R&D publique et privée, ainsi qu'aux jeunes diplômés. Le site met à disposition des informations pratiques et outils interactifs ouverts à l'échelle européenne.
Business Initiative : www.123go-networking.org
Business Initiative est une association sans but lucratif créée par la Fédération des Industriels luxembourgeois (FEDIL) et en collaboration avec la Chambre de Commerce, la Chambre des Métiers du Grand Duché de Luxembourg et Luxinnovation qui a pour objectif de transformer les potentiels économiques et les vocations latentes de la Grande Région en entreprises de demain en soutenant des idées innovantes.
Guichet Unique Transfrontalier : www.leguichet.org
Un click pour tout savoir sur les démarches à accomplir lors du démarrage de votre activité au Grand-Duché de Luxembourg, en Belgique et en France...
Société Nationale de Crédit et d'Investissement : www.snci.lu
La SNCI est un établissement bancaire spécialisé dans le financement des investissements et des exportations. Par conséquent, l'activité de la SNCI est limitée aux opérations bancaires du moyen et du long terme. Ses interventions complètent la panoplie des instruments d'ordre budgétaire et fiscal instaurés par le législateur en vue de favoriser le développement économique. La SNCI a été chargée par le législateur de la gestion des prêts d'Etat à Etat dont l'octroi est décidé par le Gouvernement.
Agence pour la Création d'Entreprises : www.apce.com
L'Agence pour la Création d'Entreprises (APCE) agit en faveur de la constitution et du développement de réseaux de soutien aux créateurs, repreneurs et cédants d'entreprises, tant au niveau local et régional que national et européen.

**ECONOMIE ET FINANCES**

ALFI : www.alfi.lu/
Luxembourg Investment Funds Association ALFI, the official trade association of

the world's 2th largest investment fund industry, strives to protect the interests of its members to promote Luxembourg as a major financial centre.
Commission de surveillance du secteur financier : www.cssf.lu/
Le site de la Commission de surveillance du secteur financier poursuit un double objectif. Il contient, d'une part, l'essentiel des informations relatives aux activités de surveillance prudentielle de la CSSF et renseigne, d'une autre part, sur les principaux aspects de l'évolution et de l'actualité de la place financière de Luxembourg.
Banque centrale du Luxembourg : www.bcl.lu
Depuis le 1er janvier 1999, la BCL conduit les opérations de l'Eurosystème à Luxembourg (l'Eurosystème comprend la BCE et les onze banques centrales nationales des pays participant à la zone euro).
Banque européenne d'investissement : http://bei.eu.int
Institution financière de l'Union européenne, la Banque européenne d'investissement a pour mission de contribuer à l'intégration, au développement équilibré et à la cohésion économique et sociale des pays membres. En dehors de l'Union, la BEI met en oeuvre les volets financiers des accords conclus dans le cadre des politiques européennes d'aide et de coopération au développement.
Banque mondiale : www.worldBank.org/
La Banque mondiale est le premier prestataire mondial d'aide au développement. Elle s'emploie aussi à coordonner son action avec celle d'autres organisations de sorte que les ressources aillent entièrement au financement du programme de développement national.
Banking in Luxembourg web resource center : www.bank.lu
Bank.lu is a web guide and resource center about the banking sector in Luxembourg. It presents a directory of companies that operate in the Luxembourg financial sector as well as additional useful and related information.
Bourse de Luxembourg : www.bourse.lu
World Competitiveness Yearbook : http://www.imd.ch/wcy/
The World Competitiveness Yearbook (WCY) is the World's leading research analyzing and ranking the ability of a nation to provide an environment that sustains the competitiveness of enterprises. It covers 47 economies using 288 criteria.
Fonds monétaire international : www.imf.org/external/fre/index.htm
The IMF is an international organization of 182 member countries, established to promote international monetary cooperation, exchange stability, and orderly exchange arrangements; to foster economic growth and high levels of employment; and to provide temporary financial assistance to countries under adequate safeguards to help ease balance of payments adjustment.
Jeune chambre économique : www.jci.lu/
L'objectif de la Jeune chambre économique du Grand-Duché de Luxembourg est d'offrir aux jeunes les possibilités de développer les aptitudes à diriger, la responsabilité sociale, la fraternité et l'esprit d'initiative.
Organisation de coopération et de développement économiques : www.oecd.org/index-fr.htm
L'OCDE rassemble 29 pays Membres au sein d'une organisation qui, avant tout, offre aux gouvernements un cadre pour examiner, élaborer et perfectionner les politiques économiques et sociales.
Organisation mondiale du commerce : www.wto.org/
L'OMC est le seul organisme international qui s'occupe des règles régissant le commerce entre les pays. Les Accords de l'OMC y occupent une place centrale et constituent les règles juridiques de base pour le commerce international et la politique commerciale.

## STATISTIQUES

STATEC : www.statec.lu
Service central de la statistique et des études économiques.
Les offices statistiques de la Grande Région : www.grande-region.lu/
Les offices statistiques rassemblent un certain nombre d'indicateurs conjoncturels sur la Grande-Région.
EUROSTAT : http://europa.eu.int/en/comm/eurostat/servfr/home.htm
Eurostat, l'Office Statistique des Communautés européennes, recueille toutes les données statistiques, collectées selon des règles uniformes, auprès des Instituts Nationaux Statistiques de chacun des 15 États membres de l'Union européenne.

## COMMERCE EXTERIEUR

Centre d'information Vector : www.saarlorlux.org
Le Centre d'information Vector réunit des informations sur la Grande-Région Saar-Lor-Lux et propose un répertoire détaillé des entreprises installées dans cette région économique.
Administration des Douanes et Accises du Grand-Duché de Luxembourg : www.etat.lu/do/
Asia-Invest : www.asia-invest.com/
Asia-Invest programme is a European Community initiative that provides financial support to facilitate business co-operation between companies from the European Union and Asia.
Base de données 'Accès aux marchés' : http://mkaccdb.eu.int/
La Commission européenne, avec le concours des groupements professionnels et de l'industrie, a rassemblé toutes les informations disponibles sur les obstacles qui affectent les exportations européennes en vue de réaliser la base de données.
Federal Trade Point Brussels : www.obcebdbh.be/tradepoint/welcome.html
The major goal of the Federal Trade Point Brussels - through the chain of Trade Points - is to broad access to international trade of local economic entities, especially small & medium enterprises, supporting them to find markets for their products and to realize more quickly and at a reasonable cost import/export operations with the help of the advanced technologies (EDI) and information networks (Internet, E-mail,...).
Gateway to Japan : http://www.eu-gateway-to-japan.be/
Lux-Development : www.lux-development.lu/
LUX-DEVELOPMENT est l'Agence Luxembourgeoise pour la Coopération au Développement du gouvernement luxembourgeois pour la quasi-totalité des projets bilatéraux financés par le Grand-Duché de Luxembourg et pour certaines interventions d'urgence ou d'aide alimentaire. Elle gère en permanence environ 70 projets financés à partir d'un budget global du Ministère des Affaires Etrangères.

## FORMATION PROFESSIONNELLE ET EDUCATION

La formation professionnelle continue au Luxembourg : www.lifelong-learning.lu
Portail luxembourgeois de la formation professionnelle continue.
Consultez le calendrier des formations de la Chambre de Commerce.
Institut de formation bancaire : www.ifbl.lu
L'institut, organe de formation de l'Association des Banques et Banquiers,

Luxembourg (ABBL), organise une multitude d'actions de formation dans le domaine bancaire, allant du simple cours de base jusqu'aux programmes les plus sophistiqués.
Office Luxembourgeois pour l'accroissement de la Productivité : www.olap.lu
L'OLAP est une association sans but lucratif, conventionné par le Ministère de l'Economie et composée d'organisations professionnelles du secteur économique. Au service de l'économie, des entreprises et des particuliers l'OLAP est organisateur agréé de cours de formations professionelles continues.
Ministère de l'Education Nationale, de la Formation Professionnelle et des Sports: www.men.lu/

Chambre des employés privés : www.cepl.lu
La Chambre des Employés Privés, qui représente les intérêts de deux catégories socioprofessionnelles obligatoirement affiliées (employés privés et agents des CFL), est un important organisme de formation professionnelle continue.
RESTENA : www.restena.lu
RESTENA (Réseau Téléinformatique de l'Education Nationale et de la Recherche) is the National Network for Education and Research of the Grand Duchy of Luxembourg. The network has been installed to serve the needs of all the institutions involved in education and research in Luxembourg.
SITec : www.sitel.lu
Le G.I.E. «Formation Continue de l'Ingénieur, SITec(r)» est le service de formation continue du Centre de Recherche public Henri Tudor.
SPIRAL : www.spiral.lu
SPIRAL est une plate-forme de transfert technologique proposant des conférences, des formations, des groupes de travail et de réflexion, des programmes de qualification et des services télématiques organisés en filières liées aux métiers de l'informatique en vue d'échanger et de diffuser les meilleures pratiques logicielles.
UNESCO : www.unesco.org/general/fre/
L'Organisation des Nations Unies pour l'éducation, la science et la culture compte 188 Etats membres.

## RECHERCHE ET DEVELOPPEMENT / INNOVATION

Portail Luxembourgeois de l'Innovation et de la Recherche : www.innovation.public.lu
Outil bilingue français/anglais entièrement gratuit, destiné aux porteurs de projets innovants, aux personnes actives dans la R&D publique et privée, ainsi qu'aux jeunes diplômés. Le site met à disposition des informations pratiques et outils interactifs ouverts à l'échelle européenne.
LUXINNOVATION : www.luxinnovation.lu
Luxinnovation is the national innovation agency. Its mission is to inform and raise awareness in the following fields : R & D (national and European support programmes), loi-cadre de développement et de diversification économiques, technological innovation and technology transfer.
Centre de Recherche Public Gabriel Lippmann : www.crpgl.lu
Le CRP - Gabriel Lippmann est un établissement public ayant pour missions la recherche scientifique appliquée et le développement technologique, le transfert de technologie et la formation permanente de haut niveau.
Centre de Recherche Public Henri Tudor : www.crpht.lu
The CRP Henri Tudor is one of the research centers in Luxembourg. Hosted by the Institute of Technology, the Public Research Centre Henri Tudor was launched at the end of 1987.

Centre de Recherche Public Santé : www.crp-sante.lu/
Le CRP-Santé est chargé de promouvoir la recherche, le développement et le transfert technologique dans les domaines concernant les différentes divisions du Laboratoire National de Santé et du Centre Hospitalier de Luxembourg.
CEPS/INSTEAD : www.ceps.lu/
Le Centre d'études de population, de pauvreté et de politiques socio-économiques fait des recherches micro-économiques et micro-sociales et crée des banques de données, dans le but de développer des approches nouvelles pour l'analyse, la programmation et la simulation de politiques socio-économiques.
IEIS - Luxembourg Institute for European and International Studies : www.ieis.lu/
The Luxembourg Institute for European and International Studies (LIEIS) provides an institutional framework for activities that were organized previously by the Luxembourg-Harvard Association in cooperation with professors, administrators and students from Harvard University.
CORDIS : www.cordis.lu/fr/home.html
Le Service d'Informations sur la Recherche et Développement de la Communauté, CORDIS, a été conçu pour aider les entreprises, et plus particulièrement les PME, dans les étapes critiques du transfert de technologie et de l'innovation.

## SOCIETE DE L'INFORMATION

Autorégulation de l'internet: http://www.autoregulation.lu/
Forum lancé par le Service de Médias et des Communications du Ministère d'Etat avec l'appui du New Media Group pour étudier la possibilité d'un système d'autorégulation de l'internet au Luxembourg.
ISPO : www.ispo.cec.be
The Information Society Promotion Office aims to promote co-operation and development in the various areas of the Information Society. ISPO acts as a bridgebuilder between Commission Services and external organizations interested in the Information Society.
Société de l'information : www.luxinfo.lu
La SIL est une association sans but lucratif de droit luxembourgeois. Son objet social comprend deux éléments : 1. la réalisation et la mise à jour régulière d'une base de données comprenant des sources d'informations officielles commentées sur le Grand-Duché de Luxembourg et l'Union européenne, 2. la formation concernant la gestion de l'information.
New Media Group : www.nmo.lu
Le New Media Group du CRP Henri Tudor a pour objet la stimulation du développement de l'industrie des nouveaux médias et le support des sociétés utilisant les technologies et les applications des nouveaux médias, et cela à un niveau national et régional

## ENVIRONNEMENT

Agence européenne de l'Environnement : http://www.eea.eu.int/
The EEA aims to support sustainable development and to help achieve significant and measurable improvement in Europe's environment through the provision of timely, targeted, relevant and reliable information to policy making agents and the public.
Certifnet : www.certifnet.com/
Le site de la certification qualité et environnement.

For additional analytical, business and investment opportunities information, please contact Global Investment & Business Center, USA at (202) 546-2103. Fax: (202) 546-3275. E-mail: rusric@erols.com

European Environment Information and Observation NETwork (EIONET) : www.eionet.eu.int/

Valorlux : www.valorlux.lu
Valorlux est une a.s.b.l. qui a comme objectif de promouvoir, coordonner et soutenir financièrement la collecte sélective, le tri éventuel et le recyclage des déchets d'emballages ménagers au Grand Duché de Luxembourg.

## AUTRES LIENS UTILES

### PORTAILS D'ENTRÉE AU LUXEMBOURG

LuxWeb : www.luxweb.lu
Luxpoint : www.luxpoint.lu
Spider : www.spider.lu

## ANNUAIRES & RÉPERTOIRES

Annuaire Professionnel : www.allo.lu
Avec un tirage de plus de 255.000 exemplaires, l'Annuaire Professionnel est l'outil incontournable des professionnels qui veulent établir des contacts commerciaux avec l'ensemble des particuliers. Une présence valorisée permet d'accroître la notoriété de toute société et de développer ses échanges commerciaux. Quelques 5000 exemplaires des Pages Jaunes sont distribués aux entreprises voisines dans la région transfrontalière.
Annuaire téléphonique du Luxembourg : www.allo.lu
Diffusé à plus de 255 000 exemplaires, cet annuaire reprend les numéros de téléphones des différents opérateurs téléphoniques, tant fixes que mobiles. Ce produit comprend également une mine d'informations utiles : les opérateurs téléphoniques, les codes postaux, les boîtes postales, les institutions luxembourgeoises et européennes, les professions médicales et para-médicales,...
Annuaire Inter Région : www.interregion.com
Le seul et unique annuaire qui constitue une zone géographique internationale en termes d'échanges économiques. Plus de 15.000 sociétés répertoriées dans la région SAAR-LOR-LUX. Outil d'échanges, de prospection et de contacts, utilisé par des professionnels qui veulent confirmer leur présence sur un marché sans frontière.
abc luxembourgeois pour le commerce et l'industrie : www.abc-d.lu/
Des informations actuelles sur des producteurs, importateurs/grossistes, exportateurs et prestataires de services aux entreprises établis au Grand-Duché de Luxembourg.
WLW Luxemburg - Wer liefert was? - Qui fourni quoi?: www.wlw.lu
Acheter et vendre au Grand-Duché. WLW Luxemburg pour trouver sans difficulté des fournisseurs et des clients. Portail uxembourgeois d'information Business to Business ; les entreprises B2B du Grand-Duché, 45.000 produits et services et 11 langues de consultation.

## TOURISME / CONGRÈS

Explorator : www.explorator.lu
Comprehensive City Guide of Luxembourg.

Foires internationales du Luxembourg : www.fil.lu
La Société des Foires Internationales de Luxembourg S.A. organise et accueille des foires et des salons spécialisés, des séminaires et des conférences ainsi que toutes autres manifestations économiques à rayonnement national et international.
ONT : www.ont.lu
Official Internet Site of the National Tourist Office and the Ministry of Tourism Luxembourg
Luxair : www.luxair.lu
Site de la compagnie aérienne luxembourgeoise Luxair
Luxembourg City Tourist Office : www.luxembourg-city.lu
Luxembourg Congres : www.luxcongress.lu
Conference facilities in the Grand-Duchy of Luxembourg
Restaurant.lu : www.restaurant.lu
An excellent resource guide listing over 400 restaurants in Luxembourg

**PRESSE ÉCRITE ET AUDIO-VISUELLE**

Luxemburger Wort : www.wort.lu
Luxembourg News : www.news.lu/
Letzebuerger Journal : www.journal.lu
Letzebuerger Land : www.land.lu
Radio Télé Luxembourg : www.rtl.lu/
Tageblatt : www.tageblatt.lu
Agefi : www.agefi.lu
IPI Presse interrégionale : www.interhost.de/ipineu/
La "Interregionale Presse - Presse Interrégionale" est une association indépendante de journalistes professionnel(le)s de la Grande Région Sarre/Lorraine/Luxembourg (Saar- Lor-Lux)/ Wallonie/Rhénanie-Palatinat. Elle est forte de 113 Mitglieder (au 09.1999).

## BASIC TITLES ON LUXEMBOURG

| Title | ISBN |
|---|---|
| Luxembourg A "Spy" Guide - Strategic Information and Developments | 1433030489 |
| Luxembourg A Spy" Guide" | 1438729758 |
| Luxembourg Banking & Financial Market Handbook | 1433030497 |
| Luxembourg Banking & Financial Market Handbook | 1438729766 |
| Luxembourg Business and Investment Opportunities Yearbook | 1433030500 |
| Luxembourg Business and Investment Opportunities Yearbook | 1438729774 |
| Luxembourg Business and Investment Opportunities Yearbook Volume 1 Strategic Information and Opportunities | 1438777213 |
| Luxembourg Business Intelligence Report - Practical Information, Opportunities, Contacts | 1433030519 |
| Luxembourg Business Intelligence Report - Practical Information, Opportunities, Contacts | 1438729782 |
| Luxembourg Business Law Handbook - Strategic Information and Basic Laws | 1438770340 |
| Luxembourg Business Law Handbook - Strategic Information and Basic Laws | 1438770340 |
| Luxembourg Business Law Handbook - Strategic Information and Basic Laws | 1433030527 |
| Luxembourg Business Law Handbook - Strategic Information and Basic Laws | 1438729790 |
| Luxembourg Constitution and Citizenship Laws Handbook - Strategic | 1438779356 |

| Title | ISBN |
|---|---|
| Information and Basic Laws | |
| Luxembourg Country Study Guide - Strategic Information and Developments | 1433030535 |
| Luxembourg Country Study Guide - Strategic Information and Developments | 1438729804 |
| Luxembourg Country Study Guide - Strategic Information and Developments Volume 1 Strategic Information and Developments | 1438774885 |
| Luxembourg Diplomatic Handbook - Strategic Information and Developments | 1433030543 |
| Luxembourg Diplomatic Handbook - Strategic Information and Developments | 1438729812 |
| Luxembourg Ecology & Nature Protection Handbook | 1433030551 |
| Luxembourg Ecology & Nature Protection Handbook | 1438729820 |
| Luxembourg Ecology & Nature Protection Laws and Regulation Handbook | 1433074257 |
| Luxembourg Economic & Development Strategy Handbook | 143303056X |
| Luxembourg Economic & Development Strategy Handbook | 1438729839 |
| Luxembourg Energy Policy, Laws and Regulation Handbook | 1433072017 |
| Luxembourg Foreign Policy and Government Guide | 1433030578 |
| Luxembourg Foreign Policy and Government Guide | 1438729847 |
| Luxembourg Immigration Laws and Regulations Handbook - Strategic Information and Basic Laws | 1438782969 |
| Luxembourg Insolvency (Bankruptcy) Laws and Regulations Handbook - Strategic Information and Basic Laws | 9781433085451 |
| Luxembourg Investment & Business Guide | 1433030586 |
| Luxembourg Investment & Business Guide | 1438729855 |
| Luxembourg Investment and Business Guide - Strategic and Practical Information | 1438768060 |
| Luxembourg Investment and Business Guide - Strategic and Practical Information | 1433030594 |
| Luxembourg Investment and Business Guide - Strategic and Practical Information | 1438768060 |
| Luxembourg Investment and Business Guide - Strategic and Practical Information | 1438729863 |
| Luxembourg Labor Laws and Regulations Handbook - Strategic Information and Basic Laws | 1438781164 |
| Luxembourg Land Ownership and Agriculture Laws Handbook | 1438759460 |
| Luxembourg Offshore Investment and Business Guide - Strategic and Practical Information | 1433030608 |
| Luxembourg Offshore Investment and Business Guide - Strategic and Practical Information | 1438729871 |
| Luxembourg Offshore Tax Guide | 1433030616 |
| Luxembourg Offshore Tax Guide | 143872988X |
| Luxembourg Recent Economic and Political Developments Yearbook | 143306328X |
| Luxembourg Recent Economic and Political Developments Yearbook | 143306328X |
| Luxembourg Recent Economic and Political Developments Yearbook | 143306328X |
| Luxembourg Tax Guide | 1433030624 |
| Luxembourg Tax Guide | 1438729898 |
| Luxembourg Taxation Laws and Regulations Handbook | 143308029X |
| Luxembourg: How to Invest, Start and Run Profitable Business in Luxembourg Guide - Practical Information, Opportunities, Contacts | 9781433083860 |
| Luxemburg Company Laws and Regulations Handbook | 1433070219 |

| Title | ISBN |
|---|---|
| Luxemburg Export-Import Trade and Business Directory | 1433030632 |
| Luxemburg Export-Import Trade and Business Directory | 1438729901 |
| Luxemburg Industrial and Business Directory | 1433030640 |
| Luxemburg Industrial and Business Directory | 143872991X |
| Luxemburg Investment and Trade Laws and Regulations Handbook | 1433076225 |
| Luxemburg Starting Business (Incorporating) in....Guide | 1433066947 |
| Luxemburg Telecommunication Industry Business Opportunities Handbook | 1433030659 |
| Luxemburg Telecommunication Industry Business Opportunities Handbook | 1438729928 |

## WORLD CONSTITUTION AND CITIZENSHIP LAWS HANDBOOK LIBRARY

***Constitution, citizenship, immigration, migration - strategic information, government programs, laws and regulations and more...***

**Price: $149 each**

| |
|---|
| Afghanistan Constitution and Citizenship Laws Handbook |
| Albania Constitution and Citizenship Laws Handbook |
| Algeria Constitution and Citizenship Laws Handbook |
| Angola Constitution and Citizenship Laws Handbook |
| Antigua and Barbuda Constitution and Citizenship Laws Handbook |
| Antilles (Netherlands) Constitution and Citizenship Laws Handbook |
| Argentina Constitution and Citizenship Laws Handbook |
| Armenia Constitution and Citizenship Laws Handbook |
| Aruba Constitution and Citizenship Laws Handbook |
| Australia Constitution and Citizenship Laws Handbook |
| Austria Constitution and Citizenship Laws Handbook |
| Azerbaijan Constitution and Citizenship Laws Handbook |
| Bahamas Constitution and Citizenship Laws Handbook |
| Bahrain Constitution and Citizenship Laws Handbook |
| Bangladesh Constitution and Citizenship Laws Handbook |
| Barbados Constitution and Citizenship Laws Handbook |
| Belarus Constitution and Citizenship Laws Handbook |
| Belgium Constitution and Citizenship Laws Handbook |
| Belize Constitution and Citizenship Laws Handbook |
| Benin Constitution and Citizenship Laws Handbook |
| Bermuda Constitution and Citizenship Laws Handbook |
| Bhutan Constitution and Citizenship Laws Handbook |
| Bolivia Constitution and Citizenship Laws Handbook |
| Bosnia and Herzegovina Constitution and Citizenship Laws Handbook |
| Botswana Constitution and Citizenship Laws Handbook |
| Brazil Constitution and Citizenship Laws Handbook |
| Brunei Constitution and Citizenship Laws Handbook |
| Bulgaria Constitution and Citizenship Laws Handbook |
| Burkina Faso Constitution and Citizenship Laws Handbook |
| Burundi Constitution and Citizenship Laws Handbook |
| Cambodia Constitution and Citizenship Laws Handbook |
| Cameroon Constitution and Citizenship Laws Handbook |
| Canada Constitution and Citizenship Laws Handbook |
| Cape Verde Constitution and Citizenship Laws Handbook |
| Cayman Islands Constitution and Citizenship Laws Handbook |

| |
|---|
| Central African Republic Constitution and Citizenship Laws Handbook |
| Chad Constitution and Citizenship Laws Handbook |
| Chile Constitution and Citizenship Laws Handbook |
| China Constitution and Citizenship Laws Handbook |
| Colombia Constitution and Citizenship Laws Handbook |
| Comoros Constitution and Citizenship Laws Handbook |
| Congo Constitution and Citizenship Laws Handbook |
| Congo, Democratic Republic Constitution and Citizenship Laws Handbook |
| Cook Islands Constitution and Citizenship Laws Handbook |
| Costa Rica Constitution and Citizenship Laws Handbook |
| Cote d'Ivoire Constitution and Citizenship Laws Handbook |
| Croatia Constitution and Citizenship Laws Handbook |
| Cuba Constitution and Citizenship Laws Handbook |
| Cyprus Constitution and Citizenship Laws Handbook |
| Czech Republic Constitution and Citizenship Laws Handbook |
| Denmark Constitution and Citizenship Laws Handbook |
| Djibouti Constitution and Citizenship Laws Handbook |
| Dominica Constitution and Citizenship Laws Handbook |
| Dominican Republic Constitution and Citizenship Laws Handbook |
| Ecuador Constitution and Citizenship Laws Handbook |
| Egypt Constitution and Citizenship Laws Handbook |
| El Salvador Constitution and Citizenship Laws Handbook |
| Equatorial Guinea Constitution and Citizenship Laws Handbook |
| Eritrea Constitution and Citizenship Laws Handbook |
| Estonia Constitution and Citizenship Laws Handbook |
| Ethiopia Constitution and Citizenship Laws Handbook |
| Falkland Islands Constitution and Citizenship Laws Handbook |
| Faroes Islands Constitution and Citizenship Laws Handbook |
| Fiji Constitution and Citizenship Laws Handbook |
| Finland Constitution and Citizenship Laws Handbook |
| France Constitution and Citizenship Laws Handbook |
| Gabon Constitution and Citizenship Laws Handbook |
| Gambia Constitution and Citizenship Laws Handbook |
| Georgia Constitution and Citizenship Laws Handbook |
| Germany Constitution and Citizenship Laws Handbook |
| Ghana Constitution and Citizenship Laws Handbook |
| Gibraltar Constitution and Citizenship Laws Handbook |
| Global Constitution and Citizenship Laws Handbook |
| Greece Constitution and Citizenship Laws Handbook |
| Greenland Constitution and Citizenship Laws Handbook |
| Grenada Constitution and Citizenship Laws Handbook |
| Guam Constitution and Citizenship Laws Handbook |
| Guatemala Constitution and Citizenship Laws Handbook |
| Guinea Constitution and Citizenship Laws Handbook |
| Guinea-Bissau Constitution and Citizenship Laws Handbook |
| Guyana Constitution and Citizenship Laws Handbook |
| Haiti Constitution and Citizenship Laws Handbook |
| Honduras Constitution and Citizenship Laws Handbook |
| Hungary Constitution and Citizenship Laws Handbook |
| Iceland Constitution and Citizenship Laws Handbook |
| India Constitution and Citizenship Laws Handbook |

| |
|---|
| Indonesia Constitution and Citizenship Laws Handbook |
| Iran Constitution and Citizenship Laws Handbook |
| Iraq Constitution and Citizenship Laws Handbook |
| Ireland Constitution and Citizenship Laws Handbook |
| Israel Constitution and Citizenship Laws Handbook |
| Italy Constitution and Citizenship Laws Handbook |
| Jamaica Constitution and Citizenship Laws Handbook |
| Japan Constitution and Citizenship Laws Handbook |
| Jersey Constitution and Citizenship Laws Handbook |
| Jordan Constitution and Citizenship Laws Handbook |
| Kazakhstan Constitution and Citizenship Laws Handbook |
| Kenya Constitution and Citizenship Laws Handbook |
| Kiribati Constitution and Citizenship Laws Handbook |
| Korea, North Constitution and Citizenship Laws Handbook |
| Korea, South Constitution and Citizenship Laws Handbook |
| Kosovo Constitution and Citizenship Laws Handbook |
| Kurdistan Constitution and Citizenship Laws Handbook |
| Kuwait Constitution and Citizenship Laws Handbook |
| Kyrgyzstan Constitution and Citizenship Laws Handbook |
| Laos Constitution and Citizenship Laws Handbook |
| Latvia Constitution and Citizenship Laws Handbook |
| Lebanon Constitution and Citizenship Laws Handbook |
| Lesotho Constitution and Citizenship Laws Handbook |
| Liberia Constitution and Citizenship Laws Handbook |
| Libya Constitution and Citizenship Laws Handbook |
| Liechtenstein Constitution and Citizenship Laws Handbook |
| Lithuania Constitution and Citizenship Laws Handbook |
| Luxembourg Constitution and Citizenship Laws Handbook |
| Macao Constitution and Citizenship Laws Handbook |
| Macedonia,Constitution and Citizenship Laws Handbook |
| Madagascar Constitution and Citizenship Laws Handbook |
| Madeira Constitution and Citizenship Laws Handbook |
| Malawi Constitution and Citizenship Laws Handbook |
| Malaysia Constitution and Citizenship Laws Handbook |
| Maldives Constitution and Citizenship Laws Handbook |
| Mali Constitution and Citizenship Laws Handbook |
| Malta Constitution and Citizenship Laws Handbook |
| Man Constitution and Citizenship Laws Handbook |
| Marshall Islands Constitution and Citizenship Laws Handbook |
| Mauritania Constitution and Citizenship Laws Handbook |
| Mauritius Constitution and Citizenship Laws Handbook |
| Mayotte Constitution and Citizenship Laws Handbook |
| Mexico Constitution and Citizenship Laws Handbook |
| Micronesia Constitution and Citizenship Laws Handbook |
| Moldova Constitution and Citizenship Laws Handbook |
| Monaco Constitution and Citizenship Laws Handbook |
| Mongolia Constitution and Citizenship Laws Handbook |
| Morocco Constitution and Citizenship Laws Handbook |
| Mozambique Constitution and Citizenship Laws Handbook |
| Myanmar Constitution and Citizenship Laws Handbook |
| Namibia Constitution and Citizenship Laws Handbook |

| |
|---|
| Nauru Constitution and Citizenship Laws Handbook |
| Nepal Constitution and Citizenship Laws Handbook |
| Netherlands Constitution and Citizenship Laws Handbook |
| New Zealand Constitution and Citizenship Laws Handbook |
| Nicaragua Constitution and Citizenship Laws Handbook |
| Niger Constitution and Citizenship Laws Handbook |
| Nigeria Constitution and Citizenship Laws Handbook |
| Northern Mariana Islands Constitution and Citizenship Laws Handbook |
| Norway Constitution and Citizenship Laws Handbook |
| Oman Constitution and Citizenship Laws Handbook |
| Pakistan Constitution and Citizenship Laws Handbook |
| Palau Constitution and Citizenship Laws Handbook |
| Palestine (West Bank & Gaza) Constitution and Citizenship Laws Handbook |
| Panama Constitution and Citizenship Laws Handbook |
| Papua New Guinea Constitution and Citizenship Laws Handbook |
| Paraguay Constitution and Citizenship Laws Handbook |
| Peru Constitution and Citizenship Laws Handbook |
| Philippines Constitution and Citizenship Laws Handbook |
| Pitcairn Islands Constitution and Citizenship Laws Handbook |
| Poland Constitution and Citizenship Laws Handbook |
| Portugal Constitution and Citizenship Laws Handbook |
| Qatar Constitution and Citizenship Laws Handbook |
| Romania Constitution and Citizenship Laws Handbook |
| Russia Constitution and Citizenship Laws Handbook |
| Rwanda Constitution and Citizenship Laws Handbook |
| Saint Kitts and Nevis Constitution and Citizenship Laws Handbook |
| Saint Lucia Constitution and Citizenship Laws Handbook |
| Saint Vincent and The Grenadines Constitution and Citizenship Laws Handbook |
| Samoa (Western) Constitution and Citizenship Laws Handbook |
| Sao Tome and Principe Constitution and Citizenship Laws Handbook |
| Saudi Arabia Constitution and Citizenship Laws Handbook |
| Senegal Constitution and Citizenship Laws Handbook |
| Serbia Constitution and Citizenship Laws Handbook |
| Seychelles Constitution and Citizenship Laws Handbook |
| Sierra Leone Constitution and Citizenship Laws Handbook |
| Singapore Constitution and Citizenship Laws Handbook |
| Slovakia Constitution and Citizenship Laws Handbook |
| Slovenia Constitution and Citizenship Laws Handbook |
| Solomon Islands Constitution and Citizenship Laws Handbook |
| Somalia Constitution and Citizenship Laws Handbook |
| South Africa Constitution and Citizenship Laws Handbook |
| Spain Constitution and Citizenship Laws Handbook |
| Sri Lanka Constitution and Citizenship Laws Handbook |
| St. Helena Constitution and Citizenship Laws Handbook |
| St. Pierre & Miquelon Constitution and Citizenship Laws Handbook |
| Sudan Constitution and Citizenship Laws Handbook |
| Suriname Constitution and Citizenship Laws Handbook |
| Swaziland Constitution and Citizenship Laws Handbook |
| Sweden Constitution and Citizenship Laws Handbook |
| Switzerland Constitution and Citizenship Laws Handbook |
| Syria Constitution and Citizenship Laws Handbook |

| |
|---|
| Taiwan Constitution and Citizenship Laws Handbook |
| Tajikistan Constitution and Citizenship Laws Handbook |
| Tanzania Constitution and Citizenship Laws Handbook |
| Thailand Constitution and Citizenship Laws Handbook |
| Togo Constitution and Citizenship Laws Handbook |
| Tonga Constitution and Citizenship Laws Handbook |
| Trinidad and Tobago Constitution and Citizenship Laws Handbook |
| Tunisia Constitution and Citizenship Laws Handbook |
| Turkey Constitution and Citizenship Laws Handbook |
| Turkmenistan Constitution and Citizenship Laws Handbook |
| Turks & Caicos Constitution and Citizenship Laws Handbook |
| Tuvalu Constitution and Citizenship Laws Handbook |
| Uganda Constitution and Citizenship Laws Handbook |
| Ukraine Constitution and Citizenship Laws Handbook |
| United Arab Emirates Constitution and Citizenship Laws Handbook |
| United Kingdom Constitution and Citizenship Laws Handbook |
| United States Constitution and Citizenship Laws Handbook |
| Uruguay Constitution and Citizenship Laws Handbook |
| Uzbekistan Constitution and Citizenship Laws Handbook |
| Vanuatu Constitution and Citizenship Laws Handbook |
| Vatican City Constitution and Citizenship Laws Handbook |
| Venezuela Constitution and Citizenship Laws Handbook |
| Vietnam Constitution and Citizenship Laws Handbook |
| Virgin Islands, British Constitution and Citizenship Laws Handbook |
| Wake Atoll Constitution and Citizenship Laws Handbook |
| Wallis & Futuna Constitution and Citizenship Laws Handbook |
| Western Sahara Constitution and Citizenship Laws Handbook |
| Yemen Constitution and Citizenship Laws Handbook |
| Zambia Constitution and Citizenship Laws Handbook |
| Zimbabwe Constitution and Citizenship Laws Handbook |

**To order and for additional analytical and marketing information, please contacts International Business Publications, USA at:**
**P.O. Box 15343, Washington, DC 20003, USA. Phone: (202) 546-210 Fax: (202) 546-32**
**E-mail: ibpusa3@gmail.com**

# WORLD COUNTRY STUDY GUIDE LIBRARY

***Strategic political, geographic, economic, business information, contacts and important developments***

**Price: $149 each**

| |
|---|
| Afghanistan Country Study Guide |
| Aland Country Study Guide |
| Albania Country Study Guide |
| Algeria Country Study Guide |
| Andorra Country Study Guide |
| Angola Country Study Guide |
| Anguilla Country Study Guide |
| Antigua and Barbuda Country Study Guide |
| Antilles (Netherlands) Country Study Guide |
| Argentina Country Study Guide |
| Armenia Country Study Guide |
| Aruba Country Study Guide |
| Australia Country Study Guide |
| Austria Country Study Guide |
| Azerbaijan Country Study Guide |
| Bahamas Country Study Guide |
| Bahrain Country Study Guide |
| Bangladesh Country Study Guide |
| Barbados Country Study Guide |
| Belarus Country Study Guide |
| Belgium Country Study Guide |
| Belize Country Study Guide |
| Benin Country Study Guide |
| Bermuda Country Study Guide |
| Bhutan Country Study Guide |
| Bolivia Country Study Guide |
| Bosnia and Herzegovina Country Study Guide |
| Botswana Country Study Guide |
| Brazil Country Study Guide |
| Brunei Country Study Guide |
| Bulgaria Country Study Guide |
| Burkina Faso Country Study Guide |
| Burundi Country Study Guide |
| Cambodia Country Study Guide |
| Cameroon Country Study Guide |
| Canada Country Study Guide |

| |
|---|
| Cape Verde Country Study Guide |
| Cayman Islands Country Study Guide |
| Central African Republic Country Study Guide |
| Chad Country Study Guide |
| Chile Country Study Guide |
| China Country Study Guide |
| Colombia Country Study Guide |
| Comoros Country Study Guide |
| Congo Country Study Guide |
| Congo, Democratic Republic Country Study Guide |
| Cook Islands Country Study Guide |
| Costa Rica Country Study Guide |
| Cote d'Ivoire Country Study Guide |
| Croatia Country Study Guide |
| Cuba Country Study Guide |
| Cyprus Country Study Guide |
| Czech Republic Country Study Guide |
| Denmark Country Study Guide |
| Djibouti Country Study Guide |
| Dominica Country Study Guide |
| Dominican Republic Country Study Guide |
| Ecuador Country Study Guide |
| Egypt Country Study Guide |
| El Salvador Country Study Guide |
| Equatorial Guinea Country Study Guide |
| Eritrea Country Study Guide |
| Estonia Country Study Guide |
| Ethiopia Country Study Guide |
| Falkland Islands Country Study Guide |
| Faroes Islands Country Study Guide |
| Fiji Country Study Guide |
| Finland Country Study Guide |
| France Country Study Guide |
| Gabon Country Study Guide |
| Gambia Country Study Guide |
| Georgia Country Study Guide |
| Germany Country Study Guide |
| Ghana Country Study Guide |
| Gibraltar Country Study Guide |
| Greece Country Study Guide |
| Greenland Country Study Guide |
| Grenada Country Study Guide |
| Guam Country Study Guide |
| Guatemala Country Study Guide |
| Guernsey Country Study Guide |
| Guinea Country Study Guide |
| Guinea-Bissau Country Study Guide |
| Guyana Country Study Guide |
| Haiti Country Study Guide |
| Honduras Country Study Guide |
| Hungary Country Study Guide |

| |
|---|
| Iceland Country Study Guide |
| India Country Study Guide |
| Indonesia Country Study Guide |
| Iran Country Study Guide |
| Iraq Country Study Guide |
| Ireland Country Study Guide |
| Israel Country Study Guide |
| Italy Country Study Guide |
| Jamaica Country Study Guide |
| Japan Country Study Guide |
| Jersey Country Study Guide |
| Jordan Country Study Guide |
| Kazakhstan Country Study Guide |
| Kenya Country Study Guide |
| Kiribati Country Study Guide |
| Korea, North Country Study Guide |
| Korea, South Country Study Guide |
| Kosovo Country Study Guide |
| Kurdistan Country Study Guide |
| Kuwait Country Study Guide |
| Kyrgyzstan Country Study Guide |
| Laos Country Study Guide |
| Latvia Country Study Guide |
| Lebanon Country Study Guide |
| Lesotho Country Study Guide |
| Liberia Country Study Guide |
| Libya Country Study Guide |
| Liechtenstein Country Study Guide |
| Lithuania Country Study Guide |
| Luxembourg Country Study Guide |
| Macao Country Study Guide |
| Macedonia,Country Study Guide |
| Madagascar Country Study Guide |
| MadeiraCountry Study Guide |
| Malawi Country Study Guide |
| Malaysia Country Study Guide |
| Maldives Country Study Guide |
| Mali Country Study Guide |
| Malta Country Study Guide |
| Man Country Study Guide |
| Marshall Islands Country Study Guide |
| Mauritania Country Study Guide |
| Mauritius Country Study Guide |
| Mayotte Country Study Guide |
| Mexico Country Study Guide |
| Micronesia Country Study Guide |
| Moldova Country Study Guide |
| Monaco Country Study Guide |
| Mongolia Country Study Guide |
| Monserrat Country Study Guide |
| Morocco Country Study Guide |

| |
|---|
| Mozambique Country Study Guide |
| Myanmar Country Study Guide |
| Namibia Country Study Guide |
| Nauru Country Study Guide |
| Nepal Country Study Guide |
| Netherlands Country Study Guide |
| New Caledonia Country Study Guide |
| New Zealand Country Study Guide |
| Nicaragua Country Study Guide |
| Niger Country Study Guide |
| Nigeria Country Study Guide |
| Niue Country Study Guide |
| Northern Mariana Islands Country Study Guide |
| Norway Country Study Guide |
| Oman Country Study Guide |
| Pakistan Country Study Guide |
| Palau Country Study Guide |
| Palestine (West Bank & Gaza) Country Study Guide |
| Panama Country Study Guide |
| Papua New Guinea Country Study Guide |
| Paraguay Country Study Guide |
| Peru Country Study Guide |
| Philippines Country Study Guide |
| Pitcairn Islands Country Study Guide |
| Poland Country Study Guide |
| Polynesia French Country Study Guide |
| Portugal Country Study Guide |
| Qatar Country Study Guide |
| Romania Country Study Guide |
| Russia Country Study Guide |
| Rwanda Country Study Guide |
| Saint Kitts and Nevis Country Study Guide |
| Saint Lucia Country Study Guide |
| Saint Vincent and The Grenadines Country Study Guide |
| Samoa (American) A Country Study Guide |
| Samoa (Western) Country Study Guide |
| San Marino Country Study Guide |
| Sao Tome and Principe Country Study Guide |
| Saudi Arabia Country Study Guide |
| Scotland Country Study Guide |
| Senegal Country Study Guide |
| Serbia Country Study Guide |
| Seychelles Country Study Guide |
| Sierra Leone Country Study Guide |
| Singapore Country Study Guide |
| Slovakia Country Study Guide |
| Slovenia Country Study Guide |
| Solomon Islands Country Study Guide |
| Somalia Country Study Guide |
| South Africa Country Study Guide |
| Spain Country Study Guide |

| |
|---|
| Sri Lanka Country Study Guide |
| St. Helena Country Study Guide |
| St. Pierre & Miquelon Country Study Guide |
| Sudan Country Study Guide |
| Sudan South Country Study Guide |
| Suriname Country Study Guide |
| Swaziland Country Study Guide |
| Sweden Country Study Guide |
| Switzerland Country Study Guide |
| Syria Country Study Guide |
| Taiwan Country Study Guide |
| Tajikistan Country Study Guide |
| Tanzania Country Study Guide |
| Thailand Country Study Guide |
| Togo Country Study Guide |
| Tonga Country Study Guide |
| Trinidad and Tobago Country Study Guide |
| Tunisia Country Study Guide |
| Turkey Country Study Guide |
| Turkmenistan Country Study Guide |
| Turks & Caicos Country Study Guide |
| Tuvalu Country Study Guide |
| Uganda Country Study Guide |
| Ukraine Country Study Guide |
| United Arab Emirates Country Study Guide |
| United Kingdom Country Study Guide |
| United States Country Study Guide |
| Uruguay Country Study Guide |
| Uzbekistan Country Study Guide |
| Vanuatu Country Study Guide |
| Vatican City Country Study Guide |
| Venezuela Country Study Guide |
| Vietnam Country Study Guide |
| Virgin Islands, British Country Study Guide |
| Wake Atoll Country Study Guide |
| Wallis & Futuna Country Study Guide |
| Western Sahara Country Study Guide |
| Yemen Country Study Guide |
| Zambia Country Study Guide |
| Zimbabwe Country Study Guide |

**To order and for additional analytical and marketing information, please contacts International Business Publications, USA at:**
**P.O. Box 15343, Washington, DC 20003, USA. Phone: (202) 546-210 Fax: (202) 546-32**
**E-mail: rusric@erols.com**

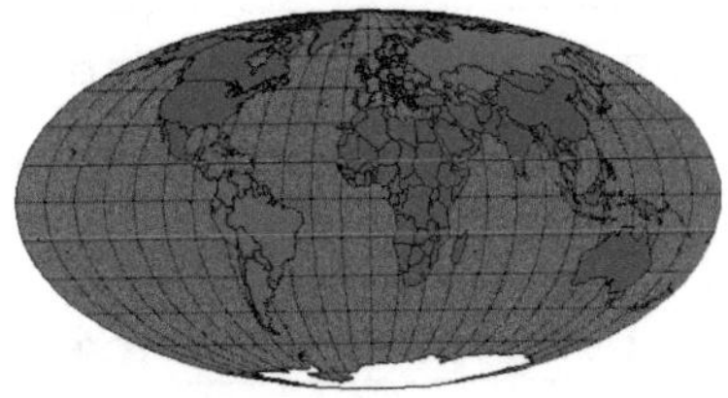

# WORLD JUSTICE SYSTEM AND NATIONAL POLICE HANDBOOK LIBRARY

## Price: $99.95 Each

| Title * |
|---|
| 1. Australia Justice System and National Police Handbook |
| 2. Austria Justice System and National Police Handbook |
| 3. Bangladesh Justice System and National Police Handbook |
| 4. Belgium Justice System and National Police Handbook |
| 5. Canada Justice System and National Police Handbook |
| 6. China Justice System and National Police Handbook |
| 7. Costa Rica Justice System and National Police Handbook |
| 8. Cuba Justice System and National Police Handbook |
| 9. Czech Republic Justice System and National Police Handbook |
| 10. Egypt Justice System and National Police Handbook |
| 11. Estonia Justice System and National Police Handbook |
| 12. Finland Justice System and National Police Handbook |
| 13. France Justice System and National Police Handbook |
| 14. Germany Justice System and National Police Handbook |
| 15. Greece Justice System and National Police Handbook |
| 16. Hungary Justice System and National Police Handbook |
| 17. India Justice System and National Police Handbook |
| 18. Indonesia Justice System and National Police Handbook |
| 19. Israel Justice System and National Police Handbook |
| 20. Italy Justice System and National Police Handbook |
| 21. Japan Justice System and National Police Handbook |
| 22. Korea, South Justice System and National Police Handbook |
| 23. Kuwait Justice System and National Police Handbook |
| 24. Laos Justice System and National Police Handbook |
| 25. Latvia Justice System and National Police Handbook |

**For additional analytical, business and investment opportunities information, please contact Global Investment & Business Center, USA at (202) 546-2103. Fax: (202) 546-3275. E-mail: rusric@erols.com**

| Title * |
|---|
| 26. Lithuania Justice System and National Police Handbook |
| 27. Malaysia Justice System and National Police Handbook |
| 28. Mexico Justice System and National Police Handbook |
| 29. Myanmar Justice System and National Police Handbook |
| 30. Pakistan Justice System and National Police Handbook |
| 31. Palau Justice System and National Police Handbook |
| 32. Palestine Justice System and National Police Handbook |
| 33. Philippines Justice System and National Police Handbook |
| 34. Russia Justice System and National Police Handbook |
| 35. Singapore Justice System and National Police Handbook |
| 36. South Africa Justice System and National Police Handbook |
| 37. Sri Lanka Justice System and National Police Handbook |
| 38. Sweden Justice System and National Police Handbook |
| 39. Taiwan Justice System and National Police Handbook |
| 40. Thailand Justice System and National Police Handbook |
| 41. Turkey Justice System and National Police Handbook |
| 42. Ukraine Justice System and National Police Handbook |
| 43. United Kingdom Justice System and National Police Handbook |
| 44. United States Justice System and National Police Handbook |

**For additional analytical, business and investment opportunities information, please contact Global Investment & Business Center, USA at (202) 546-2103. Fax: (202) 546-3275. E-mail: rusric@erols.com**